PRO TOOLS® 101

VERSION 7·4 OFFICIAL COURSEWARE

Digidesign | Frank D. Cook

Course Technology PTR

A part of Cengage Learning

Australia, Brazil, Japan, Korea, Mexico, Singapore, Spain, United Kingdom, United States

COURSE TECHNOLOGY
CENGAGE Learning™

Pro Tools 101 Version 7.4 Official Courseware Digidesign | Frank D. Cook

Publisher and General Manager, Course Technology PTR:
Stacy L. Hiquet

Associate Director of Marketing:
Sarah O'Donnell

Manager of Editorial Services:
Heather Talbot

Marketing Manager:
Mark Hughes

Acquisitions Editor:
Mark Garvey

Project Editor/Copy Editor:
Cathleen D. Small

PTR Editorial Services Coordinator:
Erin Johnson

Interior Layout Tech:
Bill Hartman

Cover Designers:
Brynn Dirksen and
Jason Lakis (Digidesign), Mike Tanamachi

DVD-ROM Producer:
Digidesign

Indexer:
Larry Sweazy

Proofreader:
Kim V. Benbow

For product information and technology assistance, contact us at
Cengage Learning Customer & Sales Support Center, 1-800-354-9706

For permission to use material from this text or product,
submit all requests online at **cengage.com/permissions**
Further permissions questions can be emailed to
permissionrequest@cengage.com

Library of Congress Catalog Card Number: 2006905036

ISBN-13: 978-1-59863-424-2

ISBN-10: 1-59863-424-0

Course Technology
25 Thomson Place
Boston, MA 02210
USA

Cengage Learning is a leading provider of customized learning solutions with office locations around the globe, including Singapore, the United Kingdom, Australia, Mexico, Brazil, and Japan. Locate your local office at: **international.cengage.com/region**

Cengage Learning products are represented in Canada by Nelson Education, Ltd.

For your lifelong learning solutions, visit **courseptr.com**

Visit our corporate website at **cengage.com**

Printed in the United States of America
4 5 6 7 11 10 09 08

This book is dedicated to musicians, sound designers, audio editors, mixing engineers, and Pro Tools enthusiasts everywhere—industry leaders of the future.

Foreword

For more than 20 years, Digidesign has been developing Pro Tools training material and making it available in different forms for a variety of purposes. Pro Tools training has been offered through venues such as Digidesign's formal Reseller Certification Programs, training sessions at tradeshow events and tours, and Avid's initial Pro Tools courses at Authorized Education Centers.

In 2001, Digidesign recognized the growing need for an official training and education program to serve the emerging education market in professional audio and post-production, as well as an industry need for Pro Tools certification. We began conducting research for the program, meeting with major audio engineering schools and audio industry leaders.

The result was the Digidesign Training & Education Program, which established comprehensive course and exam requirements for students with a choice of either a music production or a video post-production emphasis. Official training centers were established worldwide, offering two levels of certification for Pro Tools users within each emphasis: Operator certification and Expert certification. The Digidesign Training & Education Program first published the Pro Tools 101 book in 2002 for Pro Tools version 5.x. Additional Operator-level courseware was developed at the 200-level, along with Expert-level courseware at the 300-level. The courseware was published for use exclusively by Digidesign's Certified Training Partners.

The Pro Tools 101 book was updated in 2004 for Pro Tools version 6.x, followed by updates to the 200-level and 300-level courseware, each reflecting the features of the latest software update.

In 2006, Digidesign completed additional updates to address the new functionality included in Pro Tools 7 and the growing array of system configurations supported in the Pro Tools product line. The training courseware was expanded, with the addition of a new Pro Tools 110 course covering essentials of Pro Tools and the later addition of the Pro Tools 310I course covering advanced ICON mixing techniques. Digidesign teamed with Thomson Course Technology PTR and Insource Writing Solutions to rework the Pro Tools 101 book from the ground up and make it available through commercial distribution channels. For the first time, Pro Tools 101 was made publicly available and offered through retail bookstores and outlets.

In this latest edition, the Pro Tools 101 book has again been updated and improved. The material has been refreshed to address the latest software and hardware options, through the release of Pro Tools 7.4. New to this version are discussions of the Key Signature Ruler, Elastic Audio functions, the Create Click Track command, Mojo SDI features, new Track Height adjustment techniques, the new Structure Free sample player, new shortcuts and key commands, as well as a healthy complement of feature enhancements and project updates.

With more than 150 training partners in 28 different countries supporting more than 30,000 student enrollments to date, the Digidesign Training & Education Program is the leading resource for training in Pro Tools software today. The Digidesign Certification Directory at www.digidesign.com offers a searchable database of more than 2,500 certified Pro Tools Operators and Experts. Digidesign continues to work with industry leaders in major audio production facilities to promote active recruiting of graduates trained in the curriculum. We are excited to be offering this updated book to complement the Pro Tools 7.4 release, and we encourage your participation in our program.

Andy Cook
Manager, Worldwide Training & Education Programs
Digidesign
October 2007

Acknowledgments

The following individuals provided critical assistance, input, information, and material used to complete this book.

Digidesign: Alex Steinhart, Andy Cook, Andy Hagerman, Anthony Gordon, Chandra Lynn, Chris Now, Dave Lebolt, Don Falcone, Greg Robles, John Given, Mark Altin, Mark Jeffery, Paul Foeckler, Scott Church, Tim Carroll, Tim Mynett, Tom Dambly

Cheryl Panepinto at Avid

Joel Krantz, Independent Pro Tools Consultant

Ken Johnson at M-Audio

Mark Garvey at Thomson Course Technology PTR

Mark Hughes at Thomson Course Technology PTR

Rachelle McKenzie at Avid

Sean Householder at M-Audio

Shilpa Patel at Center for Pro Tools, Inc.

Special Thanks

Special thanks to Cathleen Small for diligently editing the manuscript and to William Hartman for providing continuous updates to the layout.

Extra-Special Thanks

Kudos and extra-special thanks to all of Digidesign's official training partners and certified instructors, who have tirelessly worked with us to help shape this program and who have generously provided their valuable feedback for our courseware.

About the Authors

The courseware for this book was developed by the Digidesign Training & Education department, with contributions from numerous Digidesign staff and independent contractors. Revisions and additions for this edition were provided by Frank D. Cook as part of an ongoing partnership between Insource Writing Solutions and Digidesign.

Frank D. Cook is a bass guitarist and longtime Pro Tools user. The owner of Insource Writing Solutions, Frank has worked in the technical publications industry for more than 15 years. As a writer, editor, technical publications manager, business owner, and active member of the Society for Technical Communication, Frank has authored and contributed to hundreds of guides, manuals, reports, and other publications for clients in a wide variety of industries. His company, Insource Writing Solutions, specializes in Pro Tools courseware development and provides technical writing and consulting, content management, and web-based solutions using Microsoft SharePoint and DotNetNuke.

Contents

Chapter 7: Selecting and Navigating 161

Part III: Hands-On Projects 263

Preface

Welcome to Pro Tools 101

Congratulations on entering the official Digidesign Training & Education Program. This book represents the first step on your journey toward mastery of your Pro Tools system. The information and projects you will find here apply to all Pro Tools systems (Pro Tools M-Powered, Pro Tools LE, and Pro Tools HD). Whether you are interested only in self study or you would like to pursue formal certification through the Digidesign Training & Education Program, this book will develop your core skills and introduce you to the awesome power of Pro Tools. Digidesign's award-winning technology is embraced by audio production professionals around the world. Get ready to join their ranks as you unleash the creative power and technology of Pro Tools!

About This Book

We wrote this book for the audio enthusiast with little to no Pro Tools experience. While *Pro Tools 101* can be completed through self study, Digidesign recommends obtaining hands-on experience through an instructor-led class offered by one of our official training partners. For more information on the classes offered through the Digidesign Training & Education Program, visit www.digidesign.com and click on Training, or go directly to training.digidesign.com.

Pro Tools 7.4 Edition

For this edition, *Pro Tools 101* has been refreshed and updated for Pro Tools 7.4. The material is focused to cover the basic principles you need to understand in order to complete a Pro Tools project, from initial setup to final mixdown. Whether your project involves multi-track recording of live instruments, MIDI sequencing of software synthesizers and samplers, or audio looping of REX files, *Pro Tools 101* will teach you the steps required to succeed.

The DVD at the Back of the Book

Included at the back of this book is a DVD-ROM containing *Pro Tools 101* project files and software installers for the Xpand! and Structure Free plug-ins. The disc also includes video tutorials from the Pro Tools Accelerated series.

Course Prerequisites

Most Pro Tools enthusiasts today have at least a passing familiarity with operating a computer. If you consider yourself a computer novice, however, you might want to review some basics before beginning this course. You will need to know how to complete such tasks as:

- Starting up the computer
- Using the mouse, standard menus, and keyboard commands for standard operating system commands
- Locating, moving, and renaming files and folders
- Opening, saving, and closing files

This course focuses on using Pro Tools in a digital audio recording and production environment. The work requires a basic understanding of recording techniques, processes, and equipment, such as the following:

- Miking techniques
- Mixer signal flow
- Audio monitoring equipment
- MIDI devices

If you are a beginner in the field of audio production, you can supplement this text with independently available literature on audio recording tools and techniques. Visit Digidesign's Training & Education website at training.digidesign.com for a list of selected resources.

Course Organization and Sequence

This course has been designed to familiarize you with the information and processes you will use to complete a recording project. The material is organized into four parts. Part I provides background information that will help you understand the material that is presented later and put it into context. Part II presents specific processes and techniques that you would use to complete a project, from creating a new session to completing a final mixdown. Part III provides a tutorial-style walkthrough of various tasks required to complete two hands-on projects (included on the enclosed DVD). Part IV, to be completed at any official Pro Tools training center, includes additional projects and the Pro Tools 101 final exam.

Part I: Background Information

Part I focuses primarily on background information relevant to Pro Tools and audio production. This part builds a foundation for using Pro Tools by introducing concepts of digital audio, Pro Tools hardware configurations, Pro Tools session file structures, and the Pro Tools user interface and tool set.

Part II: Working with Sessions

Part II provides information and instructions for working with Pro Tools sessions to accomplish common audio production tasks. In this part, we discuss creating sessions, creating audio and MIDI recordings, navigating within audio and MIDI recordings, and editing and mixing using Pro Tools.

Part III: Hands-On Projects

Part III is designed to provide you with experience applying the concepts of Part II. Two projects have been selected to represent typical scenarios and workflows encountered in music and post-production environments. The project tutorials follow the same progression as the chapters in Part II, with each section cross-referenced to the chapter that it supplements. The project tutorials are written so they can be completed without students having first completed Part II, enabling them to learn through hands-on experience, using Part II as a reference.

Part IV: Course Completion

Part IV of the Pro Tools 101 course can be completed in an instructor-led environment at an official Pro Tools training center. In this part of the course, students have the opportunity to work on additional projects using a variety of Pro Tools hardware. Students will also be able to complete the final exam and receive a completion certificate through the training center.

Conventions and Symbols Used in This Book

Following are some of the conventions and symbols we use in this book. We've tried to use familiar conventions and symbols whose meanings are self-evident.

Menu and Key Commands

Menu choices and keyboard commands are typically capitalized. Hierarchy is shown using the greater than symbol (>), keystroke combinations are indicated using the plus sign (+), and mouse-click operations are indicated by hyphenated strings, where needed.

Convention	Action
File > Save Session	Choose Save Session from the File menu.
Ctrl+N	Hold down the Ctrl key and press the N key.
Command-click (Mac OS)	Hold down the Command key and click the mouse button.
Right-click	Click with the right mouse button.

Icons

The following icons are used to call attention to tips, important notices, shortcuts, cross-references, and examples.

 Tips provide helpful hints, related steps, or alternative methods of working.

 Important notices include information that may affect audio, system performance, or Pro Tools session data.

 Shortcuts show useful keyboard, mouse, or controller shortcuts that can help you work more efficiently.

 Cross-references alert you to another section, book, or Pro Tools guide that provides more information on the current topic.

 Examples provide descriptions of typical situations in which a concept is applied.

Introduction to Pro Tools

Pro Tools—the most widely used application for music and post-production in the world today—is a Digital Audio Workstation (DAW) that uses the power of the personal computer to integrate hard disk audio recording, graphical audio editing, MIDI sequencing, digital signal processing (DSP), and mixing into a fast and intuitive application for personal and professional projects. Other features, such as desktop video integration and OMF/AAF file support, allow Pro Tools to fill almost any role in post-production—from home DV movie projects to feature film productions.

Creation

With the increasing popularity of software-based synthesizers and samplers, more people are using Pro Tools as a creative tool for writing and developing their projects. In the early stages of a project, Pro Tools provides a natural environment for experimentation and sound design, and its flexibility allows you to extend your creativity to every stage of a project.

Recording

Disk-based recording has opened the door to an entirely new world of audio production. The cost of hard disk storage continues to decline, while the quality of digital audio recording continues to improve with advancements in technology. Removing the restrictions of tape has changed the audio industry forever.

Editing

The impact of non-destructive editing on audio production is similar to that of the word processor on writing or of computer-aided design on architecture. Pro Tools provides straightforward audio editing features designed for efficiency, freeing up more time for you to put into the creative aspects of a project.

Mixing

Its ability to create a custom mix environment has led Pro Tools to emerge as the hub of the mixing process. A network of professional-quality plug-ins provides an ever-growing number of options to suit individual preferences. Mix automation in Pro Tools is the icing on the cake—incredibly powerful, yet amazingly simple.

Mastering

While mastering will always be an art unto itself, the benefits of Pro Tools—the highest sound quality and the ultimate in digital processing—lend themselves to the mastering process. From surround sound DVD encoding, to high-quality stereo mixes for CD, to encoding for MP3 files, Pro Tools is ideal for final preparation and delivery in a variety of formats.

The Digidesign Training & Education Program

As suggested by the title, this Pro Tools guide has been written in the form of a textbook. That is because, in addition to being an off-the-shelf guide for consumers, this book is also the official text for the first course in the Pro Tools certification program. By completing the coursework in this text and passing the Pro Tools 101 exam, you can fulfill the first of the certification requirements. And consider this: Having a certification from Digidesign just might help you land that next gig, find others with similar skills and interests, or even obtain your dream job in a major recording studio.

To become a Pro Tools certified user, you must complete additional Pro Tools coursework at a Certified Training Location or at a Pro School and then pass one of Digidesign's Certification Exams. Detailed information on current requirements is available at training.digidesign.com.

Certification Levels

Digidesign offers two levels of certification upon completion of your Pro Tools Training: Operator level and Expert level.

Operator-Level Certification

The Operator certification program prepares users to competently operate a Pro Tools|HD system in a professional environment as an assistant engineer or an entry-level editor. Students can specialize in Music Production, Post-Production, or both.

Expert-Level Certification

The Expert certification program provides users with the highest level of proficiency with Pro Tools–related hardware and software, enabling them to operate a Pro Tools|HD system in a professional, fast-paced environment at an above-average skill level. Students can specialize in Music Production, Post-Production, and/or Advanced ICON Mixing Techniques.

Courses Offered in the Training Program

Digidesign's Training & Education Partners offer three levels of coursework to help you become proficient using Pro Tools: 100-level, 200-level, and 300-level.

- 100-level courses provide you with the foundational skills you need to learn and function within the Pro Tools environment at a basic level. The goal of the courses at this level is to help individuals start working on their own projects in Pro Tools.
- 200-level courses build the fundamental skills you need to competently operate a Pro Tools|HD system in a professional environment. Coursework at this level involves a study of Pro Tools production essentials and either post-production or music production techniques. Completion of two or more 200-level courses is required for Operator certification.
- 300-level courses focus on advanced operation of Pro Tools|HD systems for music or post-production. Coursework involves working in real-world scenarios through example exercises from audio and MIDI production projects (music production track) and TV and film production projects (post-production track).

Training Program Course Configuration

The coursework for the Training Program has evolved and expanded over the years. We have recently adopted a version-specific approach to course design, enabling our training partners to teach classes based on the version of Pro Tools that meets their particular needs and training environments. We've assembled course components into a hierarchy of classes, shown on the following page, that are designed to be completed individually and in sequence. However, individual training partners may offer the same content through slightly different class configurations.

Descriptions of each of the courses offered through this program are available on the Digidesign website at training.digidesign.com.

How Can I Learn More?

If you want to learn more about the Digidesign Training & Education Program, please check out our official online resource by going to www.digidesign.com and clicking on the Training link. There you will also find information about our training partners and Operator and Expert certification.

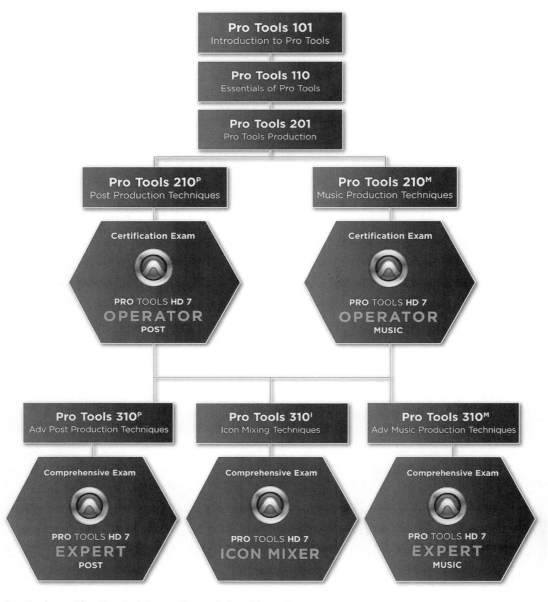

Pro Tools certification training paths and class hierarchy

PART I

Background Information

Components

- Chapter 1, Getting to Know Pro Tools

- Chapter 2, Getting Inside Pro Tools

Overview

Part I focuses on background information relevant to Pro Tools and audio production. This part builds a foundation for using Pro Tools by introducing Pro Tools' capabilities in audio, MIDI, mixing, and video post-production; describing the history of Digidesign and Pro Tools; introducing concepts of digital audio; and providing an overview of available Pro Tools system configurations. Chapter 2 introduces basic Pro Tools operations and functions, reviews the Pro Tools session file structure, and provides an overview of the Pro Tools user interface, tool set, and modes of operation.

Chapter 1

Getting to Know Pro Tools

This chapter introduces you to Pro Tools' capabilities in audio, MIDI, mixing, and video post-production. You will learn about the evolution of Digidesign and Pro Tools technology and get an introduction to factors that affect digital audio and analog-to-digital conversion. You will also learn about the many Pro Tools configurations available today and gain an understanding of cross-platform issues that affect keyboard commands and file-naming conventions.

Objectives

After you complete this chapter, you will be able to:

- Describe the advantages of recording and editing in the digital realm
- Recognize the contributions of historical developments in sampling and sound editing, MIDI technology, computer I/O, and recording technology to today's digital audio workstation
- Describe the relationship between sample rate and frequency response in digital audio
- Describe the relationship between bit depth and dynamic range in digital audio
- Recognize components of a Pro Tools M-Powered, LE, or HD system

Notes

What Is Pro Tools?

Pro Tools is the most widely used application for music and post-production (sound for film, video, and multimedia) in the world today, integrating capabilities in audio and MIDI recording, composition, editing, and mixing as well as support for desktop video. As such, Pro Tools software empowers both music and post-production professionals to easily achieve all of their production tasks within one easy-to-use interface.

More specifically, Pro Tools is a multi-track software-based digital recording and editing system. It uses the power of the personal computer to combine hard-disk audio recording, graphical audio editing, MIDI sequencing, digital signal processing (DSP), and mixing into an integrated system. With the ability to incorporate QuickTime and Avid video files, Pro Tools has also established itself as an industry choice for post-production video editing and mixing to picture.

Audio

Pro Tools works with audio that is stored electronically in digital format. The software records audio and stores it as files on your hard drive. Like a digital camera that stores a photograph as a collection of discrete pixels, Pro Tools stores recorded audio as a collection of discrete samples. Pro Tools supports audio formats of up to 24 bits and 192 kHz and has the ability to play back up to 192 tracks simultaneously.

Just as you can use an image editor to modify, enhance, and otherwise alter your digital photographs in creative new ways, so too can you use Pro Tools to take your digital audio in new directions. Working in the digital realm makes it easy to copy, paste, move, delete, modify, and otherwise manipulate your recordings. Pro Tools lets you trim waveforms, reprocess regions of audio, pitch-correct a compromised performance, replace drum sounds, rearrange song sections, and more. With the new Elastic Audio capabilities in Pro Tools 7.4, you can manipulate the speed of your audio clips in real time, allowing you to freely experiment with tempo. You can even quantize audio for quick rhythmic fixes or creative exploration.

MIDI

Using built-in sequencing technology, Pro Tools also enables you to record and edit MIDI data in the same work environment as your audio recordings. MIDI recordings differ from their digital counterparts in that they are resolution-independent, and they capture performance event data rather than sound samples. You can record MIDI signals from a keyboard or other device through a MIDI or USB interface and then edit the data using Pro Tools' intuitive graphical display.

A Pro Tools session can have up to 256 MIDI tracks in addition to its Audio tracks. Pro Tools 7.4 offers support for MIDI in Windows XP, Microsoft Vista, and Mac OS X operating systems. Available features include MIDI Time Stamping, Groove Quantize, Restore Performance, native ReWire support, tick-based and sample-based timelines, and a wide array of plug-in virtual instruments.

Mixing

Beyond recording and editing, Pro Tools provides a software-based mixing environment that provides control over signal routing, effects processing, signal levels, panning, and more. The mixing operations in Pro Tools can be automated and stored with your session, enabling you to recall, edit, and refine your mixes over time. When you save a session, all routing, automation, mixing, and effects settings remain exactly as you've left them.

Additionally, Pro Tools software can be combined with Pro Tools hardware in various configurations to provide multiple channels of simultaneous input and output for your Pro Tools sessions. Massive sessions including up to 192 simultaneous Audio tracks can be managed without audio degradation. Pro Tools systems can range from very simple to extremely advanced and powerful.

Post-Production

Pro Tools also provides a powerful platform for audio post-production tasks. You can import QuickTime movies, Avid video files, or Windows Media (VC-1 AP) clips (Windows Vista only) and use Pro Tools' fast, random-access visual reference as you "sweeten" the audio by adding and modifying sound effects, music, Foley, and dialogue. With support for multiple Video tracks and video editing capabilities in compatible configurations, you can now also perform non-destructive editing and arranging of video files and scenes within Pro Tools 7.4. When completed, you can export your finished movie file with the final audio mix embedded.

The Story of Digidesign

The art of manipulating digital audio has evolved with, and been dramatically influenced by, the evolution of Pro Tools. Introduced in 1991 by Digidesign, Pro Tools helped pioneer the concept of multi-track digital audio recording and is now recognized for having revolutionized the audio recording industry. While Pro Tools 7.4 introduces state-of-the-art new features to further enhance the product's capabilities, the core functionality of Pro Tools traces its roots to humble beginnings and the experimental work of the company's founders, Peter Gotcher and Evan Brooks.

In the Beginning

In the early 1980s, Peter Gotcher and Evan Brooks were college musicians looking for a new sound. Growing bored with the sounds offered by the EMU Drumulator drum machine they had purchased, Peter and Evan began recording their own drum sounds using live percussion instruments and various other sources—from Led Zeppelin records to the horn of a BMW. Using the tedious and labor-intensive technology that existed at the time, they began programming the sounds onto computer EPROM chips.

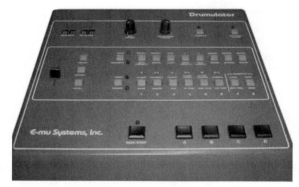

EMU Drumulator drum machine

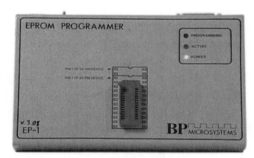

Early programmer for EPROM computer chips

Though the chips were initially created for personal use, Peter and Evan recognized a growing market in electronic music and eventually began offering their chips for retail. Sparked by interest from major music stores in New York City, Peter and Evan were soon producing multiple chip sets for retail, including Rock Drums, Electronic Drums, Latin Percussion, Sound Effects, and others.

In 1984, Peter and Evan formed Digidrums, a precursor company to Digidesign. Soon they found themselves selling their drum chips by the tens of thousands. With this success, they forged ahead into software and hardware design.

Early drum-sound chip sets

Among their software projects was a visual waveform editor initially created for editing the Digidrum sounds and developed under the name Sound Designer. As the technology matured, enabling users to edit sounds captured by a sampling keyboard, Sound Designer for EII was born. This software, which began shipping the following year, was the first to combine waveform editing with a front panel emulation/editor.

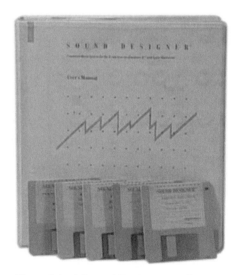

The original Sound Designer package

Evolving into Digidesign

In 1985, the company adopted a new management model led by investor Timothy Draper and CEO Paul Lego. Under this model, Peter was able to provide creative vision for the company while the CEO maintained the business focus. As the company transformed its management, the company name was also changed: Digidrums became Digidesign.

During this time, the company began designing products for working with MIDI. Digidesign created MIDI Conductor, a single-in/single-out MIDI interface for Macintosh computers, and MIDI Composer, a simple four-track sequencer for the Mac. Both products were manufactured and distributed by Assimilation, Inc.

Digidesign continued its focus on software development, releasing SoftSynth in 1986 as the first additive synthesis program for the Mac. SoftSynth enabled users to generate custom sound files that could then be loaded into a sampling keyboard.

Throughout 1986 and 1987, Sound Designer continued to mature, adding compatibility with additional systems and synthesizers. In the summer of 1987, Digidesign released two additional software packages for the Mac: FX Designer, which provided a front panel editor/librarian for the Lexicon PCM-70 effects processor, and Q-Sheet, which was a SMPTE-based MIDI sequencer that synchronized to the newly adopted MIDI Time Code (MTC) format.

Pioneering Digital Audio

Also in 1987, Digidesign began prototyping a sample playback card for digital audio. The card initially provided a single channel (mono) 16-bit output. Digidesign engineers began work on a stereo playback card later the same year. In 1988, Digidesign released Sound Accelerator, a CD-quality two-channel output card for the Mac II. This proved to be the first step toward enabling computer systems to provide professional-quality audio output.

Digidesign continued to develop software products for sampling and synthesis, including Turbosynth, a synthesis program that generated sound files for various sampling keyboards, updates to Q-Sheet adding the ability to play audio through the Sound Accelerator, and updates to SoftSynth and Sound Designer. At the same time, Digidesign began work on products designed for digital recording. This was a formative time for the company, as the technologies for sampling, waveform editing, and digital input and output began to converge.

In 1989, Digidesign released Sound Tools, a two-track hard-disk recorder. Billed as the world's first "tapeless recording studio," Sound Tools consisted of Sound Designer II software, a Sound Accelerator card, and a hardware box called the AD-In

Components of the Sound Tools system

that connected to the Sound Accelerator card, providing two analog-to-digital converters. Later the same year, the DAT I/O was released, providing an AES/EBU and S/PDIF digital interface for use with the Sound Tools system.

In 1990, the first AudioMedia card was created. AudioMedia I was a NuBus card for Macintosh computers and was the first product aimed at musicians, consumers, and independent studios. Its low cost helped drive the "democratization" of music and the recording industry, making hard-disk audio recording accessible to the masses.

The Birth of Pro Tools

The first-generation Pro Tools system was released in 1991. Initial systems supported four tracks of audio. Eventually, using an add-in board called the System Accelerator and additional cards and interfaces, these Pro Tools systems expanded to support up to 16 tracks of simultaneous recording and playback.

In 1992, Session 8 was released, providing a limited version of the Pro Tools feature set for the Windows operating system. This was Digidesign's first Windows-based product.

Early Pro Tools system

The Session 8 system for Windows NT

Two years later, Digidesign introduced Pro Tools TDM, opening the door for real-time effects plug-ins as we now know them. The Pro Tools TDM system utilized Time Division Multiplexing (TDM) technology to reliably manipulate up to 256 streams of digital audio data running between hardware cards, I/O peripherals, and the host computer. TDM technology paved the way for rapid expansion among third-party applications and plug-in developers and laid the groundwork for future plug-in software. Development of core plug-ins, non-core plug-ins, and third-party plug-ins soon followed.

By March 1995, Digidesign was recognized as having dramatically changed the economics of the recording industry, providing capabilities that formerly required million-dollar investments at prices that small studios could afford. That year, Digidesign merged with its biggest customer, Avid Technology, and has continued to operate as a division of Avid ever since.

Pro Tools Matures

In 1997, Digidesign introduced Pro Tools|24 as the next generation of Pro Tools hardware. These Pro Tools systems were the first to offer 24-bit audio capabilities. The main components included the 888|24 I/O audio interface and new cards called DSP Farms. Pro Tools|24 added an unprecedented number of inputs and outputs along with higher track counts.

Digidesign offered the first Pro Tools TDM release for Windows in 1998, expanding its platform for Windows users. The following year, Pro Tools LE was introduced, providing native audio processing based on the host computer's processor. Pro Tools LE software worked with the Digi 001 audio interface or the AudioMedia III card.

As Pro Tools systems evolved, so did the need for compatible mixing consoles and control surfaces to simplify work on large projects. By 1998, Digidesign began offering its own line of dedicated control surfaces for Pro Tools, with the introduction of ProControl. The ProControl console provided an expandable system of touch-sensitive motorized faders, LED scribbles strips, encoders for pan and send editing, and dedicated plug-in editing, utilizing Ethernet to communicate with the host CPU.

In 2001, the control surface lineup was expanded with the introduction of Control|24. This control surface featured 24 touch-sensitive, motorized faders; built-in monitoring; and microphone preamps at an affordable price. Control|24 was co-developed in a partnership between Focusrite and Digidesign.

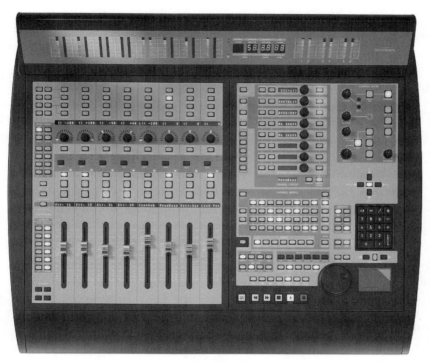

ProControl integrated control surface for Pro Tools TDM systems

The Control\24 integrated front end for Pro Tools LE and TDM systems

The influence of Pro Tools continued to spread in the professional and project studio environments as the number of available options grew. In 2001, Digidesign received a Technical GRAMMY® Award from the National Academy of Recording Arts and Sciences®. The Outstanding Technical Achievement award recognized the company with the inscription, "For breaking the boundaries of digital recording and revolutionizing the way music is produced."

In 2002, Pro Tools|HD systems were unveiled as successors to Pro Tools TDM and Pro Tools|24. These systems provided support for higher sample rates and very large mixing topologies, addressing the needs of high-end music and post-production studios.

On the opposite side of the spectrum, the Mbox was introduced as a mini "studio in a box" for use with Pro Tools LE, appealing to the needs of the hobbyist and small project studio markets. This USB-powered audio interface included two mic/line/instrument preamps and a dedicated headphone output. Mbox superseded the AudioMedia product line, which was then discontinued.

Digidesign received the 2003 Scientific and Technical Achievement Award for the Pro Tools digital audio workstation. ©Academy of Motion Picture Arts and Sciences®

The Digi 002 and Digi 002 Rack audio interface options followed, extending the capabilities of Pro Tools LE, along with numerous additional hardware components and upgrades for Pro Tools|HD systems.

In 2003, Digidesign received an Academy Award® in Scientific and Technical Achievement for the design, development, and implementation of the Digidesign Pro Tools digital audio workstation.

In the years since, Digidesign's evolution has been marked by significant developments that have included several acquisitions, the introduction of the ICON and VENUE product lines, and numerous successive Pro Tools releases and feature enhancements.

Notable Acquisitions

In August 2004, Avid acquired M-Audio, a leading provider of digital audio and MIDI solutions. Now a business unit of Digidesign, M-Audio markets its product line of computer audio peripherals, keyboard controllers, and related music and recording gear alongside Digidesign's digital audio workstations for the professional and home/hobbyist markets.

In 2005, the release of Pro Tools M-Powered software provided options for using the software with a vast array of highly portable M-Audio devices and interfaces. With three Pro Tools system configurations to choose from (M-Powered, LE, and HD), the amazing power of Pro Tools software became available to customers at all levels, from the hobbyist to the most advanced professional recording or post-production studio.

One year later, Digidesign announced the acquisition of Wizoo Sound Design, a pioneering developer of virtual instruments, sample libraries, and real-time effects. The Wizoo R&D team formed the core of the Digidesign Advanced Instrument Research (A.I.R.) group. The A.I.R. group has since focused on developing inspiring, creative virtual instrument plug-ins for Pro Tools systems, with an emphasis on tight integration and reliable performance. Popular A.I.R. plug-ins now include the Xpand! sample-playback/synthesis workstation, the Hybrid high-definition synthesizer, the Strike professional drum performance plug-in, the Velvet vintage electric piano plug-in, and the Structure professional sampling workstation.

In 2006, Sibelius Software Ltd. joined the Avid Audio family. Sibelius is the world market leader in developing software for professionals, educators, and students to write, teach, learn, and/or publish music. As a business unit of Digidesign, Sibelius continues to develop and market its own line of software, including its well-known professional music notation package. Pro Tools has begun to leverage the notation capabilities of Sibelius and now includes an option for exporting MIDI data to Sibelius software.

ICON Integrated Console Environment

Digidesign unveiled the ICON integrated console environment in 2004, featuring a D-Control worksurface. This was the first truly integrated console available for Pro Tools. Today, ICON systems offer a choice of the flagship D-Control worksurface or the medium-format D-Command worksurface, first introduced in 2005. ICON combines the console with a Pro Tools|HD Accel system as the core DSP engine and modular Pro Tools|HD audio interfaces.

The ICON integrated console for Pro Tools

ICON can be customized for rapid access to every session element, independent of the on-screen Pro Tools software interface. Operators can save mixer configurations and reduce project setup time. ICON provides full recall of every parameter within a project, allowing complex sessions to be switched out in minutes.

Both ICON options employ a modular architecture, allowing facilities to scale their system as needs dictate. Expandable to 80 physical faders, D-Control provides a central mixing environment for facilities with larger rooms. D-Control includes a comprehensive array of touch-sensitive controls and provides operators extensive hands-on control over their Pro Tools projects.

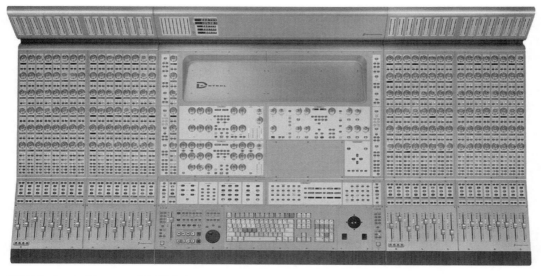

ICON D-Control layout with 32 faders (expandable to 80 faders)

The more compact D-Command worksurface is expandable to 24 physical faders, providing a similar feature set configured for single-operator facilities with smaller rooms or budgets. D-Command features dedicated panels for EQ and dynamics plug-in editing and offers similar hands-on command over Pro Tools projects as the D-Control in a smaller package.

ICON D-Command layout with 24 faders (maximum configuration)

VENUE Live Sound Environment

Digidesign introduced VENUE in 2005 as a purpose-built solution for live sound. VENUE is a state-of-the-art live sound mixing and production environment that provides a revolutionary approach to the world of sound reinforcement. Running standard Pro Tools DSP plug-ins, VENUE eliminates the need for extensive front-of-house (FOH) and monitor effects racks. VENUE also seamlessly integrates with Pro Tools for direct recording and playback of multi-track live performances.

A VENUE system consists of the flagship D-Show mixing console or its smaller sibling, the D-Show Profile, combined with an FOH mix engine, a Stage Rack I/O unit, and a multi-channel digital snake. The system is expandable up to 96 mic inputs on 27 buses and provides up to 128 tracks of simultaneous recording and playback. The mix engine provides EQ and Dynamics processing on every input channel and full support for Pro Tools plug-ins.

The base D-Show console consists of a single Sidecar and a Main Unit. A maximum of two additional Sidecars can be added, for a total of 56 input faders, allowing operators to mix large numbers of sources without banking.

The VENUE D-Show mixing console (expandable to 56 faders)

The D-Show Profile is a size-conscious alternative to the larger D-Show console, offering 24 faders and 4 fader banks that allow easy access to Profile's full 96-input capacity.

VENUE D-Show Profile

Where We Are Today

Today, Digidesign continues to expand both its hardware and software offerings for all segments of the music creation and video post-production markets, from home recording enthusiasts to large-scale motion picture sound designers and mixers. The growing Mbox 2 family of audio interfaces—Mbox 2, Mbox 2 Pro, Mbox 2 Mini— as well as the new 003 family of interfaces provide a broader range of options for Pro Tools LE users than ever before. Advanced plug-in development efforts such as the A.I.R. Structure professional sampling workstation and the Digidesign X-Form professional time stretching and pitch shifting plug-in offer unprecedented processing capabilities from within the Pro Tools environment. Digidesign's recently announced Reference Monitor Series of professional near-field monitors also marks the company's entrance into the loudspeaker market. Utilizing groundbreaking Advanced Transmission Line (ATL) technology, the two monitor designs in the series—the compact RM1 and the bigger, more powerful RM2—deliver unrivaled tonal accuracy, low distortion, accurate bass response, and incredible dynamic range.

The recent release of Pro Tools 7.4 software brings cross-platform support for the latest operating systems, expanded support for video peripherals such as Avid Mojo and Mojo SDI, the ability to work natively with high-definition video, new tools for experimenting with tempo, and a multitude of other enhancements. The Video Satellite HD option removes the video processing burden from the audio system and enables playback of unrendered Avid sequences from Avid Unity ISIS and Unity Media Network shared storage. The revolutionary Elastic Audio features in Pro Tools 7.4 allow users to modify the length of any audio event or part, be it a musical phrase, a percussive sequence, or a voice-over for a TV commercial. A variety of time compression/expansion algorithms are included, enabling users to obtain the best-sounding results for their material.

The enhanced loop-based workflows in the 7.4 release also capitalize on Elastic Audio functionality, automatically matching imported audio loops to the session tempo. The new Warp track view provides extremely fine control over each individual beat in an Elastic Audio–enabled Audio track without requiring cutting or moving elements. Enhanced ReWire support adds flexibility to Pro Tools, enabling it to accept MIDI input from ReWire-client applications—controller and note data generated in ReWire-client applications can now be sent to MIDI or Instrument tracks and recorded into your Pro Tools session.

Basics of Digital Audio

Today's Pro Tools systems give you the power to capture the subtlest details of a sound or performance and to work on digital audio with absolute precision. Becoming acquainted with the fundamentals of sound and digital audio will enable you to maximize this power by effectively utilizing the technologies that Pro Tools employs and the capabilities of your system. This section describes some of the factors that affect sound and influence the accuracy of digital audio.

 The following information provides an overview of the concepts of digital audio theory. Although you do not need to be an expert in this material, gaining exposure to these principles will enrich your understanding of many of the processes discussed later in the book.

Basic Parameters of Sound: Waveform, Frequency, and Amplitude

To work effectively with sound, it is helpful to understand a bit about what sound actually is and what gives a sound its character. When you or I hear a sound, what we actually experience are variations in the air pressure around us. These variations result from vibrations in material objects—a tabletop, a car engine, a guitar string. When a vibrating object moves through one complete back-and-forth motion (one cycle), the variation in air pressure that it produces becomes an auditory event. If the object is vibrating at a frequency that falls within the range of human hearing, we perceive it as a sound. The nature of the sound we hear is determined by the waveform, frequency, and amplitude of the vibration.

 The range of human hearing is between 20 and 20,000 cycles per second.

Waveform

The waveform of the sound pressure variations that reaches our ears creates our perception of the sound's source, whether a knock on a table, a running car engine, or a plucked guitar string. The waveform is the "shape" of the sound—or, more accurately, the shape of the vibration that produced the sound. As a vibrating object moves through its back-and-forth motions, its path is not smooth and continuous. Instead, the cycles of vibration are typically complex and jagged, influenced by factors such as the physical material that the object is composed of and resonance induced by the object's surroundings. Each object vibrates differently; the waveform of the vibration gives the sound its unique character and tone.

Frequency

The frequency of the sound pressure variations that reaches our ears creates our perception of the pitch of the sound. We measure this frequency in *cycles per second* (CPS), also commonly denoted as *Hertz* (Hz). These two terms are synonymous—15,000 CPS is the same as 15,000 Hz. Multiples of 1,000 Hz are often denoted as kilohertz (kHz). Therefore, 15,000 Hz is also written as 15 kHz.

As the frequency of vibration increases, the pitch of the sound goes up—numerically higher frequencies produce higher pitches, while numerically lower frequencies produce lower pitches. Each time the frequency doubles, the pitch raises by one octave. By way of example, the A string on a guitar vibrates at 110 Hz in standard tuning. Playing the A note on the 12th fret produces vibrations at 220 Hz (one octave higher).

Amplitude

The intensity or amplitude of the sound pressure variations that reaches our ears creates our perception of the loudness of the sound. We measure amplitude in *decibels* (dB). The decibel scale is defined by the dynamic range of human hearing, with the threshold of hearing defined as 0 dB and the threshold of sensation or pain reached at approximately 120 dB. The dB is a logarithmic unit that is used to describe a ratio of sound pressure; as such it does not have a linear relation to our perception of loudness.

As the amplitude of pressure variations increases, the sound becomes louder. Doubling the intensity of sound-pressure variations creates a gain of 3 dB; however, we do not perceive this change as doubling the sound's loudness. An increase of approximately 10 dB is required to produce a perceived doubling of loudness. By way of example, the amplitude of ordinary conversation is around 60 dB. Increasing the amplitude to 70 dB would essentially double the loudness; increasing amplitude to 80 dB would double it again, quadrupling the original loudness.

Recording and Playing Back Analog Audio

The task of a recording microphone is to respond to changes in air pressure—the waveforms, frequencies, and amplitudes that make up a sound—and translate them into an electronic output that can be captured or recorded. The continuous electrical signal produced by a microphone is an alternating current with a waveform, frequency, and amplitude that directly corresponds to, or is analogous to, the original acoustic information. Hence the term *analog audio*.

If this continuous analog signal is captured on traditional recording media, such as magnetic tape, it can be played back by directly translating the electrical waveform, frequency, and amplitude back into analogous variations in air pressure through the means of an amplifier and loudspeaker.

Analog-to-Digital Conversion

Before you can record or edit with Pro Tools, the analog audio signals relayed by a microphone, guitar pickup, or other input device must be digitized, or translated into digital (binary) numerical information that can be stored, read, and subsequently manipulated by a computer. This process is referred to as *analog-to-digital conversion*, commonly abbreviated as *A/D conversion*. Two essential factors affect the A/D process: *sample rate* and *bit depth*.

Sample Rate and Frequency Resolution

Sampling is the process of taking discrete readings of a signal at various moments in time. Each reading, or sample, is a digital "snapshot" of the signal at that particular instant. Played back in succession, these samples approximate the original signal, much like a series of photographs played back in succession approximates movement in a film or video.

The sample rate is the frequency with which these digital snapshots are collected. The sample rate required for digital audio is driven by a fundamental law of analog-to-digital conversion, referred to as the *Sampling Theorem* or the *Nyquist Theorem*.

The Nyquist Theorem states that in order to produce an accurate representation of a given frequency of sound, each cycle of the sound's vibration must be sampled a minimum of two times. If the sample rate is any lower, the system will read the incoming frequencies inaccurately and produce the wrong tones. (In concept, this is much like the effect seen in early moving pictures, where a wagon wheel will appear to rotate backward due to the low frame rates being used.) In digital audio, the false tones produced by this type of frequency distortion are known as *alias tones*.

Because the range of human hearing is generally accepted to be 20 Hz to 20 kHz, this law indicates that a sampling rate of at least 40 kHz (twice the upper range of human hearing) is required to capture full-frequency audio. Most professional digital recording devices today offer sampling rates of 44.1 kHz and 48 kHz or higher. The digital information on an audio CD is stored at a standard sample rate of 44.1 kHz.

Bit Depth and Amplitude Resolution

The useful dynamic range of speech and music is generally considered to be from 40 to 105 dB. To capture this range, an A/D converter must be able to accurately represent differences in amplitude of at least 65 dB; stated another way, it must have a minimum 65-dB dynamic range. The relative amplitude (or loudness) of a sample is captured through a process known as *quantization*. This simply means that each sample is quantified (assigned) to the closest available amplitude value.

Computers use binary digits called *bits* (0s or 1s) to quantify each sample that is taken. The number of bits used to define a value is referred to as the *binary word length*. The range of values represented by a binary word is defined by the binary word length and is equal to 2 to the *n*th power (2^n), where *n* is the number of bits in the binary word.

 The binary word length is also commonly referred to as the bit depth.

A 4-bit binary word is able to represent 16 different numeric values (2^4); used by an A/D converter to capture amplitude, this 4-bit binary word would record the amplitude continuum using 16 discrete amplitude levels. By contrast, a 16-bit digital word could define 65,536 discrete amplitude levels (2^{16}), and a 24-bit digital word could define 16,777,216 discrete amplitude levels (2^{24}).

As such, larger binary words are able to quantify variations in amplitude with much greater accuracy. Therefore, a 24-bit audio file will always more accurately reflect the dynamic range of the original sound than its 16-bit counterpart.

A very general rule of thumb can be used to calculate the dynamic range capability of an A/D system. By multiplying the word size by six, you can estimate the useful dynamic range of the system. For example, a system with an 8-bit binary word (or 8-bit quantization) would produce a dynamic range of about 48 dB, while a 16-bit system would accommodate a 96-dB dynamic range. A 24-bit system would have a theoretical dynamic range of 144 dB.

 In theoretical terms, the dynamic range (or signal-to-quantization noise ratio) increases by approximately 6 dB for each bit added to the binary word length.

A consequence of larger binary words is the higher storage capacity required to record them. Each minute of 16-bit/48-kHz stereo audio occupies about 11.4 MB of hard-drive storage space. In contrast, each minute of 24-bit/48-kHz stereo audio occupies about 17 MB of hard-drive storage space.

Recording in Digital Format

When you are recording into Pro Tools using audio that is already in a digital form (on DAT or CD, for example), you don't need to translate the audio before bringing it into the system. The process of converting from digital to analog and back to digital can introduce distortion and degrade the original signal. Therefore, unnecessary conversions should be avoided. If the audio information remains in the digital domain while being transferred between machines, it will retain its sonic integrity with no discernible signal degradation.

On the rear panel of many Pro Tools audio interfaces are two types of connections for accomplishing digital transfers. One is labeled S/PDIF, which has RCA jacks (sometimes called *coaxial jacks*), and the other, AES/EBU, which uses XLR-type connectors. S/PDIF is the Sony/Philips Digital Interface standard, a consumer format, and AES/EBU is the Audio Engineering Society/European Broadcast Union digital interface standard, a professional format. Although both formats are nearly identical in audio quality (it's virtually impossible to hear the difference), if given the choice, you should always use the AES/EBU format over the S/PDIF format because the professional format is technically more stable and filters out any copy protection encoded in the digital audio stream. Almost all digital recording or storage devices will support one or both of these formats.

Pro Tools System Configurations

The requirements for your digital audio recording projects will determine the type of Pro Tools system that you will need to use. Pro Tools software is available in three options: Pro Tools M-Powered, Pro Tools LE, and Pro Tools HD. All three options are available for both Macintosh and Windows operating systems, and all deliver the same core technology. The primary differences between the options are the hardware that each Pro Tools software option works with.

Pro Tools M-Powered and Pro Tools LE systems are host-based, meaning they use the processing power of the host computer to carry out real-time routing, mixing, and processing of audio signals. These systems use peripheral hardware to provide input and output (I/O) to the Pro Tools software. By contrast, Pro Tools|HD systems use Digidesign PCI cards with digital signal processing (DSP) power for their mixing and real-time processing operations, combined with peripheral hardware for I/O purposes.

All three Pro Tools options share the same file format, making it possible to interchange projects between these three types of systems. Pro Tools sessions are also cross-compatible between Macs and PCs.

Pro Tools M-Powered

Pro Tools M-Powered provides sampling rates of up to 96 kHz, with bit depths up to 24 bits. It will power up to 32 simultaneous Audio tracks and up to 256 simultaneous MIDI tracks. Pro Tools M-Powered software is designed for use with M-Audio hardware functioning as its audio interface. This option provides highly portable recording solutions for projects with limited I/O needs.

The Music Production Toolkit increases the Pro Tools M-Powered track count to 48 mono or stereo tracks at 96 kHz. See the "Music Production Toolkit" section later in this chapter for more details.

A variety of PCI, FireWire, and USB peripherals are available from M-Audio, providing a multitude of I/O options for Pro Tools M-Powered. Many of these peripherals can be powered by the computer's FireWire or USB bus, enabling such systems to function as completely portable Pro Tools workstations.

The following sections provide details on some of the supported interfaces for Pro Tools M-Powered. Many additional interfaces are available; check the Digidesign website for the latest list of compatible interfaces (www.digidesign.com).

The FireWire Family

- **FireWire 1814.** This is a 18-in, 14-out audio interface with XLR and ¼-inch line-level inputs, ¼-inch unbalanced outputs, and MIDI input and output. It also includes S/PDIF optical digital I/O, word clock for synchronization to other digital devices, and pass-through of surround-encoded AC-3 and DTS material.

- **FireWire 410.** This is a 4-in, 10-out audio interface with XLR and ¼-inch line-level inputs, ¼-inch unbalanced outputs, and MIDI input and output. It also includes optical and coaxial S/PDIF I/O.

M-Audio FireWire 1814 audio interface

- **FireWire Solo.** This is a 6-in, 4-out audio interface with XLR and ¼-inch inputs and two ¼-inch balanced line outputs. It also includes S/PDIF digital I/O.

FireWire Solo audio interface

- **FireWire Audiophile.** This is a 4-in, 6-out audio interface with RCA line inputs and outputs and MIDI input and output. It also includes coaxial S/PDIF I/O.

Keyboard Interfaces

- **Ozone.** This is a 25-key MIDI keyboard with a 4-in, 4-out USB audio interface, providing XLR and ¼-inch inputs, two ¼-inch unbalanced outputs, and two MIDI outputs.

- **Ozonic.** This is a 37-key MIDI keyboard with a 4-in, 4-out FireWire audio interface, providing XLR and ¼-inch analog inputs, four ¼-inch analog outputs, and MIDI input and output.

M-Audio Ozonic keyboard with audio interfaces

PCI Cards with Breakout Cables

- **Audiophile 192.** This PCI card provides a 4-in, 4-out 24-bit/192 kHz audio interface with ¼-inch balanced analog inputs and outputs and MIDI input and output. It also includes coaxial S/PDIF I/O.

Audiophile 2496 audio interface

- **Audiophile 2496.** This PCI card provides a 4-in, 4-out 24-bit/96 kHz interface with RCA line inputs and outputs and MIDI input and output. It also includes coaxial S/PDIF I/O.

- **Delta 1010LT.** This PCI card provides a 10-in, 10-out audio interface with mic and RCA inputs, RCA outputs, and MIDI input and output. It also includes coaxial S/PDIF I/O.

Delta 1010LT audio interface

PCI Cards with External Box

- **Delta 44.** This is a 4-in, 4-out interface providing four ¼-inch instrument inputs and four ¼-inch outputs.

- **Delta 66.** This is a 6-in, 6-out interface providing four ¼-inch instrument inputs and four ¼-inch outputs as well as coaxial S/PDIF I/O.

M-Audio Delta 44 audio interface

- **Delta 1010.** This is a 10-in, 10-out audio interface providing eight ¼-inch inputs, eight ¼-inch outputs, and MIDI input and output. It also includes coaxial S/PDIF I/O.

Delta 1010 audio interface

Mobile Interfaces

- **MobilePre USB.** This unit combines a preamp with a 2-in, 2-out USB audio interface, providing XLR microphone inputs as well as ¼-inch and ¼-inch inputs and outputs.

- **Fast Track USB.** This USB audio interface is designed for guitarists, providing an XLR microphone input, a ¼-inch instrument/line input, and two RCA outputs. It includes GT Player Express software, providing effects and virtual stomp boxes.

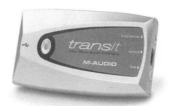

M-Audio MobilePre USB audio interface

- **Fast Track Pro.** This USB audio interface provides two front-panel mic/line inputs with phantom power, a ¼-inch headphone jack, ¼-inch and RCA outputs, and MIDI input and output.

- **Transit.** This is a USB audio interface with a ¼-inch stereo analog/optical digital input, a ¼-inch headphone/line output, and a TOSLINK optical digital output.

Transit audio interface

JamLab audio interface

- **JamLab.** This compact interface features a ¼-inch input for guitar and a ¼-inch headphone/line output. It includes GT Player Express software, providing effects and virtual stomp boxes.

Other Interfaces

- **Black Box.** This unit combines amp modeling, beat-synced effects, and a drum machine with a USB audio interface, providing an XLR mic input, a ¼-inch instrument input, and two ¼-inch balanced line outputs. It also includes S/PDIF digital output.

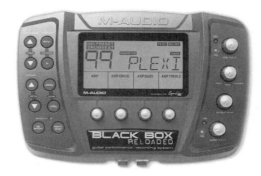

M-Audio Black Box audio interface

- **ProjectMix I/O.** This mixer combines a control surface with an 18 × 14 audio interface, providing eight ¼-inch balanced and XLR microphone inputs, 8 × 8 ADAT Lightpipe, 2 × 2 S/PDIF, and word clock. It also includes a MIDI interface, two ¼-inch headphone outputs, and two stereo output pairs for flexible routing.

- **NRV10.** This 8 × 2 analog mixer provides a 10 × 10 FireWire audio interface and includes five XLR mic inputs, an integrated effects processor, a headphone jack, and XLR and ¼-inch outputs. It includes the NRV10 interFX application.

- **Torq Conectiv.** This digital DJ system includes a 4 × 4 USB audio interface with a ¼-inch microphone input, four RCA inputs and outputs, and a ¼-inch headphone jack with volume control. It includes Torq DJ software.

M-Audio ProjectMix I/O control surface with audio interface

M-Audio Torq Conectiv

Pro Tools LE

Pro Tools LE provides sampling rates of up to 96 kHz, with bit depths up to 24 bits. It will power up to 32 simultaneous Audio tracks and up to 256 simultaneous MIDI tracks. Pro Tools LE software is designed to use external Digidesign hardware, such as an Mbox 2 or 003, as its audio interface. Pro Tools LE systems provide up to eight channels of simultaneous analog input (up to 18 channels of total simultaneous I/O) and are commonly used in home and project studios.

 The Music Production Toolkit increases the Pro Tools LE track count to 48 mono or stereo tracks at 96 kHz. See the "Music Production Toolkit" section later in this chapter for more details.

Pro Tools LE systems work with Digidesign interfaces including the original Mbox, the Mbox 2 family, the Digi 002 and Digi 002 Rack, and the 003 family.

The Mbox 2 Family

The core of the Mbox 2 family consists of the compact Mbox 2, the ultra compact Mbox 2 Mini, and the larger-format Mbox 2 Pro. The Mbox 2 family interfaces are designed to provide ease of use and portability while maintaining professional sound quality at an affordable price. Like the original Mbox that they have replaced, Mbox 2, and Mbox 2 Mini feature powered USB connectivity and support up to 24-bit/48-kHz audio resolution.

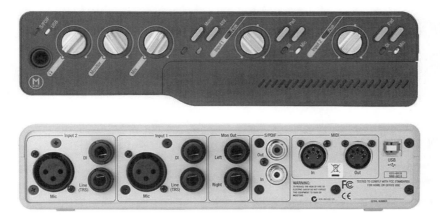

Digidesign Mbox 2 audio interfaces

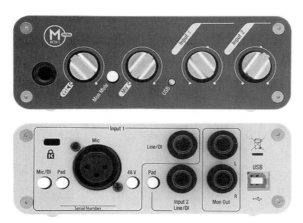

Mbox 2 Mini audio interfaces

Mbox 2 includes microphone, line, and direct input (DI) jacks for each of its two inputs; two ¼-inch unbalanced outputs; S/PDIF I/O; and MIDI input and output connectors. Mbox 2 Mini includes a single XLR microphone input, two ¼-inch inputs for line- or DI-level sources, and two ¼-inch outputs.

Mbox 2 Pro is a FireWire-powered interface that provides high-definition audio and MIDI in a portable package. It features support for audio resolutions up to 24 bits/96 kHz. Mbox 2 Pro includes two XLR/¼-inch combo inputs, two ¼-inch inputs, two front panel DI inputs, six ¼-inch outputs, two channels of S/PDIF digital I/O, and MIDI input and output.

Digidesign Mbox 2 Pro audio interface

The 003 Family

The 003 family consists of the 003 and 003 Rack FireWire-enabled interfaces, which are successors to the Digi 002 and Digi 002 Rack. Both units provide up to 18 channels of simultaneous I/O. The 003 provides I/O by way of an integrated control surface with eight motorized, touch-sensitive faders in a portable $8 \times 4 \times 2$ digital mixer. The 003 Rack provides the same I/O functionality in a rack-mounted unit. Both units provide 24-bit, 96-kHz audio and include the following I/O features:

- Eight 24-bit analog inputs
- Eight ¼-inch 24-bit analog outputs
- Four professional mic preamps with gain controls and high-pass filter switches
- Stereo ¼-inch TRS monitor outputs with level control
- Eight channels of 24-bit ADAT Optical I/O or two channels of S/PDIF Optical I/O
- Two channels of 24-bit S/PDIF digital I/O
- One MIDI input port and two MIDI output ports (16 channels in, 32 channels out)
- Dual headphone outputs with individual level controls

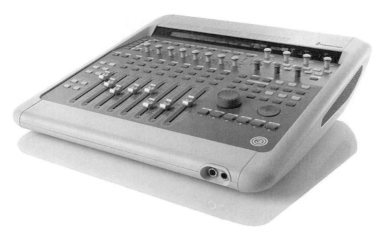

Digidesign 003 audio interface

Digidesign 003 Rack audio interface

Pro Tools|HD

Pro Tools|HD systems provide sampling rates of up to 192 kHz, with bit depths up to 24 bits. They will power up to 192 simultaneous Audio tracks (record and playback) and up to 256 simultaneous MIDI tracks. Pro Tools|HD systems provide the most robust Pro Tools option, utilizing Digidesign's dedicated DSP hardware and TDM II technology to carry out real-time routing, mixing, and processing of multiple audio signals. The TDM II bus architecture design provides support for extremely large mixing configurations.

Pro Tools|HD systems are designed for professional studios and provide up to 160 channels of simultaneous I/O. Pro Tools HD 7 software provides a total available track count of 192 Audio tracks, 160 aux inputs, 128 instrument tracks, and 256 MIDI tracks, as well as additional tracks for Master Faders.

Pro Tools|HD Core Configurations

Pro Tools HD software can be used to run a variety of Pro Tools|HD systems. All HD systems have a common basic configuration, which includes the following core components:

- Pro Tools HD software
- One or more Pro Tools|HD Core cards

The basic configuration can be expanded by adding one or more Pro Tools|HD Accel cards to the core system. Older expanded Pro Tools|HD core systems may include one or more HD Process cards (the predecessor of the HD Accel card).

In addition to the core components, all Pro Tools|HD systems require the presence of at least one Digidesign HD audio interface.

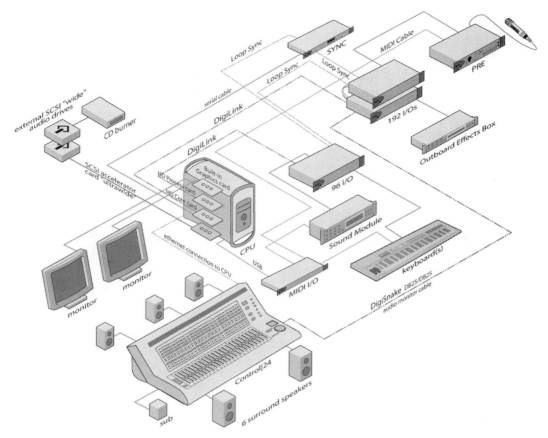

HD Music system

HD Core Card

The HD Core card is the main card of an HD system. It provides up to 96 simultaneous tracks of 16- or 24-bit direct-to-disk audio recording or playback, as well as DSP power for mixing and plug-in processing. The HD Core card supports 24-bit sessions at up to 192 kHz.

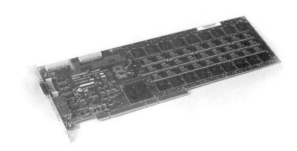

HD Core card

A single HD Core card provides 32 channels of I/O to the system, supporting up to two 16-channel HD-series audio interfaces. Expansion cards, such as the HD Accel card, can be added as needed to provide additional I/O channels and increase the record-and-playback track count.

Accel Cards

Additional cards, such as the HD Accel card, add recording and playback track count to a core system, up to the maximum of 192 tracks. Each HD Accel card adds 32 channels of I/O capacity to the system and DSP power for mixing and plug-in processing.

Pro Tools|HD 7 allows you to connect up to 10 HD audio interfaces to a system through the use of multiple HD Accel cards.

HD Accel card

Pro Tools|HD Audio Interfaces

Each core system requires at least one Pro Tools|HD–series audio interface—192 I/O, 192 Digital I/O, 96 I/O, or 96i—for handling the input and output (I/O) of audio signals.

192 I/O and 192 Digital I/O Audio Interfaces

The distinguishing characteristic of the 192 I/O and 192 Digital I/O is their ability to provide 192-kHz sample rates for recording, processing, and playback in Pro Tools|HD systems.

The 192 I/O supports up to 16 channels of analog and digital input and output and features a wide range of analog and digital I/O options to choose from, including eight channels of analog I/O, eight channels of AES/EBU, eight channels of TDIF, 16 channels of ADAT, and two additional channels of AES/EBU or S/PDIF digital I/O.

The 192 I/O also includes an I/O option bay, which can be used for an expansion card to add more inputs or outputs to the unit. Available expansion cards include the 192 AD card, the 192 DA card, and the 192 Digital card.

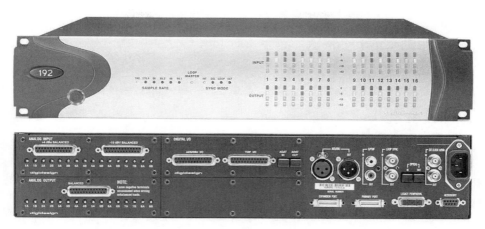

Digidesign 192 I/O audio interface (front and back panels)

The 192 Digital I/O is specifically designed to facilitate digital input from a variety of sources into the Pro Tools|HD environment and features a wide range of digital I/O options, including up to 16 channels of AES/EBU, TDIF, and ADAT I/O, along with S/PDIF I/O.

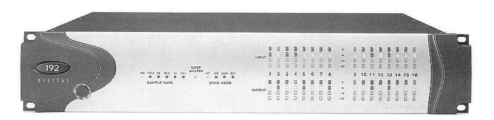

Digidesign 192 Digital I/O audio interface (front and back panels)

96 I/O and 96i I/O

The 96 I/O and 96i I/O provide sample rates of up to 96 kHz for recording, processing, and playback in Pro Tools|HD systems.

The 96 I/O is a 16-channel audio interface featuring a wealth of I/O options, including eight channels of analog I/O, eight channels of ADAT optical I/O, two channels of AES/EBU and S/PDIF I/O, and Word Clock I/O.

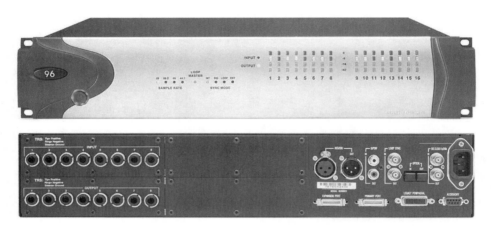

Digidesign 96 I/O audio interface (front and back panels)

The 96i I/O is designed as an interface for third-party outboard gear—keyboards, samplers, effects, and other line-level equipment. It includes 16 analog inputs for balanced or unbalanced A/D conversion and a S/PDIF port capable of 24-bit digital I/O for connecting professional DAT recorders, CD players, and other digital recording devices.

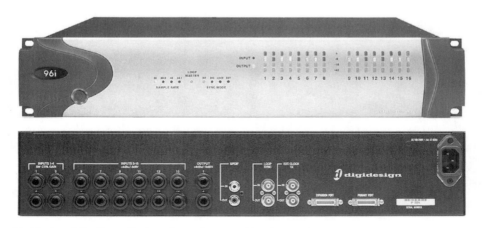

Digidesign 96i I/O audio interface (front and back panels)

Other Pro Tools System Options

Other external hardware units that can be configured in a Pro Tools|HD system include the Digidesign PRE, MIDI I/O, and SYNC I/O.

Digidesign PRE

Digidesign PRE is an eight-channel preamp that provides a transparent signal path designed specifically for the Pro Tools|HD environment. PRE accepts microphone, line, and direct instrument (DI) level inputs on all eight channels and can be placed anywhere in the studio.

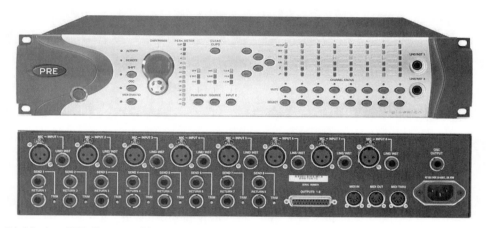

Digidesign PRE (front and back panels)

Digidesign MIDI I/O

MIDI I/O is a multi-port MIDI peripheral that provides 10 MIDI inputs and outputs for a total of 160 channels. Any number of inputs can be patched to any number of the unit's outputs without passing though the computer. MIDI I/O connects to the computer via a self-powered USB connection.

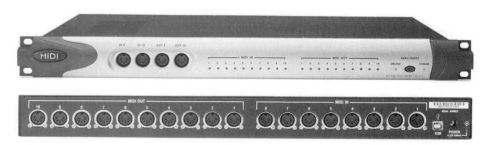

Digidesign MIDI I/O (front and back panels)

Digidesign SYNC I/O

Digidesign's SYNC I/O is a multi-purpose synchronization peripheral for synchronizing Pro Tools to a variety of devices, locking to time code or Bi-Phase/Tach signals with near-sample accurate synchronization. SYNC I/O supports all major industry-standard clock sources and time-code formats.

Digidesign SYNC I/O (front and back panels)

Add-Ons for Pro Tools M-Powered and Pro Tools LE

The capabilities of any Pro Tools system can be expanded with numerous Digidesign and third-party plug-ins, providing everything from EQ, dynamics, and effects processing to amplifier and analog tape simulations to synthesizers, drum kits, and other virtual instruments. Aside from plug-in components, additional software options and peripheral devices are available that extend the capabilities and functionality of Pro Tools M-Powered and Pro Tools LE systems, including the Music Production Toolkit, DV Toolkit 2 (Pro Tools LE only), and Mojo SDI (Pro Tools LE 7.4 only).

Music Production Toolkit

Digidesign's Music Production Toolkit is an optional software add-on for Pro Tools LE and Pro Tools M-Powered systems. The Music Production Toolkit offers a selection of tools that expand the capabilities of the base system. The Toolkit includes a collection of plug-ins, a multi-track version of the Beat Detective rhythm analysis and correction tool, and track counts up to 48 mono or stereo tracks at up to 96 kHz (interface permitting). The Music Production Toolkit also provides the ability to export mixes as MP3 files.

Extensive Plug-In Collection

The Music Production Toolkit includes powerful plug-ins that are ideal for creating and producing music.

- **Hybrid.** Developed by Digidesign's Advanced Instrument Research group, Hybrid is a high-definition synthesizer that combines the warmth of classic analog waveforms with digital wavetables to produce the sounds of legendary synths or something completely unique.
- **TL Space Native Edition.** The TL Space convolution reverb delivers the pristine sound of real reverberant spaces with a comprehensive library of reverb and effect impulses and the ability to add impulses easily.
- **Smack! LE.** This professional compressor/limiter plug-in is designed for anyone who requires a great-sounding, flexible, and easy-to-use compression tool for music or other audio material.
- **SoundReplacer.** SoundReplacer lets users replace drum sounds or other audio easily and automatically while retaining the feel and dynamics of the original performance.
- **Digidesign Intelligent Noise Reduction (DINR) LE.** This AudioSuite version of the award-winning DINR TDM plug-in effectively reduces unwanted noise—from guitar-amp buzz to tape hiss—for cleaner, more professional-sounding audio.

Multi-Track Beat Detective with Enhanced Resolution Algorithm

The multi-track version of the Beat Detective rhythm analysis and correction tool works across multiple Audio and MIDI tracks at the same time—a major time-saving capability otherwise available only on Pro Tools|HD systems.

Additionally, with Pro Tools 7.4, the Music Production Toolkit enables the new Enhanced Resolution analysis option in Beat Detective, producing the best results for the widest variety of audio material.

More Audio Tracks

The Music Production Toolkit expands a Pro Tools LE or Pro Tools M-Powered system to up to 48 mono or stereo tracks at up to 96 kHz for creating larger, more complex mixes.

Pro Tools MP3 Option

By including the Pro Tools MP3 Option, the Music Production Toolkit makes it easy to listen to a new mix on a portable device or quickly share it with other band members without having to use a separate application.

DV Toolkit 2

Digidesign's DV Toolkit 2 is an optional software add-on for Pro Tools LE systems. Building on the original DV Toolkit option for Pro Tools LE, DV Toolkit 2 provides a further expanded collection of post-production tools for producing high-end sound for film and video projects. DV Toolkit 2 includes a collection of post-production plug-ins, track counts up to 48 mono or stereo tracks at up to 96 kHz (interface permitting), and a full range of post-production features otherwise available only on Pro Tools|HD systems, including the ability to have multiple Avid Video or QuickTime clips and multiple Video tracks in the same session.

Essential Post-Production Plug-Ins

DV Toolkit 2 includes three powerful plug-ins that are ideal for working with sound for picture.

- **TL Space Native Edition.** The TL Space convolution reverb can instantly add realism to a film or video project. It offers a full range of authentic acoustic environments through a comprehensive library of reverb and effect impulses and the ability to add impulses easily.
- **DINR LE.** This AudioSuite version of the award-winning DINR TDM plug-in effectively reduces unwanted noise—from street sounds to air-conditioner rumble—for cleaner audio. DINR analyzes and subtracts noise entirely within the digital realm for results that are virtually free of side effects.
- **Synchro Arts VocALign Project for Pro Tools.** VocALign Project for Pro Tools stretches or squeezes one audio signal to match the timing patterns of another. The plug-in can be used to synchronize dialogue to video, dub foreign language films, tighten Foley and sound effects tracks, fine-tune the timing of music tracks, or achieve a perfectly lip-synched performance for a music video.

DigiBase Pro

DigiBase Pro—an advanced version of DigiBase previously available only with Pro Tools|HD systems—allows customers to create and share custom catalogs for quick and easy access to sounds or files associated with a project. This is a valuable tool for working with the large collections of files and volumes that are common on many film and video projects.

DigiTranslator 2.0

DigiTranslator 2.0 simplifies the process of file interchange by seamlessly converting and exchanging OMF, AAF, and MXF files between Pro Tools systems and Avid workstations—as well as other OMF 2.0-, AAF-, and MXF-capable audio and video applications.

Extended Pro Tools Functionality

DV Toolkit 2 adds key capabilities to Pro Tools LE software for working with sound for film or video. Many of the added features are familiar to post-production pros and provide a seamless transition from Pro Tools|HD to Pro Tools LE systems.

- Time Code and Feet + Frames functions
- Replace Region and Edit to Timeline selection commands
- Scrub Trim tool
- Export session text
- Continuous scrolling
- Universe window
- Automation snapshots
- Enhanced Import Session Data features

More Audio Tracks

DV Toolkit 2 expands a Pro Tools LE system to up to 48 mono or stereo tracks at up to 96 kHz for creating larger, more complex mixes.

Pro Tools MP3 Option

By including the Pro Tools MP3 Option, DV Toolkit 2 makes it easy to listen to a new mix on a portable device or quickly share it with other members of the project team without having to use a separate application.

Mojo SDI

The Avid Mojo SDI is a hardware video peripheral device that provides complete integrated Avid Video support within Pro Tools. Pro Tools LE 7.4 users with an Mbox 2 or 003 interface can now take advantage of the Avid Mojo SDI to bring the professional Avid video format into Pro Tools LE for the first time. This also provides desktop post-production professionals a seamless interchange between LE and HD systems.

Avid Mojo SDI

Pro Tools LE with an Avid Mojo SDI lets you import, play back, and edit Avid video files in the Timeline and supports the following video features:

- Multiple Video tracks in the Timeline (only one can be played back at a time)
- Multiple QuickTime movies on an individual Video track
- Multiple playlists for Video tracks
- Multiple codecs on an individual Video track
- Ability to store video files in the Region List and drag them from the Region List to the Timeline
- General video editing capabilities, including non-destructive editing with all Edit modes and Edit tools (except Time Compression/Expansion and the Pencil tools); multiple undos; selecting and editing across multiple tracks; capturing, separating, and healing regions; region looping, and more.
- Video region groups

Cross-Platform Issues

Each Pro Tools configuration is available for both Mac OS and Windows systems. Most Pro Tools controls, tools, procedures, and menus are similar on both systems. There are, however, some differences in keyboard commands and file-naming conventions that can impact your work when moving sessions between different platforms.

Keyboard Commands

Many keyboard commands in Pro Tools use *modifier keys*, which are keys pressed in combination with other keys or with a mouse action. In addition, other equivalent keys have different names on each platform. The following table summarizes equivalent keys on Mac OS and Windows:

Mac OS	Windows
Command key ⌘	Ctrl (Control) key
Option key	Alt key
Ctrl (Control) key	Start (Win) key
Return key	Enter key on main (not numeric) keypad
Delete key	Backspace key

File-Naming Conventions

A few differences exist in the way files are named and recognized by Mac OS and Windows.

File Name Extensions

For cross-platform compatibility, all Pro Tools files in a session must have a three-letter file extension added to the file name. Pro Tools 7.x sessions use the extension ".ptf." Sessions created in earlier versions of Pro Tools may use the extension ".pts" or ".pt5." WAV files have the ".wav" file extension, and AIFF files have the ".aif" file extension.

Incompatible ASCII Characters

Pro Tools file names cannot use ASCII characters that are incompatible with a supported operating system. The following characters should be avoided in order to maintain cross-platform compatibility:

/   (slash)
\   (backslash)
:   (colon)
*   (asterisk)
?   (question mark)
"   (quotation marks)
'   (apostrophe)
<   (less-than symbol)
>   (greater-than symbol)
| (vertical line or pipe)

You should also avoid any character typed with the Command key on the Macintosh.

Chapter 2

Getting Inside Pro Tools

This chapter covers basic Pro Tools operations and functions. It introduces the user interface as well as common tools and modes of operation.

Objectives

After you complete this chapter, you will be able to:

- Explain the basic Pro Tools session file structure
- Power up a Pro Tools M-Powered or LE system
- Navigate the Pro Tools menu system to locate common commands
- Recognize and work in the main Pro Tools windows
- Understand the Edit tools and Edit modes
- Work with Time Scales, Timebase Rulers, and MIDI Controls

Notes

Introduction

This chapter presents an overview of basic Pro Tools operations and functions. You will be introduced to the filing structure that Pro Tools uses for its sessions and back-ups, the steps required to start up a Pro Tools system, the primary elements of the Pro Tools interface, and some of the common tools and modes you will use to work in Pro Tools.

Target Systems

Although most of the concepts discussed in this book are applicable to all Pro Tools systems, the book is specifically targeted at Pro Tools M-Powered and LE users running software version 7.4. Certain menus, commands, and functionality may be slightly different on other systems. Pro Tools|HD users and LE/M-Powered users with the Music Production Toolkit or DV Toolkit 2 will also have access to additional features.

New features introduced in the Pro Tools 7.4 release are generally identified as such in the text. All descriptions are based on the user interface in Pro Tools M-Powered and Pro Tools LE 7.4 systems, unless otherwise noted. Screenshots represent Pro Tools LE 7.4 running on Windows XP with an Mbox 2 interface, unless otherwise noted.

Pro Tools File Structure

Before you create or edit a recording project, or *session*, in Pro Tools, it is helpful to understand how the software works with the various files that are related to a project. Rather than storing a session as a single file, Pro Tools stores various session components separately and maintains a roadmap to the files it uses in a session file. All of the files used for a project are grouped together in a session folder.

File Organization

When you create a Pro Tools session, the system sets up a standard hierarchy for the session and its associated files by automatically creating folders for each type of file. When you record, convert on import, or edit material, specific files will appear in each of these folders.

Pro Tools keeps related files together in this hierarchy to facilitate backups of sessions and transfers of all files between sessions and Pro Tools systems.

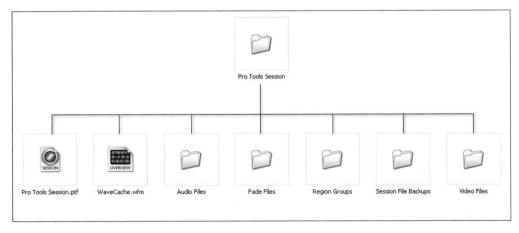

Pro Tools session file hierarchy

File Types

The types of files that Pro Tools stores in each folder in the hierarchy are described in the following sections. These files are typically created by Pro Tools as you work on a project.

Pro Tools Session File

A session file is the document that Pro Tools creates when you start a new project. A session file contains a map of all the audio tracks, audio and video files, settings, and edits associated with your project. Session documents can be saved and reopened, recalling a given project with all of its associated audio, edit information, and input/output assignments. You can easily copy and rename session documents, allowing you to save alternate versions of a project without changing the source audio. Pro Tools 7.x files are named with a .ptf extension.

WaveCache File

In Pro Tools 7.0 and later, each session creates a WaveCache.wfm file. This file stores all of the waveform display data for the session and enables it to open more quickly. The WaveCache file can be included whenever a session is transferred to another Pro Tools 7.x system.

Pro Tools also maintains a distinct WaveCache file inside the local Digidesign Databases folder (C:\\Digidesign Databases), which retains waveform data for all files used on the system. Additional WaveCache files are created on each external hard drive attached to your system and are stored in the Digidesign Databases folder on each drive.

 WaveCache files can be deleted without harming the session or your system. If the WaveCache is missing, Pro Tools will recalculate the session waveform data, causing the session to open more slowly.

Audio Files

When audio is recorded into a Pro Tools session, each take of the audio recording is stored as a separate file inside the corresponding session's Audio Files folder. Pro Tools is compatible with audio files in the WAV, AIFF, or SD II (Mac OS only) formats. However, for compatibility purposes, WAV is the default file format for both Mac OS and Windows Pro Tools systems.

Fade Files

The Fade Files folder contains separate fade file documents, which are created automatically by Pro Tools to apply volume fade-ins, fade-outs, and crossfades generated while editing a session. In the event that you move or copy a session and lose fade files, Pro Tools can recreate them automatically.

MIDI Files

MIDI files exported from Pro Tools using the Send to Sibelius command are saved in an auto-created MIDI Files folder in the Pro Tools session folder. MIDI files are named after the session, or if only one track is exported, named after the track.

If you do not use the Send to Sibelius command, no MIDI Files folder will be created in the session folder.

Region Groups

The Region Groups folder is the default directory that Pro Tools 7.0 and later uses for any region groups you export from your Pro Tools session. If you do not *export* any region groups, this folder will remain empty and will be removed when you close the session; region groups used in your session are not stored in this folder unless they've been exported.

Rendered Files

Pro Tools 7.4 creates temporary files for Rendered Elastic Audio processing. These files are kept in a new, auto-created Rendered Files folder in the session folder. If you commit Rendered Elastic Audio processing to a track, a new file is written to disk in the Audio Files folder, and the temporary rendered file is deleted from the Rendered Files folder.

If you do not use Rendered Elastic Audio processing in your session, no Rendered Files folder will be created in the session folder.

Session File Backups

If you enable the AutoSave function in Pro Tools, the Session File Backups folder will be created automatically, and autosaved session files will be stored in this location.

Video Files

The Video Files folder is created only when you digitize a movie into Pro Tools using AVoption|V10 or Avid Mojo. When you import a movie that is already in digital form (such as a QuickTime or Avid video file) into Pro Tools, the session references that movie in its stored location and does not copy it into your current Pro Tools session folder.

 For maximum session portability, you might want to create a Video Files folder, if it does not already exist, and copy existing movies into it prior to importing them into your session.

Starting Pro Tools

Because Pro Tools systems are composed of both hardware and software, preparing your system for use might involve more than simply turning on your computer and launching the Pro Tools application. The larger the system, the more important it becomes to follow a specific startup sequence.

Powering Up Your Hardware

When starting your Pro Tools hardware, it's important to power up the system components in the proper order. Starting components out of sequence could cause a component to not be recognized, prevent the software from launching, or cause unexpected behavior.

The recommended sequence for starting the Pro Tools hardware is as follows:

1. Make sure all your equipment (including your computer) is off.

2. Turn on any external hard drives and wait about 10 seconds for them to spin up to speed.

3. Turn on any MIDI interfaces and MIDI devices (including any MIDI Control surfaces) and synchronization peripherals.

4. Turn on your Pro Tools audio interfaces. Wait at least 15 seconds for the audio interface to initialize.

5. Start your computer.

6. Turn on your audio monitoring system, if applicable.

 Some Pro Tools M-Powered and LE interfaces, such as the Fast Track USB and Mbox 2, get their power from the computer; these interfaces do not need to be powered up in advance.

 Additional steps will be required for Pro Tools\HD system startup. Consult the Getting Started guide that came with your system for details.

Using the PACE iLok System

Most Digidesign and third-party software products are protected with an iLok key. Using an iLok for Pro Tools enables you to use a single key for all of your plug-ins and software options.

The iLok is a USB smart key that contains licenses for your protected software products. A single iLok can store more than 100 separate licenses from multiple software vendors. The iLok enables you to carry your software licenses with you wherever you go in a portable, convenient, and hassle-free key. Details and tools for managing your iLoks and licenses are available at www.ilok.com.

Before launching your Pro Tools software, you need to insert your iLok key into an available USB port on your computer.

The PACE iLok key

Launching Pro Tools

Pro Tools software can be launched by double-clicking on the application icon on the system's internal drive or by double-clicking on a shortcut to the application. In Windows systems, the application is typically installed under C:\Program Files\Digidesign\Pro Tools, and a shortcut is placed on the Desktop. In the Mac OS, the application is typically placed under Applications\Digidesign\Pro Tools.

Pro Tools application icons

 On Windows systems, Pro Tools may also be available from the Start menu at the lower-left corner of the display.

Mac OS users might want to create a shortcut to the Pro Tools application on the Dock. To do so, simply drag the application icon onto the Dock.

When you launch Pro Tools, the application starts with no session open. From this point, you can change settings that affect the application's overall performance, depending on your needs.

Optimizing Host-Based Pro Tools Performance

Pro Tools M-Powered and LE systems take advantage of the computer's processing capacity (called *host-based processing*) to carry out operations such as recording, playback, mixing, and real-time effects processing. Pro Tools|HD systems use dedicated DSP hardware for most of their audio processing power; however, they can also use host-based processing capacity for real-time effects processing.

While the default system settings are adequate for most processing tasks, Pro Tools lets you adjust the performance of a system by changing settings that affect its host-based processing capacity (the Hardware Buffer Size and the CPU Usage Limit).

Hardware Buffer Size

The Hardware Buffer Size (H/W Buffer Size) controls the size of the hardware cache used to handle host-based tasks, such as Real-Time AudioSuite (RTAS) plug-in processing.

- Lower Hardware Buffer Size settings reduce monitoring latency and are useful when you are recording live input.
- Higher Hardware Buffer Size settings allow for more audio processing and effects and are useful when you are mixing and using more RTAS plug-ins.

 The H/W Buffer Size setting does not affect TDM processing (Pro Tools|HD systems).

CPU Usage Limit

The CPU Usage Limit controls the percentage of the computer's processing power allocated to Pro Tools host processing tasks.

- Lower CPU Usage Limit settings limit the effect of Pro Tools processing on other processing-intensive tasks, such as screen redraws, and are useful when you are experiencing slow system response or when you are running other applications at the same time as Pro Tools.
- Higher CPU Usage Limit settings allocate more processing power to Pro Tools and are useful for playing back large sessions or using more RTAS plug-ins.

Modifying Hardware Buffer Size and/or CPU Usage Limit Settings

Adjustments to the Hardware Buffer Size and CPU Usage Limit can be made in the Playback Engine dialog box, as follows:

1. Choose SETUP > PLAYBACK ENGINE.
2. From the H/W Buffer Size pop-up menu, select the audio buffer size in samples—lower the setting to reduce latency; raise it to increase processing power for plug-ins.
3. From the CPU Usage Limit pop-up menu, select the percentage of CPU processing to allocate to Pro Tools—lower the setting to increase system response; raise it to increase processing power for Pro Tools.
4. Click **OK**.

 Additional details on the Playback Engine dialog box are covered in the Pro Tools 110 course.

Pro Tools 7.4 Playback Engine dialog box (Mbox 2)

 The Mix knob on the Mbox 2 and Mbox 2 Mini enables you to monitor ana-
log input signals while recording with zero latency. You can use this knob to
blend and adjust the monitor inputs between your latency-free live inputs
and Pro Tools playback. For zero-latency monitoring, turn the Mix knob
fully left.

The Pro Tools Software Interface

Before beginning to work on a session, you should have some basic familiarity with
the Pro Tools software interface. The software interface is displayed once you create
or open a session by choosing FILE > NEW SESSION, FILE > OPEN SESSION, or FILE >
OPEN RECENT. Details on creating and opening sessions are provided in Chapter 3,
"Creating Your First Session."

This section will introduce you to the menu structure, the Edit window, the Mix window, and the Transport window for Pro Tools 7.4.

The Menu Structure

Among the first things you will see after opening a Pro Tools session for the first
time are the menus. Learning how the menus are organized will save you a lot of
time when you are trying to find a specific Pro Tools function. Following is a brief
description of each menu.

File Menu

File menu commands let you create and maintain Pro Tools sessions. The File menu includes options for opening, creating, and saving sessions; bouncing tracks; and importing and exporting session components.

Edit Menu

Edit menu commands allow you to edit and manipulate the current selection and to affect data in the timeline. The Edit menu includes options for copying and pasting; duplicating, repeating, and shifting selections; trimming, separating, and healing regions; and performing similar operations.

View Menu

View menu commands control the display of Pro Tools windows, tracks, and track data. Some View menu commands toggle the display of various components or data in Pro Tools windows. Select the command to display the component or data; deselect the command to hide it.

Track Menu

Track menu commands let you set up and maintain tracks in a Pro Tools session. The Track menu includes options for creating, duplicating, grouping, deleting, and otherwise modifying tracks and track settings.

Region Menu

Region menu commands allow you to work with Pro Tools *regions*, or "pointers" to available audio or MIDI files or file segments. The Region menu includes options for arranging, grouping, looping, quantizing, warping, and otherwise modifying regions and region settings.

 In Pro Tools HD and Pro Tools LE with DV Toolkit 2 or a Mojo SDI, certain Region menu commands are also available for working with Video regions.

Event Menu

The Event menu contains commands for modifying the time and tempo settings of your Pro Tools session, for working with MIDI and audio events and operations, and for adjusting various properties of MIDI recordings.

AudioSuite Menu

The AudioSuite menu allows you to access all AudioSuite plug-ins currently installed in your system's Plug-Ins folder. AudioSuite plug-ins use Digidesign's proprietary non-real-time, file-based processing plug-in format for Pro Tools. AudioSuite processing applies a plug-in effect permanently, replacing a selection with a new audio file.

Options Menu

The Options menu commands let you select several editing, recording, monitoring, playback, and display options. From this menu, you can enable loop recording, set pre- and post-roll, engage Dynamic Transport mode, set scrolling options, and make other similar choices.

Setup Menu

The Setup menu lets you configure various Pro Tools hardware and software parameters. It includes options for configuring your peripheral devices, such as audio interfaces; configuring host-based processing options; setting disk allocations; mapping I/O settings; configuring session and MIDI settings; configuring Click/Countoff behavior; and modifying your Pro Tools preferences.

Window Menu

Window menu commands allow you to display various Pro Tools windows and palettes. The Window menu includes commands for toggling the Edit, Mix, and Transport windows; the Pro Tools Task Manager; the Workspace and Project browsers; and the Window Configurations, Automation, Memory Locations, Video, Color Palette, Undo History, and other displays.

Help Menu

The Help menu provides links to important Pro Tools documentation, including Keyboard Shortcuts, the DigiRack Plug-Ins Guide, the Pro Tools Menus Guide, and the Pro Tools Reference Guide.

Main Pro Tools Windows

Pro Tools software provides a host of windows and palettes you can use to perform a variety of tasks and functions. The three main windows that you will need to be familiar with to begin working with Pro Tools are the Edit window, the Mix window, and the Transport window.

Edit Window

The Edit window provides a timeline display of audio, MIDI data, video, and mixer automation for recording, editing, and arranging tracks. It displays an audio waveform for each audio track in your session and is the window that you will use to work directly with the audio, MIDI, and video files in your session. Each audio and MIDI track displayed in the Edit window has controls for Record Enable, Solo, Mute, and Automation Mode.

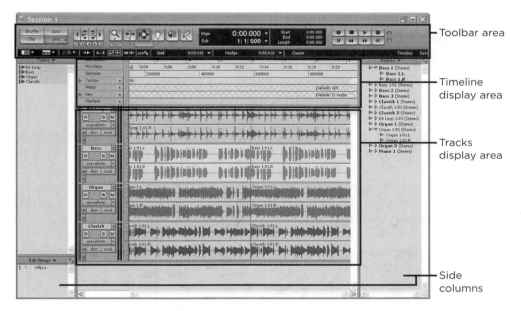

Pro Tools 7 Edit window

Edit Tools

Pro Tools provides several Edit tools in the toolbar area at the top of the Edit window. The Edit tools are used to select, move, trim, and otherwise modify regions in Pro Tools. The functionality of each Edit tool is described in the "Edit Tool Functions" section later in this chapter.

Edit tool buttons

Edit Modes

Pro Tools provides selector buttons in the toolbar area at the top of the Edit window for activating each of its four Edit modes. The Edit modes (Shuffle, Spot, Slip, and Grid) affect the movement and placement of audio and MIDI regions (and individual MIDI notes). The Edit modes also affect how commands such as Copy and Paste function and how the various Edit tools (Trim, Selector, Grabber, and Pencil) work. The Edit modes are described in the "Edit Mode Features" section later in this chapter.

Edit mode buttons

Edit Window Side Columns

The Edit window includes columns on the left and right side that provide additional view and display options for your session data. Along the left side of the Edit window is a vertical column that contains the Track List and Edit Group List. The Track List is at the top of the column and contains a pop-up menu used to display and sort tracks. Directly beneath the Track List is the Edit Group List, where the track grouping status is displayed. (Track grouping is covered in the Pro Tools 110 course.) Both

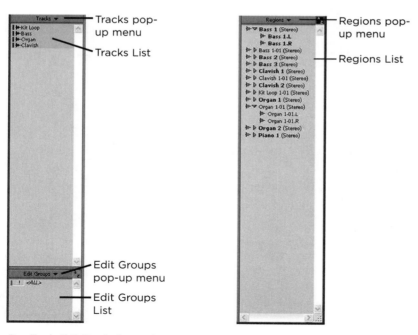

Pro Tools 7 Edit window columns

lists in the left-side column contain display areas and pop-up menus for their respective functions.

Along the right side of the Edit window is a separate vertical column that contains the Region List. The Region List contains a pop-up menu and display area for the audio and MIDI files and file segments (regions) that are currently available in the session. On Pro Tools|HD systems and LE systems with DV Toolkit 2 or an Avid Mojo SDI, the Region List will also display Video files and regions.

Pro Tools lets you customize the display of Edit window side columns to accommodate your needs at any given point in your project. You can show and hide the left and right columns independently or adjust their display widths and heights as needed. By sizing or hiding these columns, you can control the amount of horizontal display area available for your track views in the Edit window, as well as simplify the Edit window view.

To show or hide either the left or right column, do the following:

- Click the double arrow located in the bottom corner beneath the corresponding column you want to show or hide. The double arrow will change and point in the opposite direction, and the column will slide into or out of view.
- Click the corresponding double arrow again to return to the previous view.

To adjust column width or height, follow these steps:

1. Position your pointer over the column separator; the cursor will change into a double-headed arrow.
2. Click and drag on the column separator to adjust its position as needed.

Ruler Views

Rulers are horizontal displays that appear in the Timeline display area of the Edit window, just above your audio, MIDI, and video tracks. Pro Tools' Rulers provide a variety of useful display increments. You can display or hide any combination of the following Rulers in the Edit window:

- **Bars:Beats.** This Ruler is useful for music editors, composers, and musicians.
- **Min:Sec.** This Ruler is useful for radio or those who need absolute time.
- **Samples.** This Ruler displays the system's smallest editing resolution.
- **Time Code and Time Code 2.** These Rulers are primarily used for video and film post-production and some professional music applications (Pro Tools HD or LE with DV Toolkit only).

- **Feet+Frames.** This Ruler is also used for video and film post-production work.
- **Tempo.** This Ruler indicates changes in tempo within the session.
- **Key Signature.** This Ruler indicates key changes within the session.
- **Meter.** This Ruler indicates changes in meter within the session.
- **Markers.** This Ruler displays markers for important track locations within the session.

Additional information on Rulers is provided in the "Time Scales and Rulers" section later in this chapter.

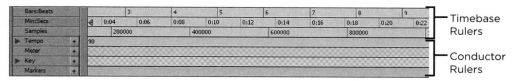

Ruler Views with all Rulers displayed

Mix Window

The Mix window provides a mixer-like environment for recording and mixing audio. In the Mix window, tracks appear as mixer strips (also called *channel strips*). Each track displayed in the Mix window has controls for inserts, sends, input and output assignments, Automation Mode selection, panning, and volume. The channel strips also provide buttons for enabling record, toggling solo and mute on and off, and selecting voice assignments and mix groups.

Signal Routing Controls

The top portion of each channel strip in the Mix window provides controls for routing signals into and out of the track. These controls include Insert selectors, Send selectors, Input selectors, and Output selectors. Insert selectors can be used to add real-time effects processing to a track using one of your loaded plug-ins. Send selectors can be used to route a track's signal to an available bus path or output path. The Input and Output selectors are used to route input and output signals from your audio interface for recording or playback.

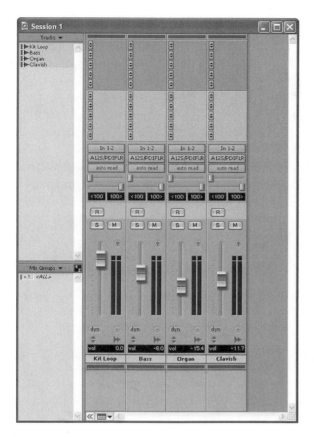

Pro Tools 7 Mix window

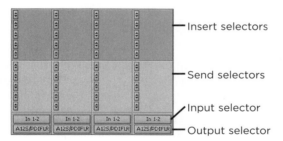

Insert selectors

Send selectors

Input selector

Output selector

Signal routing controls

Record and Playback Controls

Immediately beneath the signal routing controls in the Mix window is a series of controls that are used to set record and playback options. These controls include the Automation Mode selector; the Pan Slider; the Track Record Enable, Solo, and Mute buttons; and the Volume Fader. The Automation Mode selector can be used to enable various recording options for Pro Tools' automatable parameters. The Pan Slider can be used to position the output of a track within a stereo field (or output pair). The buttons for Track Record Enable, Solo, and Mute can be used to activate and deactivate each of these functions for a track during record and playback operations. The Volume Fader can be used to adjust the playback/monitor level of a track.

 The Volume Fader in the Mix window does not affect the input gain (record level) of a signal being recorded. The signal level must be set appropriately at the source or adjusted using a preamp or gain-equipped audio interface.

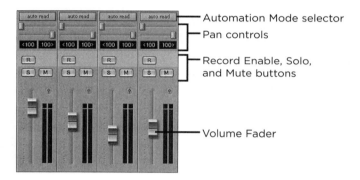

Record and playback controls

Mix Window Side Column

The Mix window includes a single column located on the left side that provides additional view and display options for your session data. The Mix window side column contains the Track List and Mix Group Lists. The Track List is at the top of the column and is used to display and sort tracks. Directly beneath the Track List is the Mix Group List, where the track grouping status is displayed. (Track grouping is covered in the Pro Tools 110 course.) Both lists in the Mix window side column contain display areas and pop-up menus for their respective functions.

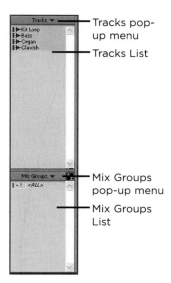

Tracks pop-up menu

Tracks List

Mix Groups pop-up menu

Mix Groups List

Pro Tools 7 Mix window column

As with the Edit window side columns, Pro Tools lets you customize the display of the Mix window side column as needed. You can show and hide the side column, adjust the display width, and adjust the relative height of the lists.

To show or hide the side column, do the following:

- Click the double arrow located in the bottom corner beneath the side column. The double arrow will change and point in the opposite direction, and the column will slide into or out of view.

- Click the double arrow again to return to the previous view.

To adjust column width or height, follow these steps:

1. Position your pointer over the column separator; the cursor will change into a double-headed arrow.

2. Click and drag on the column separator to adjust its position as needed.

Transport Window

Though it is referred to as the Transport window, in many ways this portion of the Pro Tools interface functions more like a control palette than a window. The Transport window provides buttons for various transport functions that operate similarly to the transport controls on a CD player. This window can also be set to display counters (Location Indicators) and MIDI Controls. The Location Indicators in the Transport window typically mirror the Main and Sub Counters at the top of the Edit window.

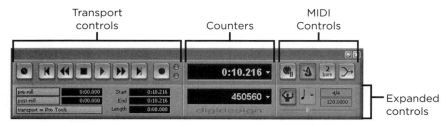

The Transport window, showing transport controls, counters, and MIDI Controls

Counters

Enabling the counters in the Transport window displays the Location Indicators to the right of the transport controls. The Location Indicators provide information for navigation and editing via a Main Location Indicator and a Sub Location Indicator. The Main and Sub Location Indicators can be set for different Time Scale formats (such as Samples, Bars:Beats, or Minutes:Seconds).

The Main Location Indicator in the Transport window provides a convenient way to navigate to a specific time location. To navigate with the Main Location Indicator, follow these steps:

1. Click in the MAIN LOCATION INDICATOR.
2. Type in a location.
3. Press ENTER (Windows) or RETURN (Macintosh). The Timeline insertion point will automatically move to the new location.

MIDI Controls

The Transport window includes a MIDI Controls section, providing options for playing back your session and recording MIDI data. The MIDI Controls let you set options for triggering MIDI recording, playing metronome clicks, overdubbing MIDI, using a tempo map, and setting the tempo and meter. The functions of the MIDI Controls are described in more detail in the "Transport Window MIDI Controls" section later in this chapter.

Tool Tips and Additional Help

The Help menu provides links to various PDF files that are installed with Pro Tools, which you can use as reference sources.

In addition to the Help menu, the Pro Tools 7 interface provides Tool Tips in all main windows to help you solve any question that you may come across in Pro Tools.

When you park the cursor for a few seconds over an abbreviated name (such as a track name or an output assignment) or over an unlabeled icon or tool, Pro Tools will display the full name of the item or its function.

Tool Tips are an optional display element controlled via the Tool Tips Display options in the Display Preferences pane (SETUP > PREFERENCES, DISPLAY tab). Tool Tips settings provide two options: Function shows the basic function of the item, and Details shows the complete name of an abbreviated name or item. Tool Tips can be set to display either or both of these options or they can be turned off altogether.

Edit Tool Functions

The Edit tools located in the toolbar area at the top of the Edit window provide access to Pro Tools' powerful audio and MIDI editing functions. The Edit tools include the Zoomer tool, the Trim tool, the Selector tool, the Grabber tool, the Scrubber tool, the Pencil tool, and the Smart Tool.

Zoomer Tool

Use the ZOOMER tool to zoom in and out on a particular area within a track. Zooming in is often helpful to examine a region or waveform closely.

Normal Zoom mode

The Zoomer tool offers two modes: Normal and Single Zoom mode.

- In Normal Zoom mode, the Zoomer tool remains selected after zooming.
- In Single Zoom mode, the previously selected tool is automatically reselected after zooming.

Single Zoom mode

To use the Zoomer tool, select it and click on the desired point within the track onto which you want to zoom in. Each click zooms all tracks in by one level, and the Edit window is centered on the zoom point.

To zoom in on a particular area in the Edit window, drag with the Zoomer tool over the area you want to view. As you drag, a gray box will appear, indicating the range on which you will be zooming in. Release the mouse to fill the window with the selected portion of the waveform.

 You can also use the Zoomer tool for Marquee Zooming, allowing you to zoom in on a waveform both horizontally and vertically. To use Marquee Zooming, Ctrl-drag (Windows) or Command-drag (Mac OS) with the Zoomer tool.

To zoom out, hold **ALT** (Windows) or **OPTION** (Macintosh) while clicking with the **ZOOMER** tool.

 *Double-click on the **ZOOMER** tool to get a full track view that fills the Edit window with the longest track in the session.*

Zoom Toggle Button

The Zoom Toggle button is located immediately beneath the Zoomer tool in the toolbar area. Use the **ZOOM TOGGLE** button to toggle the view between the current zoom state and a preset/defined zoom state.

Zoom Toggle button

When Zoom Toggle is enabled, the Edit window displays the stored zoom state. Any subsequent changes made to the view while Zoom Toggle is active are also stored in the zoom state. When Zoom Toggle is disabled, the Edit window reverts to the pre–Zoom Toggle view.

Zoom Toggle behavior varies depending on the settings selected in the Zoom Toggle preferences (**SETUP > PREFERENCES, EDITING** tab).

Trim Tool

Use the **TRIM** tool to trim excess audio, MIDI, or video content from the beginning or end of a region. The Trim tool modifies regions non-destructively, leaving the underlying source audio or video files unchanged. This tool allows you to quickly shorten or expand a region, up to the entire length of the source file. The first time you trim a region, Pro Tools automatically adds it to the Region List as a new region (not applicable to video files in Pro Tools LE or M-Powered), with a name derived from the original in order to differentiate it.

Standard Trim tool

 The Trim tool button also provides access to the Time Compression/ Expansion (TCE) Trim tool, the Loop Trim tool, and the Scrub Trim tool (Pro Tools HD only). These additional Trim tools are covered in detail in the Pro Tools 201, 210M, and 210P courses.

Selector Tool

Use the SELECTOR tool to position the playback cursor or to select an area in a track for playback or editing. To position the playback cursor, click with the Selector tool at the point where you want playback to begin. To select an area for playback or editing, drag with the Selector tool across any area on one or more tracks. To add to or remove from an existing selection, hold the SHIFT key and click or click and drag to the left or right.

Selector tool

The Selector tool selects horizontally and vertically, allowing selections across multiple tracks in a single operation. Selected areas appear highlighted in the Edit window. In addition, the selection is displayed in dark gray in the Timeline area at the top of the window.

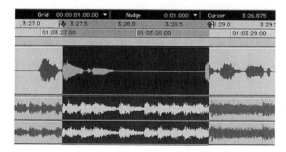

Selection across multiple tracks

You can use the Selector tool to quickly make a lengthy selection, as follows:

1. Click with the SELECTOR tool to position the playback cursor where you want the selection to start.
2. Scroll to the desired endpoint using the scroll bar at the bottom of the Edit window.
3. Shift-click at the desired endpoint to complete the selection.

Grabber Tool

Use the GRABBER tool to select an entire region with a single mouse click, to move regions along the timeline within their current tracks, and to move regions between tracks.

Grabber tool button

To select a region, click anywhere on the region in the Edit window using the GRABBER tool. To move a region along the timeline, click anywhere on the region and drag to the left or right with the GRABBER tool. Dragging a region vertically with the Grabber tool will move the region to another track in your session.

The Grabber tool can be used to position regions in a variety of ways, depending on the Edit mode that is currently selected. Regions can be moved freely along the time-line in Slip mode or can be positioned numerically via a dialog box using Spot mode. Regions can also be made to snap to other regions or to timeline increments using Shuttle or Grid mode, respectively. The Edit modes are discussed in more detail in the "Edit Mode Features" section later in this chapter.

 The Grabber tool button also provides access to the Separation Grabber and Object Grabber tools. These additional Grabber tools are covered in the Pro Tools 201 course.

Scrubber Tool

Use the SCRUBBER tool to "scrub" slowly across Audio tracks in the Edit window to find a particular moment or audio event. Scrubbing originated in tape editing as a process of rocking the tape back and forth past the play head to locate a precise position (usually for the sake of performing a splice). By scrubbing back and forth over an audio waveform in Pro Tools, you can listen closely and zero in on an exact edit point.

To scrub audio in Pro Tools, click on a track in the Edit window with the **SCRUBBER** tool and drag left or right to begin playback at that point. Playback speed and direction vary with mouse movement. Scrubbing becomes smoother as the magnification of the screen increases.

Scrubber tool

 Dragging the Scrubber tool between two adjacent mono or stereo Audio tracks allows you to scrub the two tracks together.

Pencil Tool

Use the **PENCIL** tool to destructively "redraw" waveform data. This tool is most commonly used to repair a pop or click in an audio file. A pop or click appears as a sudden sharp spike in a waveform. This tool becomes active only when the Edit window is zoomed in to the sample level.

Pencil tool

The Pencil tool is also useful for creating and editing MIDI data. The Pencil tool shapes (Freehand, Line, Triangle, Square, and Random) can be used to enter pitches with varying durations and velocities. (Note velocities are determined by the Pencil shape.) The various Pencil tool shapes can be particularly useful for drawing and editing different types of MIDI Control data—common examples include using Line for volume, Triangle for pan, Freehand for pitch bend, and Square or Random for velocity.

 The Pencil tool can also be used for drawing automation breakpoints. Automation editing is covered in the Pro Tools 110 course.

Smart Tool

Use the SMART TOOL to provide instant access to the Selector, Grabber, and Trim tools, and to perform fades and crossfades. The position of the cursor in relation to a region or note or within an automation playlist determines how the Smart Tool functions.

Smart Tool in the Edit window

To use the Smart Tool as a Selector, position the tool over the middle of an audio region, in the upper half. To use it as a Grabber, position it in the lower half. For the Trim tool, position the SMART TOOL near the region's start or end point.

To use the Smart Tool for a fade-in or fade-out, position the tool near an audio region's start or end point, near the top. Once the Fade cursor appears, drag into the region to set the fade length. The fade is created automatically using the Default Fade Settings (from the Editing Preferences tab).

For a crossfade, position the SMART TOOL between two adjacent audio regions, near the bottom. Once the Crossfade cursor appears, drag left or right to set the crossfade length. The crossfade is created automatically using the Default Fade Settings (from the Editing Preferences tab).

Edit Mode Features

Pro Tools has four Edit modes: Shuffle, Spot, Slip, and Grid. The Edit mode is selected by clicking the corresponding mode button on the left side of the toolbar area in the Edit window.

Edit mode buttons

 You can also use function keys F1 (Shuffle), F2 (Slip), F3 (Spot), and F4 (Grid) to set the Edit mode.

The Edit mode affects the movement and placement of audio regions, MIDI regions and notes, and video regions or clips. It also affects how commands, such as Copy and Paste, function, as well as how the various Edit tools work (Trim, Selector, Grabber, and Pencil).

Shuffle Mode

In Shuffle mode, you can move, trim, cut, or paste regions within a track or among tracks, but their movement is constrained by other regions, and the changes you make will affect the placement of subsequent regions on the track. All regions to the right of an edit move back and forth along the timeline in train-car fashion to make space for added material or to close a gap when material is removed.

Use Shuffle mode as a convenient way to make regions line up next to each other neatly, without overlapping or leaving silence between them.

Slip Mode

In Slip mode, you can move, trim, cut, or paste regions freely within a track or among tracks without affecting the placement of other regions on the track. In this mode, it is possible to place a region so that there is space between it and other regions in a track. When the track is played back, this space is silent. It is also possible to move a region so that it overlaps or completely covers another region.

Use Slip mode when you want the Trim, Selector, Grabber, and Pencil tools to work without any restrictions to placement in time.

Spot Mode

In Spot mode, you can move or place regions within a track at precise locations by specifying a destination location in a dialog box. As in Slip mode, edit operations do not affect the placement of other regions on the track.

When Spot mode is enabled, Pro Tools prompts you with a dialog box when working with regions, allowing you to specify the start, end, duration, or other relevant parameters.

Use Spot mode when you want to control the placement or duration of a region using precise numerical values.

Grid Mode

In Grid mode, regions and MIDI notes that are moved, trimmed, or inserted will snap to the nearest time increment using the currently selected Time Scale and Grid size.

Grid mode can be applied using either Absolute or Relative positioning options. (See Chapter 8 for details.)

Use Grid mode for making precise edits and aligning regions and selections using precise time intervals.

Time Scales and Rulers

Every Pro Tools session uses a Main Time Scale and a Sub Time Scale. The Main Time Scale determines the time format used for Transport functions and Grid and Nudge values. The Sub Time Scale provides additional timing reference.

Pro Tools also provides various Rulers to help you navigate along the timeline. Rulers can be displayed for a variety of time formats, including but not limited to the time formats used for the Main Time Scale and Sub Time Scale. Ruler Views appear in the Timeline display area at the top of the Edit window.

Main Time Scale

The Main Time Scale in a Pro Tools session is set to Min:Sec by default, meaning that timeline locations are represented in minutes and seconds relative to the start point of the session. The Main Time Scale determines the timebase units used for the following:

- The Main Counter in the Edit window
- The Main Location Indicator in the Transport window
- Selection Start, End, and Length values
- Pre- and Post-Roll amounts
- Initial Grid and Nudge values

The Main Time Scale can be set to Bars:Beats, Minutes:Seconds, or Samples. The additional Time Scales Time code, Time code 2, and Feet+Frames are available in Pro Tools HD or Pro Tools LE with DV Toolkit 2. To set the Main Time Scale, do one of the following:

- Select the desired timebase using the VIEW > MAIN COUNTER menu.

Main Counter menu

- Select the desired timebase from the MAIN TIME SCALE pop-up menu for the Main Counter at the top of the Edit window.

Main Time Scale pop-up menu

- If a Ruler is displayed for the desired timebase, click on its name so it becomes highlighted.

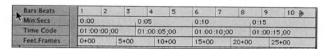

Switching the Main Time Scale using Rulers

Sub Time Scale

The Sub Time Scale in a Pro Tools session is set to Samples by default, meaning that timeline locations are represented as sample-based values, relative to the start point of the session. The Sub Time Scale provides a convenient secondary timing reference.

Like the Main Time Scale, the Sub Time Scale can be set to Bars:Beats, Minutes:Seconds, or Samples (or Time code, Time code 2, or Feet+Frames in Pro Tools HD or Pro Tools LE with DV Toolkit 2). To set the Sub Time Scale, select the desired timebase from the Sub Time Scale pop-up menu for the Sub Counter at the top of the Edit window.

Sub Time Scale pop-up menu

Ruler Display Options

Pro Tools provides two types of Rulers that can be displayed in the Edit window: Timebase Rulers and Conductor Rulers. The Pro Tools Timebase Rulers include the following:

- Bars:Beats
- Min:Sec
- Samples
- Time code (Pro Tools HD or LE with DV Toolkit 2 only)
- Feet+Frames (Pro Tools HD or LE with DV Toolkit 2 only)
- Time code 2 (Pro Tools HD or LE with DV Toolkit 2 only)

 Timebase Rulers are commonly referred to as Timelines in the industry.

The Pro Tools Conductor Rulers include the following:

- Tempo
- Meter
- Markers
- Key Signatures

You can customize your sessions to display only the Timebase and Conductor Rulers you want to work with. To display a Ruler, do one of the following:

- Choose VIEW > RULERS and select the desired Ruler View.
- Click the RULER VIEW SELECTOR and select the desired Ruler from the pop-up menu.

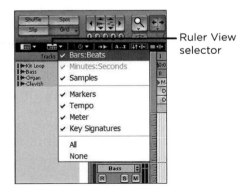

Ruler View selector and pop-up menu

To remove a Ruler from the display, do one of the following:

- Choose VIEW > RULERS and click on a checked Ruler View to deselect it.
- Alt-click (Windows) or Option-click (Mac OS) directly over the Ruler's name in the Timeline display area.

Alt-clicking/Option-clicking on a Ruler name in the Timeline display area

- From the Ruler View selector pop-up menu, click on a checked item to deselect it.

Clicking on a Ruler to deselect it (Pro Tools LE with DV Toolkit 2)

 The Ruler that corresponds to the session's Main Time Scale cannot be deselected. (The Main Time Scale Ruler is indicated by blue highlighting in the Ruler name.)

You also have the option to change the display order of the Rulers, arranging them as needed to best fit your work style. To change the display order for the Rulers, do the following:

- Click directly on the Ruler's name and drag up or down to the desired location.

In the following example, the Time Code Ruler was moved to the top display position:

Rulers before and after moving Time Code display (Pro Tools LE with DV Toolkit 2)

Transport Window MIDI Controls

The Transport window provides access to various MIDI Controls with options for playing back your session and recording MIDI data. The available MIDI Controls include Wait for Note, Metronome Click, Countoff, MIDI Merge Mode, Tempo Ruler Enable, Tempo Resolution selector Meter, and Tempo.

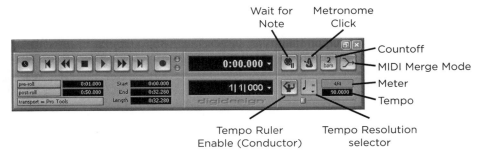

MIDI Controls in the Transport window

Wait for Note

When Wait for Note is selected, recording does not begin until a MIDI event is received. This ensures that you begin recording when you're ready to play and that the first MIDI event is recorded precisely at the beginning of the record range.

 You can set a preference in the MIDI Preferences page to use the F11 key for Wait for Note.

Metronome Click

When Metronome Click is selected, a metronome will sound during playback and recording, as specified by the settings in the Click/Countoff Options dialog box (SETUP > CLICK/COUNTOFF).

To modify the click settings, choose SETUP > CLICK/COUNTOFF or double-click the METRONOME CLICK button in the Transport window. Enter the desired settings in the Click area of the Click/Countoff Options dialog box.

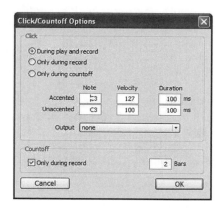

Click/Countoff Options dialog box

 With the Numeric Keypad mode set to Transport, you can press 7 to enable the Click.

 To set the mode of the Numeric Keypad, choose Setup > Preferences > Operation. Select the mode under "Numeric Keypad" in the Transport section.

Countoff

When Countoff is selected, Pro Tools counts off a specified number of measures before playback or recording begins. The number of measures used for countoff is indicated on the face of the Countoff button.

To change the Countoff settings, choose SETUP > CLICK/COUNTOFF or double-click the COUNTOFF button in the Transport window. Enter the desired settings in the Countoff area of the Click/Countoff Options dialog box.

 With the Numeric Keypad mode set to Transport, you can press 8 to enable the Countoff.

MIDI Merge Mode

When MIDI Merge Mode is selected (Merge mode), recorded MIDI data will be merged with existing track material, overdubbing the track. When deselected (Replace mode), recorded MIDI data will replace existing track material.

To engage Merge mode, click on the MIDI Merge Mode button in the Transport window. Click a second time to return to Replace mode.

 With the Numeric Keypad mode set to Transport, you can press 9 to enable MIDI Merge.

Tempo Ruler Enable

When selected, Pro Tools uses the tempo map defined in the Tempo Ruler to control the tempo during playback and recording. When deselected, Pro Tools switches to Manual Tempo mode and ignores the tempo map.

In Manual Tempo mode, you can enter a BPM value in the Tempo field or tap in the tempo as follows:

1. Click the TEMPO RULER ENABLE button (aka the CONDUCTOR button) so it becomes unhighlighted.
2. Click in the TEMPO field so it becomes highlighted.
3. Tap the T key on your computer keyboard repeatedly at the new tempo.

To compute the new tempo, Pro Tools averages the last eight (or fewer) taps to determine the correct tempo. The computed BPM value appears in the Transport's Tempo field.

The tempo can also be adjusted by moving the Manual Tempo Slider or by typing a value directly into the Current Tempo field when you are in Manual Tempo mode.

Tempo Resolution Selector

The Tempo Resolution selector button is used to set the note value that gets the beat. (The default value is a quarter note.) Changing this value will change the song playback tempo, in that note durations will change while BPM remains constant.

To change the note value assigned to a beat, click on the Tempo Resolution selector button and choose a new note value from the drop-down list.

Meter Display

The Current Meter display indicates the session's current meter based on the play location. Double-click the Current Meter display to open the Meter Change dialog box.

Tempo Field

The Current Tempo field displays the session's current tempo based on the play location. In Manual Tempo mode, you can enter a BPM value directly into this field. In addition, when the Tempo field is selected, you can tap in a tempo from a MIDI controller.

PART II

Working with Sessions

Overview

Part II provides information and instructions for working with Pro Tools sessions to accomplish common audio production tasks. In the early chapters, you will learn processes for creating and configuring sessions, creating audio and MIDI recordings, and keeping session files organized. As you progress through the chapters, you will learn how to import audio and movie files, how to set up virtual instrument plug-ins, how to use selection and navigation techniques to work with audio and MIDI recordings, and how to edit your work using Edit modes, edit commands, and moving and trimming operations. In the final chapters, you will learn about Pro Tools' mixing and automation functions, plug-in operations, and mixdown and bouncing operations, as well as processes for burning a completed mix on CD from your operating system.

Chapter 3

Creating Your First Session

This chapter covers the basics of working with Pro Tools sessions. It introduces session configuration options, playback and navigation options, and session saving and opening operations.

Objectives

After you complete this chapter, you will be able to:

- Choose appropriate session parameters for a project
- Create and name tracks
- Navigate your session for playback and editing
- Save, locate, and open sessions on available hard drives

Notes

Introduction

Before you can begin working with audio or MIDI in Pro Tools, you need to have a Pro Tools session open. This chapter covers the basics of creating a session, adding tracks to your session, navigating your session, and saving and reopening sessions.

Configuring a Pro Tools Session

With your Pro Tools software running, you can begin a new recording project by creating a new session document. As discussed in Chapter 2, creating a session sets up a standard hierarchy of folders for the session and its associated files. The characteristics of your recording will be determined by the settings you choose for the session and for the tracks you add to the session.

Choosing Session Parameter Settings

To create a new Pro Tools session, choose FILE > NEW SESSION. The New Session dialog box will appear, asking you to name the session and configure the session parameters. The New Session dialog box includes selections for audio file type, sample rate, I/O settings, and bit depth.

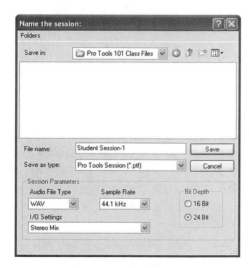

The New Session dialog box

Audio File Type

Pro Tools stores audio as WAV, AIFF, or SD II (Mac OS only) files. WAV is the default file type on all platforms. Use the default (WAV) format unless you intend to work primarily with imported files that are in one of the other formats.

Sample Rate

Pro Tools supports 44.1- or 48-kHz sample rates on all systems. Sample rates of 88.2 and 96 kHz are available with an Mbox 2 Pro, a Digi 002 or Digi 002 Rack, or any 003 family interface, while HD-series systems also support sample rates of 176.4 and 192 kHz. To optimize the file sizes in your session, choose the lowest sample rate that meets the needs of the project.

 The SD II (Sound Designer II) file format (available on Mac OS only) does not support sample rates above 48 kHz.

A sample rate of 44.1 kHz, the industry standard for audio CDs, is typically adequate for home- and small-project studio recordings. Higher sample rates can be chosen for demanding projects to capture a greater frequency response from the source audio and to minimize sound degradation throughout the project lifecycle. However, with higher sample rates come greater disk space requirements for your session (see Table 3.1 in the "Bit Depth" section of this chapter).

For more details on sample rates, see the "Sample Rate and Frequency Resolution" section in Chapter 1.

I/O Settings

Pro Tools provides preset input and output configurations for Stereo Mix or various surround sound options (Pro Tools HD only), such as 5.1 Mix I/O. You can also choose Last Used to load the settings from your last session. Use the settings that match the intended output of your final mix. For the Pro Tools 101 course, we will use the Stereo Mix setting only.

 Use the STEREO MIX setting whenever you are recording music or other audio intended for a general consumer market, such as music to be burned to audio CDs or to be posted as MP3 files.

Bit Depth

Pro Tools allows you to record in 16-bit or 24-bit audio resolution. Note that 24-bit audio is available when using hardware that supports 24-bit digital I/O, even if it does not support 24-bit conversion for analog I/O. The 16-bit option generates smaller files and is typically adequate for basic recordings destined for audio CDs. The 24-bit option provides a greater dynamic range in your recorded audio (see the "Bit Depth and Amplitude Resolution" section in Chapter 1) and lowers the noise floor. This option should be used for high-end recordings that include very quiet passages (such as a classical orchestra piece), recordings that require intensive processing, and recordings intended for media that support higher resolution audio, such as DVD.

 For highest quality audio, record at 24 bits and properly dither down, if needed, during the final mix. Dithering is covered in the Pro Tools 110 course.

Table 3.1 shows the relationship between sample rate, bit depth, and hard disk space consumption for the configurations supported in Pro Tools 7.x.

Table 3.1 Audio Recording Storage Requirements

Session Sample Rate	Session Bit Depth	Megabytes/Track Minute (Mono)	Megabytes/Track Minute (Stereo)
44.1 kHz	16-bit	5 MB	10 MB
44.1 kHz	24-bit	7.5 MB	15 MB
48 kHz	16-bit	5.5 MB	11 MB
48 kHz	24-bit	8.2 MB	16.4 MB
88.2 kHz	16-bit	10 MB	20 MB
88.2 kHz	24-bit	15 MB	30 MB
96 kHz	16-bit	11 MB	22 MB
96 kHz	24-bit	16.5 MB	33 MB
176.4 kHz	16-bit	20 MB	40 MB
176.4 kHz	24-bit	30 MB	60 MB
192 kHz	16-bit	22 MB	44 MB
192 kHz	24-bit	33 MB	66 MB

Creating the Session

After choosing your session parameters, enter a name for the new session, navigate to a valid audio drive for your session, and click SAVE to save your session-related files to the current directory. The new Pro Tools session will open, with no tracks in the Edit and Mix windows.

 You can configure Pro Tools to automatically add a click track to new sessions. Choose SETUP > PREFERENCES and select the MIDI tab. Enable the option for AUTOMATICALLY CREATE CLICK TRACK IN NEW SESSIONS.

Adding Tracks

Once you've created a new session, you will need to create and name new tracks. In Pro Tools, tracks are where audio, MIDI, and automation data are recorded and edited. Audio and MIDI data can be edited into regions that are copied or repeated in different locations to create loops, to rearrange sections or entire songs, or to assemble material from multiple takes. You add tracks to a Pro Tools session using the New Tracks dialog box.

The New Tracks dialog box

To add tracks to your session, choose TRACK > NEW to open the New Tracks dialog box, then choose the number of tracks and track format, type, and timebase using the dialog box controls.

 Numerous shortcuts are available for working with the New Tracks dialog box, including the following:

Change track format	*Ctrl+left/right arrow (Windows) or Command+left/right arrow (Mac OS)*
Change track type	*Ctrl+up/down arrow (Windows) or Command+up/down arrow (Mac OS)*
Change track timebase	*Ctrl+Alt+up/down arrow (Windows) or Command+Option+up/down arrow (Mac OS)*
Add/Remove rows	*Ctrl+Shift+up/down arrow (Windows) or Command+Shift up/down arrow (Mac OS)*

Track Number

The New Tracks dialog box allows you to add multiple tracks to your session simultaneously. To add multiple tracks with the same format, type, and timebase, enter the number of tracks to add in the TRACK TOTAL field. To add multiple tracks using different configurations, click on the ADD ROW button (plus sign).

You can simultaneously add as many tracks with as many different configurations as your session will allow.

 Tracks will be added to your session in the order shown in the New Tracks dialog box. To rearrange the track order, click on the MOVE ROW control and drag the row to a new position.

Arranging tracks using the Move Row control

Track Format

Within the New Tracks dialog box, you can choose a format for the track or tracks you are adding to your session. Available options include mono, stereo, or multi-channel formats, depending on the type of track you are adding and the type of system you are using. (Multi-channel formats are available on Pro Tools|HD systems only.) Stereo tracks provide the added benefit of automatically linking both channels for editing, mixing, and region renaming, although control over each individual channel of the stereo pair is not possible.

Track Type

Track types supported in Pro Tools 7.4 include:

- Audio tracks
- MIDI tracks
- Instrument tracks
- Video tracks
- Auxiliary inputs
- VCA Masters (Pro Tools HD only)
- Master faders

Any combination of the supported track types can be added using the New Tracks dialog box.

 Pro Tools M-Powered and Pro Tools LE without the DV Toolkit 2 or a Mojo SDI do not include Video tracks in the New Tracks dialog box, since they can have only a single Video track, which is created when you import video into your session.

Audio Tracks

Audio tracks allow you to import/record and edit an audio signal as a waveform. Audio tracks can be mono, stereo, or any supported multi-channel format.

Pro Tools LE and M-Powered systems can create up to 32 voiceable tracks in a session, while Pro Tools|HD systems can create up to 256 such tracks; however, the session sample rate, the number of voices your hardware supports, and the continuity of your audio will determine how many tracks you can actually play back and record simultaneously.

MIDI Tracks

MIDI tracks store MIDI note and controller data. Pro Tools includes an integrated MIDI sequencer that lets you import/record and edit MIDI data in much the same way that you perform these operations when working with audio files. MIDI data appears in tracks in the Pro Tools Edit window, referencing the same timeline as audio tracks.

Note that you do not specify a track format for MIDI tracks, since no audio passes through the track; MIDI tracks are data-only.

Instrument Tracks

Instrument tracks combine the functions of MIDI tracks and auxiliary inputs (see the "Auxiliary Inputs" section below) into a single track type, making them ideal for composing with soft synths, sound modules, and all your other MIDI devices.

Video Tracks

Video tracks let you add or import video to the Timeline. Pro Tools M-Powered and LE let you add or import one Video track per session and use a single video clip on the track. Pro Tools HD and Pro Tools LE with DV Toolkit 2 or a Mojo SDI let you add multiple Video tracks to the Timeline and use multiple video files and video regions on each Video track. Only one Video track can be active, or *online*, at any time.

Auxiliary Inputs

An Auxiliary Input track can be used as an effects send, a destination for a submix, an input to monitor or process live audio (such as audio from a MIDI source), or a control point for any other audio routing task. Auxiliary Inputs can be mono, stereo, or any supported multi-channel format.

VCA Master Tracks

VCA Master tracks are available in Pro Tools HD only. These tracks emulate the operation of voltage-controlled amplifier channels on analog consoles. Traditional VCA channel faders are used to control, group, or offset the signal levels of other channels on the console. In similar fashion, a Pro Tools VCA Master track is associated with a Mix group, and the controls of the tracks in the Mix group can then be modified by the controls on the VCA Master.

 VCA Masters are covered in depth in the Pro Tools 310I course.

Master Faders

A Master Fader is a single fader used to control hardware output levels and bus paths. Master Fader tracks control the overall level of the audio tracks that are routed to the session's main output paths or buses. In Pro Tools, you can create a Master Fader track for mono, stereo, or any supported multi-channel format.

 Example: *Suppose you have 24 tracks in a session with tracks 1 through 8 routed to Analog Output 1–2, tracks 9 through 16 routed to Analog Output 3–4, and tracks 17 through 24 routed to Analog Output 5–6. You might want to create three Master Faders, one to control each of the output pairs.*

Timebase

The Track Timebase can be set to Samples or Ticks. In Pro Tools 7.0 and later, all track types can be set to either sample-based or tick-based, with different tracks set to different timebases, as needed.

Audio tracks are sample-based by default, meaning that audio regions and events have absolute locations on the timeline, regardless of tempo or meter changes specified in the session. By contrast, MIDI and Instrument tracks are tick-based by default, meaning that MIDI regions and events are fixed to Bar and Beat locations and move relative to the sample timeline as meter and tempo changes occur.

Pro Tools 7.4 introduces the ability to enable audio tracks for Elastic Audio processing. Sample-based Elastic Audio–enabled tracks let you apply real-time or rendered Elastic Audio processing by editing in Warp view, applying Quantize functions, and using the TCE Trim tool. Tick-based Elastic Audio–enabled tracks can also automatically adjust to match tempo changes in your session and conform to the session's tempo map.

You select whether a track is sample-based or tick-based when you create it; however, you can change timebases later as needed.

 Sample-based editing and tick-based editing are covered in more detail in the Pro Tools 110 and 210M courses.

Naming Tracks

When you create tracks in Pro Tools, they are added to the session using generic names, such as Audio 1, Audio 2, MIDI 1, and so on. To change a track name to something more meaningful, double-click the track name within the Edit window or the Mix window. A dialog box will appear, allowing you to rename the track.

The Track Name dialog box

 In Pro Tools 7.2 and later you can also name a track by right-clicking on the track name and choosing RENAME from the pop-up menu.

Using the Track Name dialog box, you can also add comments to a track and cycle through the tracks in your session, renaming and adding comments to each, using the Next and Previous buttons. Comments you add will be displayed in the Comments area at the bottom of the channel strip (Mix window).

 Press CTRL+LEFT/RIGHT ARROW (Windows) or COMMAND+LEFT/RIGHT ARROW (Mac OS) in the Track Name dialog box to cycle through your tracks and rename each without leaving the keyboard.

Deleting Tracks

When you delete tracks, your audio or MIDI region data will remain in the Region List, but your arrangement of the regions on the deleted track (the track's playlist) will be lost. This is also true of video regions in Pro Tools HD or Pro Tools LE with DV Toolkit 2 or a Mojo SDI.

 The Track Delete command cannot be undone.

To delete a track, follow these steps:

1. Click the name of the track to select it; Shift-click or Ctrl-click to select multiple tracks.
2. Choose TRACK > DELETE.
3. If all selected tracks are empty, they will be deleted immediately; if any tracks contain data, you will be prompted with a verification dialog box. Click DELETE to permanently remove the selected tracks from the session.

 In Pro Tools 7.2 and later, you can also right-click on a track name and choose DELETE from the pop-up menu to remove all selected tracks.

Adding Audio to Your Session

Once you have created one or more audio tracks in your session, you can begin adding audio, either by recording to your track(s) or by importing existing audio files. When you record audio or import audio from a hard drive (or other volume) into tracks in your session, Pro Tools also places the audio files in the Region List.

Audio recording is covered in Chapter 4, "Making Your First Audio Recording," and audio importing is covered in Chapter 5, "Importing Media into Your Session."

The Playback Cursor and the Edit Cursor

The Edit window displays two different cursors: a playback cursor and an edit cursor. The two cursors are linked by default; however, you can unlink them to meet the needs of a particular situation. When unlinked, the different cursors allow you to play and edit two entirely different areas of a session simultaneously. This can be useful when you are working with a film or video scene or when you are editing a region within a loop.

Throughout this book, we will assume that the playback and edit cursors remain linked, unless otherwise noted.

 Workflows that involve unlinking the edit and playback cursors are included in the Pro Tools 210M and 310M courses.

To link or unlink the playback and edit cursors, choose OPTIONS > LINK TIMELINE AND EDIT SELECTION. The option should be checked (linked) for this course.

Playback Cursor

The playback cursor is a solid, non-blinking line that moves across the screen during playback and indicates where the current playback point is. The playback cursor's exact time location is displayed in the Main and Sub Counters/Location Indicators in the Edit window and Transport window, as well as in the Big Counter window (accessed via the Window menu).

Edit Cursor

The edit cursor is a flashing line that appears when you click the Selector tool in a track. The blinking edit cursor indicates the starting point for any editing tasks that you perform. By making a selection with the edit cursor, you define an area for Pro Tools to perform a desired editing task.

With the Edit and Timeline selections linked and the Pro Tools transport stopped, the playback cursor's location will always match the edit cursor's location.

Setting the Playback Point

With the Edit and Timeline selections linked, you can set the playback point using the Selector tool by clicking directly on a track. To set the playback point on a track using the Selector tool, follow these steps:

1. In the Edit window, click the SELECTOR tool. The cursor will turn into an I-beam.
2. Click and release the mouse button at any point in an existing track.
3. Press the SPACE BAR to begin playback from this point.
4. To stop playback, press the SPACE BAR again.
5. To move to a different playback point in the track, click the SELECTOR at the new position, and press the SPACE BAR again.

You can also set the playback point with any tool selected by clicking on any Ruler in the Timeline display area of the Edit window. This allows you to set the playback point without changing tools. Clicking on a Timebase Ruler provides a common way to set the playback point regardless of whether the Edit and Timeline selections are linked.

Scrolling Options

Pro Tools offers several different display options that determine how the contents of the Edit window are displayed during playback and recording. The three options available on all Pro Tools systems are discussed in the following sections. Two additional options that provide continuous scrolling are available on Pro Tools|HD systems only.

No Scrolling

Scrolling can be turned off by choosing OPTIONS > SCROLLING > NO SCROLLING. This option prevents Pro Tools from scrolling the Edit window during playback and recording as the playback cursor moves off screen, and it does not reposition the window when playback or recording is stopped.

After Playback

To prevent scrolling during playback but have the Edit window reposition to the stop point during playback and recording, use the After Playback scrolling option. To select this option, choose OPTIONS > SCROLLING > AFTER PLAYBACK.

Page

To scroll the Edit window one screen (or "page") at a time as the playback cursor moves across the Timeline, enable the Page scrolling option. To select this option, choose OPTIONS > SCROLLING > PAGE.

When Page scrolling is enabled, the playback cursor moves across the Edit window until it reaches the right edge of the window. Each time the playback cursor reaches the right edge, the entire contents of the window are scrolled, one screen at a time, and the playback cursor continues from the left edge of the Edit window.

 When the zoom magnification of the Edit window is too high, Page scrolling will not function. If you experience problems, decrease the zoom magnification to enable Page scrolling.

Locating the Playback Cursor

At times, the playback cursor might be difficult to find in a session. For example, if the No Scrolling option is selected, the playback cursor will move off screen after it has played past the location currently visible in the Edit window.

To make navigation easier, Pro Tools provides a Playback Cursor Locator, which you can use to jump to the playback cursor when it is off screen.

If the playback cursor is not visible in the Edit window, the Playback Cursor Locator will appear in the Main Timebase Ruler, as follows:

- On the left if the playback cursor is located before the visible area
- On the right if the playback cursor is located after the visible area

Playback Cursor Locator

Playback Cursor Locator

The Playback Cursor Locator is red when any track is record-enabled and blue when no tracks are record-enabled.

To locate the playback cursor when it is off screen, click the **PLAYBACK CURSOR LOCATOR** in the Main Timebase Ruler. The Edit window's waveform display will jump to the playback cursor's current onscreen location.

Saving, Locating, and Opening Existing Sessions

As with most software applications, Pro Tools provides commands for saving and opening your files under the File menu. The following sections describe the options for saving, locating, and opening your session files and other files related to your Pro Tools projects.

Saving a Session

While working in Pro Tools, it is important to save your work often. When you save a session using the two commands explained in the following sections, you are saving only the Pro Tools session file, not its associated files. (A session's audio and fade files are written directly to disk, so you don't have to save them independently.) Consequently, even very large sessions can be saved quickly.

Save Command

Saving can be done manually by choosing the Save command from the File menu. This saves the changes you have made since the last time you saved and writes the session in its current form over the old version. You cannot undo the Save command.

Save As Command

The Save As command is useful for saving a copy of the current session under a different name or in a different hard drive location. Because the Save As command closes the current session and lets you keep working on the renamed copy, it is particularly useful if you are experimenting and want to save successive stages of a session. This way, you can save each major step under a different name, such as Student Session-2, Student Session-2A, and so on. By working this way, you can always retrace your steps if you should want to go back to an earlier version.

To use the Save As feature, follow these steps:

1. Choose FILE > SAVE AS.
2. Type a new name for the session.
3. Click SAVE.

The renamed, newly saved session will then remain open for you to continue your work.

 A third Save command, Save Copy In, is discussed in Chapter 10.

Locating and Opening a Session

Pro Tools provides specialized windows, called *DigiBase browsers*, that you can use to quickly locate, manage, and open Pro Tools sessions and compatible files. DigiBase browsers provide more meaningful search, navigation, file information, and audition capabilities than a standard Explorer or Finder window in your operating system.

If you know the location of the session you want to open, you can do so directly from the File menu (choose FILE > OPEN SESSION). For recently used sessions, choose FILE > OPEN RECENT and select the session that you wish to open from the submenu. In other cases, you can use the DigiBase Workspace browser to help locate a session on your system.

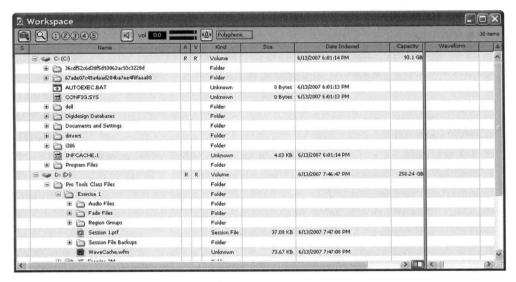

The DigiBase Workspace browser window

Locating a Session

The DigiBase Workspace browser has a powerful search tool that lets you search for Pro Tools file types, such as session files, audio files, and video files.

To search for Pro Tools sessions in the DigiBase Workspace browser, follow these steps:

1. Choose WINDOW > WORKSPACE.

2. In the Workspace window, click the FIND button (magnifying glass) to show the search tools.

3. Select the volumes or folders you want to search by selecting the appropriate check boxes in the Workspace window. Note that you can navigate through the file system by clicking the plus (+) icons (Windows) or arrow icons (Mac OS) to expand or collapse volumes and folders.

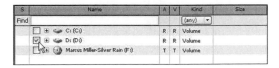

4. Click the drop-down button in the Kind column and select SESSION FILE.

5. Click the SEARCH button. The search results will be shown in the bottom half of the Workspace browser.

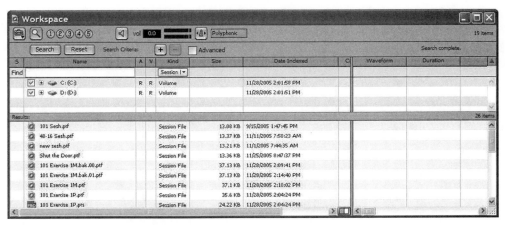

Search results shown in the Workspace browser

Opening a Session

Once you have located the session you are interested in, you can open the session directly from the DigiBase Workspace browser window. (You can also open Pro Tools sessions from the computer's hard drive by double-clicking on the session file or by using the FILE > OPEN SESSION or FILE > OPEN RECENT commands within Pro Tools.)

 Pro Tools can have only one session open at a time. If you attempt to open a session while another session is open, Pro Tools will prompt you to save the current session and close it before opening the selected session.

To open a Pro Tools session using a DigiBase browser, follow these steps:

1. Locate the session file you want to open in the Workspace browser.
2. Double-click the session file.

The Pro Tools session will open with all windows and display options appearing exactly as saved. Any previously created tracks will appear in the Edit and Mix windows, and all audio and MIDI regions associated with the session will appear in the Region List at the right of the Edit window.

 If the Edit or Mix window is not displayed in a session you have opened, you can display it by choosing the corresponding command in the Window menu.

Chapter 4

Making Your First Audio Recording

This chapter covers the steps you will need to take to prepare for and begin recording audio in your Pro Tools sessions. It also describes the types of audio regions your session will include and covers processes for keeping your regions and audio files organized.

Objectives

After you complete this chapter, you will be able to:

- Set up Pro Tools hardware and software for recording audio
- Record audio onto tracks in your session
- Organize your regions and audio files after recording to minimize clutter and optimize your session

Notes

Introduction

Many Pro Tools projects require extensive audio recording. After all, multi-track recording is a cornerstone of what Pro Tools is all about. Whether your projects involve a simple setup in a home studio or an elaborate system in a professional environment, knowing how to get your audio onto tracks in Pro Tools is the first step to creating a successful recording.

Before Recording

Before you begin recording in a session, you should ensure that your system has enough storage space for the project. The amount of storage space consumed by audio regions in a project will vary, depending on the bit depth and sample rate of the session. (See the "Analog-to-Digital Conversion" section in Chapter 1 for a detailed discussion of bit depth and sample rate.)

Audio Storage Requirements

Pro Tools records all audio using sample rates ranging from 44.1 kHz to 192 kHz, with bit depths of 16-bit or 24-bit. At a sample rate of 44.1 kHz, each track consumes 5 megabytes (MB) of disk space per minute for 16-bit audio (mono) and 7.5 MB per minute for 24-bit audio (mono). With increasing bit depth and sample rates, hard disk space consumption increases correspondingly; recording at a sample rate of 88.2 kHz, therefore, consumes twice as much space as recording at 44.1 kHz. Similarly, recording in stereo consumes twice the space of recording in mono.

 Table 3.1 in Chapter 3 shows storage consumption at the different data rates supported by Pro Tools.

Disk Space Window

With a session running, you can monitor storage space and estimate the amount of available record time remaining for your project using the Disk Space window.

To access the Disk Space window, choose WINDOW > DISK SPACE.

The Disk Space window shows the number of continuous track minutes available on each mounted hard drive, using the current session's sample rate and bit depth.

Disk	Size	Avail	%	44.1 kHz 24 Bit Track Min.
C: (C:)	9.3G	507.8M	5.3%	67.1 Min
D: (D:)	18.6G	1.8G	9.8%	245.4 Min

Disk Space window

Preparing to Record

Once you have created a session, added an audio track (or tracks) to record onto, and verified that you have adequate disk space available for your project, you will need to prepare your hardware and software for recording. The general processes you will use to prepare for recording audio are as follows:

1. Check the hardware connections.
2. Record-enable the audio track(s).
3. Set the track input path, level, and pan.
4. Set up a click track (optional).

Checking Hardware Connections

Recording audio involves connecting an instrument, microphone, or other sound source to your Pro Tools system. Most audio interfaces have inputs designated for different sound sources and input types. Before starting to record, you should verify that your sound source is connected to the appropriate inputs of the audio interface and that the signal is being passed through correctly. For basic recording of a single sound source or stereo pair, use the lowest available inputs on your audio interface that match your input device(s) (for example, Inputs 1 and 2 for a stereo pair).

If necessary, check the configuration of your audio interface and/or the hardware setup of your system to ensure correct routing of inputs or to change existing settings. Depending on your audio interface, you can use physical controls or switches, the controls in the Hardware Setup dialog box, or a separate control panel to define which physical inputs and outputs on your audio interface are routed to available inputs and outputs in Pro Tools.

 Example: Suppose you are using an Mbox 2 with a keyboard connected to the direct input (DI) connectors on Inputs 1 and 2 and a microphone connected to each of the Mic input connectors on Inputs 1 and 2. Using the DI-Mic toggle switches on the face of the Mbox 2, you can choose which source is routed to your Pro Tools inputs.

To verify system input routing using the Hardware Setup feature, do the following:

1. Choose SETUP > HARDWARE.
2. Ensure that the input assignments correspond as intended to each of the physical input connections you've made on the system's audio interface.

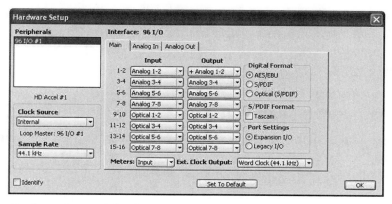

Hardware Setup dialog box (Pro Tools HD 7)

Record-Enabling Tracks

To set up a Pro Tools audio track for recording, click the track's RECORD ENABLE button in either the Edit window or the Mix window. The button will flash red when the track is record-enabled.

When a track has been record-enabled, the Track Fader turns red, indicating that it is now functioning as a record monitor level control.

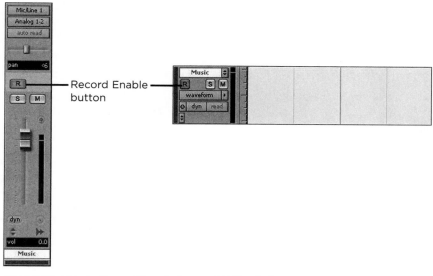

Record Enable buttons: Mix window and Edit window

To record-enable multiple audio tracks, click the RECORD ENABLE buttons on additional tracks. To record-enable all tracks of a particular type in the session, Alt-click (Windows) or Option-click (Mac OS) on any track's RECORD ENABLE button.

Setting Input Path, Level, and Pan

With your sound source connected to the inputs of your Pro Tools interface, you are now ready to set Pro Tools to receive a signal from your source and to pass the signal through the system for recording and monitoring purposes.

Input Path

To set the incoming signal, do the following:

1. Locate the channel strip for the track you will record to in the Mix window.
2. Verify that the input displayed on the Input Path selector matches the input that your sound source is plugged into on your audio interface.

The Input Path selector in the Mix window

3. If necessary, click the INPUT PATH SELECTOR to make changes, selecting the correct input path from the pop-up menu. (Note: Stereo tracks will have a pair of inputs routed to the track.)

Input Path selector pop-up menu

 Example: *Suppose you are recording a vocalist with an acoustic guitar accompaniment onto tracks 1 and 2 of your session, respectively, using an Mbox 2. The vocalist's mic is plugged into Input 1 of your Mbox 2, and the guitar mic is plugged into Input 2. In the Pro Tools Mix window, you should have the Input Path selector for your first track set to* **IN 1 (MONO)** *(to receive signal from Mbox Input 1) and the Input Path selector for your second track set to* **IN 2 (MONO)** *(to receive signal from Mbox Input 2).*

Input Level

As a general rule, input levels should be adjusted to obtain a strong, clean signal without clipping. Unlike when recording to tape, however, you do not need to record at the highest possible level in Pro Tools. Recording too hot may actually raise the noise floor in your final mix long before you begin clipping, degrading your audio quality. For best results, aim for an average input level around –6 dB, keeping the track meter in the yellow range. To do this, adjust the level of your analog source while monitoring the indicator lights on your onscreen track meter.

Adjusting the input level will typically require you to change the source volume, adjust the microphone placement, or modify the incoming signal strength using a mixer or pre-amplifier because record levels cannot be adjusted within Pro Tools. Note that although a track's Volume Fader can be used to increase or decrease play-back levels, the Volume Fader does not affect record levels.

All Pro Tools LE systems and certain M-Audio I/O devices provide pre-amplifier gains for their inputs. For all other Pro Tools I/O devices, record levels are set entirely from the source or pre-I/O signal processing.

In the case of direct digital recording, which involves a one-to-one transfer, the source levels are copied directly to Pro Tools, typically with no level adjustment possible. (Some digital playback devices support digital output gain adjustment, allowing levels to be modified at the source.)

Pan Position

To set the pan position of the incoming signal (the placement of the signal in the stereo field), change the position of the Pan Slider for the track in the Mix window. The Pan Slider is initially set to >0<, signifying the center of the stereo field. The Pan Slider ranges from <100 (hard left) to 100> (hard right). Setting the pan affects the stereo placement of a signal for monitoring and playback purposes only; it has no effect on how the audio files are actually recorded.

Creating a Click Track (Optional)

When you're working with a song or other composition that is bar- and beat-based, you might want to record tracks while listening to a MIDI-generated metronome click in Pro Tools. This ensures that recorded material, both MIDI and audio, will align with your session's bar and beat boundaries.

Aligning track material with beats allows you to take advantage of many useful MIDI editing functions in Pro Tools. It also enables you to arrange your song in sections by copying and pasting measures in Grid mode.

To set up a click track in Pro Tools 7.3 and later, use the CREATE > CLICK TRACK command. This command inserts the Click plug-in on a new auxiliary input track. The Click plug-in is a mono plug-in that creates an audio click during session playback. You can use this audio click as a tempo reference when performing and recording. The Click plug-in receives its tempo and meter data from the Pro Tools application, enabling it to follow any changes in tempo and meter that have been set in a session. Several click sound presets are included for you to choose from.

To create a click track, do the following:

- Choose CREATE > CLICK TRACK. A new click track will be created in your session.

To configure the Click plug-in, do the following:

1. Choose OPTIONS > CLICK to enable the Click option, if not already active (or enable the Metronome Click button in the Transport window).
2. From the Insert panel for the click track (Mix or Edit window), click on the CLICK insert nameplate. The Click plug-in window will open.

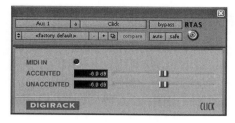

The Click plug-in window

 Details on inserts and plug-ins are presented in Chapter 9, "Basic Mixing Techniques."

3. Click on the drop-down labeled <FACTORY DEFAULT> to select a click sound preset, and set other options as desired.

   • **Accented.** Controls the output level of the accented beat (beat 1 of each bar) of the audio click.

   • **Unaccented.** Controls the output level of the unaccented beats of the audio click.

4. Click the CLOSE icon in the upper-right corner (Windows) or upper-left corner (Mac OS) to exit the Click plug-in window.

5. Choose SETUP > CLICK/COUNTOFF to open the Click/Countoff Options dialog box; set the Click and Countoff options as desired.

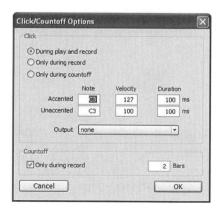

Click/Countoff Options dialog box

 The Note, Velocity, Duration, and Output options in this dialog box are used with MIDI instrument–based clicks and do not affect the Click plug-in.

When you begin playback, a click is generated according to the tempo and meter of the current session and the settings in the Click/Countoff Options dialog box.

Recording and Managing Audio

With your sound source routed to one or more tracks and the desired tracks record-enabled, you are ready to begin recording audio. Pro Tools offers a variety of recording modes that can be used in different audio recording situations. We will use the default mode (Nondestructive Record) for all work done in this course, unless otherwise noted.

 Other record modes are covered in the Pro Tools 110, 201, and 210M courses.

To begin recording audio, do the following:

1. Display the Transport window, if it is not already showing (**WINDOW > TRANSPORT**).

2. To display or hide the expanded view, click the **EXPANDED VIEW** toggle button in the upper-right corner (Windows) or upper-left corner (Mac OS) of the Transport window.

3. Verify that one or more tracks have been record-enabled (see the "Record-Enabling Tracks" section earlier in this chapter).

4. Click the **RECORD** button in the Transport window to enter Record Ready mode. The button will turn red and begin to flash.

The Transport window in Record Ready mode

5. When you're ready, click **PLAY** in the Transport window to begin recording (or press the SPACE BAR).

 You can also press **CTRL+SPACE BAR** *(Windows),* **COMMAND+SPACE BAR** *(Mac OS), or* **F12** *to start recording immediately without first entering Record Ready mode.*

6. When you have finished your record take, click the **STOP** button in the Transport window (or press the SPACE BAR).

Organizing after Recording

You should complete several housekeeping steps immediately after making a successful audio recording to stay organized and to prevent accidents while editing.

Return to Playback Mode

Returning record-enabled tracks to Playback mode will prevent unintended recording onto those tracks during subsequent operations in your session. To return a track to Playback mode and adjust the playback settings, do the following:

1. Click the RECORD ENABLE button on the audio track to take it out of Record Ready mode. The track's Volume Fader will now function as a playback level control rather than as an input-monitoring level control.
2. Click PLAY in the Transport window.
3. Adjust the playback level and panning as necessary.

 If you have overloaded your audio inputs during recording and caused clipping, the topmost indicator on the level meter will stay lit. Click the indicator light to clear it.

Organize Audio Files and Regions

Each time you record audio into Pro Tools, you create a single audio file that appears in both the Region List and the Track Playlist. An *audio file* is an entire unedited, continuous audio recording. Audio files—or *whole-file regions*, as they are known in Pro Tools—are written and stored externally from your session file and have a maximum file size of two gigabytes. Organizing audio files involves maintaining information both within the Pro Tools session and within the external files.

 When you record audio into Pro Tools, the audio files are stored in your session's Audio Files folder by default.

As you begin to edit, you also create smaller, more manageable pieces of the original sound file, called *subset regions*, or simply *regions*. An audio subset region is an electronic pointer, normally stored within the session document, that references some portion of an audio file. Regions can range in length from one sample up to a maximum of two hours. Regions do not store audio information directly, but instead store information used to display, edit, and play back audio information contained in the whole-file region. Organizing audio subset regions is generally internal to Pro Tools only.

Recognizing Audio Files and Regions

The Region List in the Edit window shows all whole-file regions and subset regions that have been used in your session. Pro Tools lists all whole-file regions in boldface type and all subset regions in normal type. When sound files are recorded onto stereo audio tracks, in addition to appearing in boldface type, the word *stereo* is shown in parentheses at the end of the file name. Examples of these file and region types are shown in the following figure.

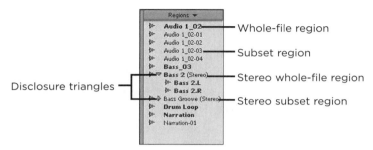

Audio files and regions in the Region List

Note that regions on stereo audio tracks also allow you to view both left and right channels of the region separately by clicking the disclosure triangle.

Audio regions are the smallest pieces of audio data that can be moved or edited within Pro Tools. They are created during normal editing, either by the user or automatically by Pro Tools, and can refer to any type of audio, such as music, dialogue, sound effects, Foley, or automated dialogue replacement (ADR).

Whole-file regions and subset regions can also appear in the Track Playlist. As shown in the following figure, audio regions are displayed on tracks inside Pro Tools using a solid rectangle to clearly delineate their boundaries.

Audio regions as displayed in a Track Playlist

Naming Audio Files and Regions

During recording and editing, Pro Tools gives your audio files and regions default file names. You might want to change the names of the files and/or regions in your session to make them easier to recognize and more meaningful for your purposes.

Default Naming Conventions

When you record audio on a track, Pro Tools names the resulting file (a whole-file region) using the name of the audio track followed by an underscore and the take number for that track (a sequential number determined by the number of times you've recorded on that track). Following are examples of the file names Pro Tools automatically creates after recording for the first time on a mono track and on a stereo track:

Audio 1_01	Where *Audio 1* is the mono track name and *01* is the take number
Music 1_01 (Stereo)	Where *Music 1* is the stereo track name and *01* is the take number

When you edit a whole-file region on a track, Pro Tools retains the original file and creates a new, edited region, appending a hyphen followed by the edit number onto the end of the region name (a sequential number determined by the number of different edits you have created from that whole-file region). Following are examples of the region names Pro Tools automatically creates for the first edit to whole-file regions on a mono track and on a stereo track:

Audio 1_02-01	Where *Audio 1_02* is a whole-file region on a mono track and *01* is the edit number for that region
Music 1_02-01 (Stereo)	Where *Music 1_02* is a whole-file region on a stereo track and *01* is the edit number for that region

Changing File and Region Names

You can change the default name that Pro Tools assigns to a whole-file region or a subset region at any time. To rename a region, double-click the file or region in the Edit window (with the Grabber tool) or in the Region List. The Name dialog box will open.

The Name dialog box

*In Pro Tools 7.2 and later, you can also rename a region by right-clicking on the region in the Edit window or the Region List with any tool and choosing **RENAME** from the pop-up menu.*

When renaming a whole-file region, you can select from the following options in the Name dialog box:

- **Name Region Only.** Renames the file region in Pro Tools but leaves the original file name on the hard drive unchanged.
- **Name Region and Disk File.** Renames the region in Pro Tools and renames the file on the hard drive as well.

Note that when you rename a stereo file or region, both corresponding left and right channels are renamed accordingly.

Removing Audio Regions and Deleting Audio Files

Pro Tools makes an important distinction between removing regions from a session and deleting files from a hard drive:

- When you remove a region from a session, the parent audio file remains on the hard drive and can be used in other regions elsewhere in the session or in other sessions.
- When you delete an audio file from the hard drive, all regions referring to that file are removed from the session, and the file is permanently deleted.

Removing Audio Regions

As your Region List grows in your session, you might want to periodically remove the audio regions you no longer need, in order to reduce the clutter. However, because removing audio regions does not delete the audio files, it will have no effect on hard drive usage of the session.

To remove unwanted audio regions from the Region List, do the following:

1. Select the regions in the Region List that you want to clear. To select multiple regions, Ctrl-click (Windows) or Command-click (Mac OS) on regions individually; to select a continuous range, Shift-click on the top and bottom of the range.

2. Choose **CLEAR** from the Regions pop-up menu.

Regions pop-up menu

3. In the resulting Clear Regions dialog box, click **REMOVE** to remove the regions from the session, while leaving the audio files of any whole-file regions that are cleared on the hard drive.

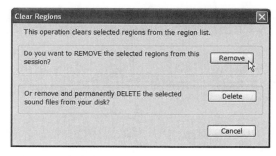

The Clear Regions dialog box

Pro Tools requires that all regions used on any Track Playlist, in the Undo queue, or on the clipboard remain in the Region List. If you attempt to remove a region that has been placed on a track, on the clipboard, or in the Undo queue, the following warning appears:

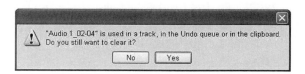

Choose one of the following:

- **Yes.** This option clears the region from the Region List and the corresponding track, Undo queue, or clipboard.
- **No.** This option cancels the Clear command.

Deleting Audio Files

As you work on your session, you will probably accumulate unwanted whole-file regions from test recordings or unusable takes. As you reduce clutter in your Region List, you might want to delete the audio files for such whole-file regions from your hard drive.

By removing audio files from the hard drive, you can free up additional drive space and reduce the overall storage requirements of your session. In addition to utilizing hard drive space more effectively, this will also help reduce the file backup time of your sessions.

To remove regions from the Region List and delete any associated audio files from the hard drive permanently, do the following:

1. Complete Steps 1 and 2 in the "Removing Audio Regions" section earlier in this chapter.
2. In the Clear Regions dialog box, click **DELETE** to remove the selected regions from the Region List *and* permanently delete the files for any selected whole-file regions from your hard drive.

 The Delete option permanently and irreversibly deletes audio files from your hard drive for the current session and all other sessions that reference the audio file. It cannot be undone. Use this command with caution.

Just like when you are removing audio regions, if you attempt to delete a file that has been placed on a track, on the clipboard, or in the Undo queue, you will receive a warning message.

- Click **YES** to permanently remove the file from the session and from the hard drive.
- Click **No** to leave the file untouched in the session and on the hard drive.

Pro Tools will prevent you from permanently deleting an audio file that is referenced by subset regions within the same session. If you attempt to delete an audio file that is referenced by other regions in the session, the following dialog box will appear:

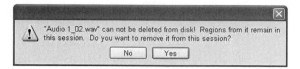

- Click **YES** to remove the whole-file region from the Region List, while leaving the audio file on the hard drive.
- Click **No** to leave the whole-file region untouched in the Region List.

If no other confirmation dialog box appears first, Pro Tools will prompt you with the following warning before completing the Delete command:

- Click **YES** to permanently remove the file from the session and from the hard drive.
- Click **No** to leave the file untouched in the session and on the hard drive.

 To bypass multiple warnings when you are clearing or deleting multiple files or regions, Alt-click (Windows) or Option-click (Mac OS) on the **YES** *or* **No** *button. This will prevent multiple warnings from appearing.*

Chapter 5

Importing Media into Your Session

This chapter introduces various processes for importing audio and video files into a Pro Tools session. It describes file formats and types that can be imported, explains the functions of the Import Audio dialog box and other methods of importing audio, and discusses importing video files.

Objectives

After you complete this chapter, you will be able to:

- Determine whether the bit depth, sample rate, and format of an audio file are compatible with your session
- Explain the functions of each part of the Import Audio dialog box
- Import audio files to the Region List or to Audio tracks in the Edit window
- Import video files to a Video track in the Edit window

Notes

Introduction

Many music and post-production projects require you to work with media files that have been created outside of your current session. Whether you need to add music tracks recorded by others, copy audio sound effects files from a CD, or place a video clip in your session, you will need to know how to use the import options provided in Pro Tools.

Considerations Prior to Import

Pro Tools allows you to import audio and video files that already reside on a hard drive (or other volume) into your session. You can import media using one of several techniques, depending upon the type of media you are importing. Pro Tools can read various file formats directly and can convert certain audio formats on import. Prior to importing a file, you should understand whether the file can be read by your session and how the file will change if it needs to be converted.

Bit Resolution, Sample Rate, and File Format

The types of media files that you can successfully import into a Pro Tools session will depend in part on how the session was originally configured. Some important considerations for audio files include the bit resolution, sample rate, and native file format of your session and of the files you plan to import. Important considerations for video files include the file format, frame rate, and sample rate.

Audio Bit Depth and Sample Rate

The bit depth (or bit resolution) of a Pro Tools session will be either 16-bit or 24-bit, and the sample rate may be any of the following, depending on the system: 44.1 kHz, 48 kHz, 88.2 kHz, 96 kHz, 176.4 kHz, or 192 kHz. These settings are specified when a session is created (see the "Choosing Session Parameter Settings" section in Chapter 3). The bit depth and sample rate of an imported file must match those of the current session in order to play back correctly.

Audio File Formats

The native audio file format used in a Pro Tools session will be one of the following: Sound Designer II (SD II) (available on Mac OS systems only), Audio Interchange File Format (AIFF), or Waveform Audio File Format (WAV), as specified when the session was created (see the "Choosing Session Parameter Settings" section in Chapter 3).

 To determine the bit depth, sample rate, and native file format of an open session, choose SETUP > SESSION.

Pro Tools recognizes compatible file formats that match the sample rate and bit depth of your session, allowing you to add them to the Region List without requiring any file translation. Pro Tools will convert files on import, if necessary. Pro Tools can import many common audio file formats, including the following:

- **Sound Designer II (SD II).** SD II is an Avid and Digidesign proprietary monophonic or stereo interleaved file format supported on Macintosh systems only. This format supports only 44.1- and 48-kHz sample rates and can be imported into a compatible session without requiring conversion.

- **Audio Interchange File Format (AIFF).** This file format is used primarily on Macintosh systems, although the Windows versions of Pro Tools also support this file format. AIFF files can be recorded directly or imported without requiring conversion. The AIFF file format is commonly used with multimedia software programs for Macintosh, such as Final Cut, and is the standard audio file format used by Apple's QuickTime software.

- **Audio Interchange File Compressed (AIFC).** An updated variant of the original AIFF audio file standard for the Macintosh, AIFC allows users to apply audio compression standards to AIFF files. In Avid systems, AIFC file compression is usually turned off; as such, there is essentially no difference between the Avid AIFC format and the standard AIFF file format.

- **Waveform Audio File Format (WAVE/WAV).** Pro Tools reads and plays back any standard WAVE (WAV) format files. However, it records and exports WAV files exclusively in the Broadcast WAV or BWF format. (Like other WAVE files, BWF files are denoted by the .WAV extension.) BWF files store their timestamps in a consistent way that makes them ideal for file interchange operations. BWF is the default file format for both Macintosh and Windows-based Pro Tools systems. BWF/WAV files can be recorded and played back directly (without conversion) on both Macintosh and Windows systems, allowing seamless audio file exchange between these two platforms.

- **MP3 (MPEG-1 Layer-3).** This file format has become the most popular audio file format on the Internet. MP3 files are supported on all common computer platforms and employ file compression of 10:1, while still maintaining good audio quality. Because of their small size and cross-platform support, they are well-suited for use in e-mail messages, web publishing, bulk file transfer, and storage. MP3 files must be converted for import to a Pro Tools session.

- **Windows Media Audio (WMA).** The original WMA Standard format is becoming increasingly widespread and is now second only to MP3 in popularity for compressed audio. The newer WMA Professional format offers higher quality and scales well at smaller file sizes; this format also supports multi-channel surround-sound files, sample rates up to 96 kHz, and 24-bit resolution. Pro Tools converts WMA files on import.

Video File Formats

Pro Tools can import video files in the QuickTime format. Pro Tools HD and Pro Tools LE with DV Toolkit 2 or a Mojo SDI can also import Avid video files. Windows Vista systems also have the ability to import Windows Media (VC-1 AP) files.

Before you import a video file, you should verify the correct frame rate and sample rate, when applicable.

 QuickTime software is required for working with QuickTime files in Pro Tools. If you do not have the software installed on your system, you can obtain a free download from the Apple website (www.apple.com).

Configuration of Stereo Files

No universal stereo file configuration standard exists for software programs on Macintosh and Windows systems. However, two main stereo file configuration formats are common on both platforms: split stereo and interleaved stereo.

These two stereo file formats have no audible difference between them. Instead, the difference is mainly in how the audio is stored in the files. Either format can be imported into Pro Tools, although Pro Tools treats the two formats differently.

- **Split stereo.** In split stereo files, the stereo information is split between separate left and right channel mono files. The split stereo file format is supported on Pro Tools systems (and Avid picture-editing systems); files in this format can be imported directly into a session. The split stereo file format is primarily used for Sound Designer II, AIFF/AIFC, and WAV/BWF files.

- **Interleaved stereo.** In an interleaved stereo file, the stereo information is combined (interleaved) into one single file that contains both left and right channel information. The stereo interleaved file format is not directly compatible with Pro Tools. When interleaved stereo files are imported into a session, Pro Tools rewrites (or translates) the file into corresponding split stereo files. Stereo interleaved files are primarily used for MP3 files and by software programs such as Adaptec/Roxio Toast, Apple Final Cut Pro, and QuickTime.

Importing interleaved stereo sound files is a non-destructive process, meaning it will not destroy or overwrite the original file. Instead, Pro Tools copies the left and right channel information from the original interleaved file into separate split stereo mono file pairs. These files are then placed in the Region List as stereo file pairs, with a corresponding notation of .L and .R appended to each file name.

Importing Audio

When you import audio from a hard drive (or other volume) to your session, Pro Tools places the audio files in the Region List. Pro Tools provides several options for importing audio into a session.

Import Audio Dialog Box

Audio files and regions can be imported directly to the Region List or imported to new tracks using the Import Audio dialog box. This dialog box can be used to add, copy, and/or convert audio files for use in your session.

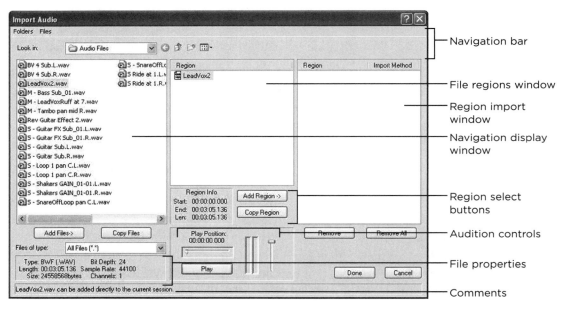

Import Audio dialog box (Windows XP)

The Import Audio dialog box includes seven main areas.

- **File navigation.** A standard navigation bar at the top of the dialog box combined with the navigation display window on the left side allows you to locate and select audio files within an available hard drive or other volume.

- **File properties.** The area below the navigation window lists the file type, length, size, bit depth, sample rate, and number of channels (1=mono, 2=stereo interleaved) for the file selected in the navigation window.

- **Comments.** The area along the bottom of the dialog box describes how the selected file can be imported into the session and provides other information about the file's use in the session.

- **File regions.** The file regions window in the middle of the dialog box shows the currently selected file and lists the whole file region (parent soundfile) and the internal regions (pointers to portions of the parent soundfile) that have been created from the original source file. Two types of icons can appear in the window, indicating whether the item is an audio file or an audio region.

  - **Audio file.** An icon that looks like a document with the upper-left corner turned down and dual audio waveforms is used to identify an audio file.

  - **Audio region.** An icon that looks like reverse highlighted dual audio waveforms is used to identify an audio region.

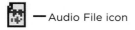 —Audio File icon

 —Audio Region icon

File and Region icons in the Import Audio dialog box

- **Region select buttons.** The Add Region and Convert Region/Copy Region buttons below the file regions window are used to select audio to add, copy, or convert for use in your session. Clicking one of these buttons adds the selected audio file or region to the region import window on the right side of the dialog box.

- **Audition controls.** The controls beneath the region select buttons allow you to start, stop, rewind, and fast-forward playback of the currently selected file or region.

- **Region import.** The area on the right side of the dialog box displays the audio files and regions that you have selected to import to the Region List of your current session and the import method that will be used. You can remove regions from this list using the buttons beneath the display window.

Importing Audio with the Import Command

Audio files can be imported to tracks or directly to the Region List, making the files available to be placed into tracks later.

To import audio, follow these steps:

1. Choose FILE > IMPORT > AUDIO. The Import Audio dialog box will appear.

2. Select an audio file in the navigation window to display its properties and any regions it contains.

3. Place a file or region in the region import window by clicking any of the following buttons:

   - **Add/Add All.** Use these buttons to add files or regions that match the format, bit rate, and sample rate of your session to the Region List. Regions that do not match the sample rate of the current session can also be added using these buttons, but they will not play back at the correct speed and pitch.

 The Add and Add All buttons reference the original audio file(s) and do not copy them into your session's Audio Files folder. If the original file is moved or becomes unavailable, the session may no longer be able to play the file.

   - **Copy/Copy All.** Use these buttons to copy and add files or regions that match the format, bit rate, and sample rate of your session to the Region List. The Copy/Copy All buttons change to Convert/Convert All buttons when the selected audio region does not match the sample rate or bit rate of the current session.

   - **Convert/Convert All.** Use these buttons to copy and convert files or regions that do not match the format, bit rate, or sample rate of your session. All converted files will automatically be copied into new files that match the file format, bit rate, and sample rate of your session, with the correct speed, length, and pitch.

4. Click DONE to begin importing the audio to your session.

5. If any audio files or regions are being copied or converted, a dialog box will appear, prompting you to select a target destination for the newly created files. In the Choose a Destination Folder dialog box, the Audio Files folder for the current session will be selected by default; you can choose an alternate folder or directory location, if desired. Navigate to the desired folder location and choose USE CURRENT FOLDER.

6. When the Audio Import Options dialog box appears, do one of the following:

   - Select **NEW TRACK** and choose a start location from the drop-down list. New audio tracks will be created for each separate region you import, and each region will be placed at the specified location on its track. The imported audio will also appear in the Region List.

   - Select **REGION LIST** to import the audio to the Region List for later use. The imported audio will appear in the Region List in the session but will not be added to any tracks.

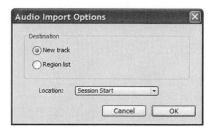

The Audio Import Options dialog box

Importing Audio with DigiBase Browsers

As discussed in Chapter 3, Pro Tools provides specialized *DigiBase browsers* that you can use to quickly locate, manage, and open Pro Tools sessions and compatible files. DigiBase browsers provide powerful search, navigation, file information, and audition capabilities for Pro Tools.

You can import audio into Pro Tools by dragging files into a session from a DigiBase browser window. All files imported in this manner are automatically converted to match the file format, bit depth, and sample rate of the session. If no conversion is necessary, the original files will be referenced and not copied.

Like the Import Audio dialog box, the DigiBase Workspace browser can be used to import audio directly into the Region List or to import audio into new tracks in a session.

Importing to the Region List

To import audio directly into the Region List using the DigiBase Workspace browser, follow these steps:

1. Choose **WINDOW** > **WORKSPACE**.
2. To refine file choices so you can pick from only audio files in specific locations, follow these steps:

   a. In the Workspace window, click the **FIND** button (magnifying glass).

Clicking the Find button in the Workspace browser

   b. Select the volumes and/or folders you want to search by selecting the appropriate check boxes. Note that you can drill down through the file system by clicking the plus (+) icons (Windows) or arrow icons (Mac OS) to expand volumes and folders.

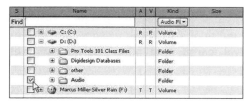

Selecting a volume to search

   c. Click the drop-down button in the **KIND** column and select **AUDIO FILE**.

   d. Click the **SEARCH** button. The search results will be shown in the bottom half of the Workspace browser.

3. Drag the audio files you want to import from the Workspace browser onto the Region List.

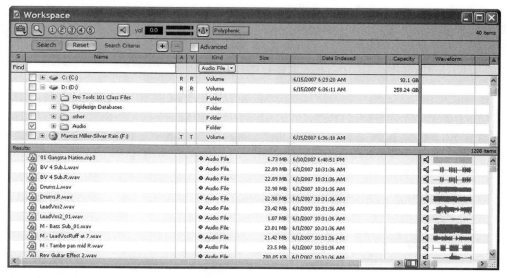

Search results displayed in the Workspace browser

The files are automatically converted to the file format, bit depth, and sample rate of the session, if necessary, and appear in the Region List.

 Imported audio that matches the session sample rate and bit depth will be referenced in its original location and not copied into the current session's Audio Files folder. To force copy a file, Alt-drag (Windows) or Option-drag (Mac OS) the file to the Region List.

Importing to Tracks

To import audio to tracks using the DigiBase Workspace browser, follow these steps:

1. Choose WINDOW > WORKSPACE and use the Workspace browser to locate the audio files you want to import. (See Step 2 in the preceding "Importing to the Region List" section.)

2. Drag the audio files from the browser onto an existing track or tracks in the Pro Tools Edit window.

The files will be automatically converted to the file format, bit depth, and sample rate of the session, if necessary, and will appear on the selected track or tracks.

To create new tracks for audio when importing from the Workspace browser, Shift-drag the audio files from the Workspace browser to the Edit window, or drag the files to empty space at the bottom of the window, if available. Each of the imported audio files will appear at the beginning of a new track.

Batch Importing Audio

With a Pro Tools session open, you can quickly import multiple audio files directly into the session. Selected files that have a different file type, bit depth, or sample rate from the session will be automatically converted on import.

To batch import files, follow these steps:

1. With a Pro Tools session open, browse the files on available volumes using your operating system's Explorer or Finder window.
2. Locate the audio files you want to import and drag them onto the Pro Tools application icon or its alias/shortcut.

Each of the files will appear in the Region List in the session.

Importing Audio from an Audio CD

Pro Tools lets you import tracks from an audio CD using the DigiBase drag-and-drop feature. Since the transfer is made in the digital domain, there is no signal loss. The sample rate for audio CDs is 44.1 kHz. Therefore, if your session's sample rate is set to 48 kHz or higher, Pro Tools will convert the sample rate for the imported audio. Before importing CD audio, set the Sample Rate Conversion Quality Preference accordingly (choose SETUP > PREFERENCES and select the PROCESSING tab).

To transfer audio from an audio CD using a DigiBase browser, follow these steps:

1. Insert the audio CD into your CD-ROM drive.
2. From within your Pro Tools session, choose WINDOW > WORKSPACE.
3. Browse to the CD and select the audio track(s) you want to import.
4. Drag the file(s) onto the Region List of the current session. (You can also place files directly onto tracks by dragging them onto the Edit window.)

Importing Video

To import a video file into Pro Tools, follow these steps:

1. Check the time code settings of the session to make sure they match those of the movie you want to import, and save the session.

2. Choose FILE > IMPORT > VIDEO. A dialog box will open, allowing you to select the video file to import.

3. Navigate to and select the desired QuickTime movie or other video file that is compatible with your system.

4. Click OPEN. The Video Import Options dialog box will appear.

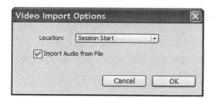

The Video Import Options dialog box

5. Select the desired import options as follows:
   - Select a start location from the LOCATION drop-down list.
   - If you wish to import audio embedded in a QuickTime movie, select IMPORT AUDIO FROM FILE.

6. Click OK.

Pro Tools will import the movie and display it in its own Video track in the Edit window as well as in a floating Video window. The first frame of the movie will be automatically placed at the selected start time in your session. If you chose to import audio, you will be prompted to choose a destination folder for the audio file. After you've selected the desired folder, the audio will appear in a new Audio track in the session.

Depending on the setting of your Video track view, the movie will display in the Edit window as blocks or as a picture-icon (picon) "thumbnail" overview of the frames of the movie it represents. The Video track will show greater or lesser detail, depending on your current zoom level in the Edit window—the closer in you zoom, the greater the number of individual frames that are displayed in the Video track; the farther out you zoom, the fewer the number of individual frames that are visible.

The Video track behaves much like a Pro Tools Audio or MIDI track in that you can move the Video region with the Grabber or other editing tools. This allows you to offset the movie to any start point. You can also edit the Video track by trimming the clip or deleting sections from within it.

In Pro Tools M-Powered and LE, only one video file can be associated with a session at a time. If you want to import a different movie into a session, repeat the preceding steps. The new movie will replace the original in the session.

Pro Tools HD and Pro Tools LE with DV Toolkit 2 or a Mojo SDI let you use multiple Video tracks in your session and add multiple video files and Video regions to each Video track. However, only one Video track can be active at any time.

In Pro Tools M-Powered and LE, the Video track will take its name from the imported video file. Video tracks can subsequently be renamed, in the same manner as other tracks in your session. (See the "Naming Tracks" section in Chapter 3 for details.) However, if you later import a new video file, the track will be renamed to match the imported file.

 Using Frames view to view movie content in the Video track may cause your computer to exhibit reduced or sluggish performance. If this happens, switch the Video track view to Blocks mode. You can also hide the Video track to further optimize performance, if necessary.

Chapter 6

Making Your First MIDI Recording

This chapter covers the basics of recording and working with MIDI data in Pro Tools. It describes how to set up and record onto MIDI-compatible tracks, how to use virtual instrument plug-ins, and how to select different views for the MIDI data on your tracks.

Objectives

After you complete this chapter, you will be able to:

- Identify the two types of MIDI-compatible tracks that Pro Tools provides
- Describe the difference between sample-based operation and tick-based operation
- Prepare a system to record MIDI data
- Set up a virtual instrument to play MIDI data recorded on an Instrument track

Notes

Introduction

Recording and editing MIDI data is similar to working with audio; many of the tools, modes, and menu functions work in a like fashion. However, MIDI data is fundamentally different from audio, and thus some of the processes and operations you use to work with this data will be different. This chapter will introduce additional Pro Tools features that will allow you to record and edit MIDI data in ways that are specific to this protocol.

MIDI Basics

MIDI, or Musical Instrument Digital Interface, is a protocol for connecting electronic instruments, performance controllers, and computers so they can communicate with one another. MIDI data is different from data in an audio file in that it does not store actual sound; instead, it contains information about a performance, such as the pitch, duration, volume, and order of notes to be played.

MIDI devices transmit performance data via MIDI messages, which are composed of 8-bit numbers (encompassing a range of values from 0 to 127) that can include information such as *pitch number* (which indicates an individual note in a scale) and *velocity* (which typically affects an individual note's volume). Up to 16 separate channels of MIDI information can be sent over a single MIDI cable, allowing a single cable path to control multiple MIDI devices or to control a single device that is capable of multi-channel (also known as *multi-timbral*) operation.

Many other kinds of information can be conveyed via MIDI messages, such as pan and general MIDI volume information for instruments that support these, as well as program change events, or commands that tell MIDI instruments which of their available sounds, or *patches*, to use.

A *MIDI sequencer* allows you to store, edit, and play back MIDI information that can be used to control MIDI-compatible devices, such as synthesizers, sound modules, and drum machines. These devices don't necessarily have to be external hardware devices—a growing number of software synthesis and sampling packages are available, enabling you to add internal devices to your host computer.

MIDI in Pro Tools

Pro Tools includes an integrated MIDI sequencer that lets you import, record, and edit MIDI in much the same way that you work with audio. MIDI data appears in tracks in the Pro Tools Edit window, referencing the same Timeline as your Audio tracks. Corresponding channel strips appear in the Pro Tools Mix window and include familiar mixer-style controls that affect MIDI data in the track.

As you learned in Chapter 3, Pro Tools provides two types of tracks for working with MIDI data: MIDI tracks and Instrument tracks.

- A *MIDI track* stores MIDI note, instrument, and controller data only; no audio can pass through a MIDI track. MIDI tracks are often used in conjunction with Auxiliary Input tracks for monitoring and playing back the audio associated with MIDI data.

- An *Instrument track* provides MIDI and audio capability in a single channel strip. Like MIDI tracks, Instrument tracks store note, instrument, and controller data. Instrument tracks can also route audio signals for monitoring and playing back the MIDI events on the track. This capability simplifies the process of recording, editing, and monitoring MIDI data.

Creating MIDI-Compatible Tracks

If your session does not already contain them, you will have to create one or more MIDI-compatible tracks for your MIDI recording. The type of track you use (MIDI track or Instrument track) will depend on how you will work with your MIDI devices, whether you will be using a virtual instrument on the track (see the "Using Virtual Instruments" section later in this chapter), and the complexity of your setup. For basic MIDI recording or working with virtual instruments, you will probably find Instrument tracks easier to use, due to the simplified manner in which they allow you to route audio from your MIDI devices through your session.

To add MIDI-compatible tracks, do the following:

1. Chose **TRACK > NEW** to open the New Tracks dialog box.
2. Input the number of desired tracks in the **TRACK TOTAL** field.
3. Select either **MIDI TRACK** or **INSTRUMENT TRACK** in the Track type drop-down list. The Track Time Base drop-down will default to Ticks.
4. For Instrument tracks, choose between **MONO** and **STEREO** in the Track format drop-down list (additional multi-channel formats are available on Pro Tools|HD systems).
5. Click **CREATE**.

When you create a track for working with MIDI data, the track timebase defaults to Ticks, indicating that the track uses tick-based timing (also known as bar-and-beat-based timing). MIDI operations are typically bar-and-beat-based, whereas audio operations are typically sample-based.

Sample-Based Operation versus Tick-Based Operation

The differences between sample-based operation and tick-based operation are essentially the differences between how audio data is stored and how MIDI data is stored.

Sample-Based Operation

In sample-based operation, recorded information is tied to fixed points in time relative to the beginning of the session. In Chapter 4, you learned how to record audio in Pro Tools. Recorded audio data is stored in audio files as individual audio samples. In Pro Tools, the corresponding audio regions are represented on sample-based tracks by default. Audio material that resides on sample-based tracks is located at particular sample locations on the Timeline. You can think of these sample-based locations as *absolute locations* in time, measured by the number of samples that have elapsed since the beginning of the session. The audio material will not move from its absolute locations in time if the session tempo is later modified—though the audio regions' *relative* bar and beat locations in the session will change.

Audio tracks can also be set to tick-based operation to perform specialized functions, such as tempo matching for REX-type region groups or Elastic Audio. For the purposes of this course, whenever we discuss recording and editing audio, we will assume sample-based operation unless otherwise stated.

Tick-Based Operation

In tick-based operation, recorded information is tied to specific bar|beat locations in an arrangement. When you record MIDI data, Pro Tools uses tick-based timing to determine the locations of your MIDI events. MIDI events are recorded relative to particular bar|beat locations within the composition (such as bar 16, beat 1), and their absolute locations adjust based on the session tempo—if the tempo increases, the MIDI data plays back faster and individual events occur earlier in time; if the tempo decreases, the MIDI data plays back slower and the same events occur later in time. The Elastic Audio capabilities introduced in Pro Tools 7.4 provide the same functionality for audio on tick-based tracks, enabling audio regions to automatically compress or expand to conform to the session tempo.

Pro Tools subdivides the bars and beats in your session into ticks, with 960 ticks comprising a quarter note. Timing can thus be specified with a precision (or resolution) of up to 1/960th of a quarter note when using tick-based operation. You can think of the tick-based locations as *relative locations* in time, measured by the number of bars, beats, and ticks that have elapsed since the beginning of the session. A tick-based event will not move from its rhythmic location relative to other tick-based events in the song if the session tempo is later modified—but a tempo change will cause the event to occur earlier or later in *absolute* time, thereby changing its location relative to any sample-based audio in the session.

Tick-based tracks and data can coexist with sample-based tracks and data within the same Pro Tools session.

 Pro Tools displays relationships between audio and MIDI accurately in the Edit window at all zoom levels, with MIDI event durations drawn proportionally to the timeline, according to tempo.

Though MIDI tracks are typically tick-based, they can also be set to sample-based to perform specialized functions. For the purposes of this course, whenever we discuss MIDI recording and editing, we will assume tick-based operation, unless otherwise stated.

 Sample-based MIDI operations are discussed in the Pro Tools 110 and 310M courses.

Time Scale and Rulers for Working with MIDI

When you are working with MIDI data in a session, you will frequently reference the Bars:Beats Time Scale. This Time Scale can be displayed in the Location Indicators at the top of the Edit window and is represented on the Bar:Beat Ruler. You will also commonly work with tempo, meter, and key signature settings, which are displayed in the Tempo, Meter, and Key Signature Rulers, respectively.

Setting the Timebase Ruler and Main Time Scale

For MIDI recording and editing, you will find it helpful to display the Bar:Beat Timebase Ruler and to set the Main Time Scale to Bars:Beats. This will let you reference any recorded material, track selections, and edits to the bar numbers and beats of the project.

To set the Timebase Ruler and Main Time Scale, do the following:

1. Display the Bar:Beat Ruler by choosing VIEW > RULERS > BARS:BEATS.
2. Set the Main Time Scale to Bars:Beats by doing one of the following:
   - Click on BARS:BEATS in the Ruler View area of the Edit window.
   - Select VIEW > MAIN COUNTER > BARS:BEATS.
   - Click on the MAIN COUNTER SELECTOR in either the Edit window or the Transport window and select BARS:BEATS from the drop-down list.

Main Counter selector in the Edit window

Refer to Chapter 2 for more information on the Main Time Scale.

The Bars:Beats Time Scale displays information in the following format:

1|1|000 (Bar Number|Beat Number|Tick Number)

The first number in this format represents the bar number with respect to the zero point on the session timeline. The second number represents the beat number within the current bar. The final number represents the tick number within the current beat, based on the division of 960 ticks per quarter note.

Tempo, Meter, and Key Signature Rulers

The Tempo, Meter, and Key Signature Rulers allow you to specify the default tempo, meter, and key signature for your session, and to set tempo, meter, and key changes at any point along the session Timeline. To display the Tempo, Meter, and Key Signature Rulers, choose VIEW > RULERS > TEMPO, VIEW > RULERS > METER, and VIEW > RULERS > KEY SIGNATURE, respectively.

Preparing to Record MIDI

Once you have added MIDI-compatible tracks to your session, you will next need to prepare your MIDI device and software for recording. The general processes you will use to prepare for recording MIDI are as follows:

1. Connect a MIDI device.
2. Enable input from the MIDI device.
3. Check the track inputs/outputs.
4. Record-enable the track(s).
5. Set record options.

Connecting a MIDI Device

Recording MIDI data typically involves connecting a keyboard, drum machine, or other MIDI device as an input to your Pro Tools system. Before starting to record, you should verify that the MIDI device you will use for input (also called a *MIDI controller*) is connected to your system through an input on your MIDI interface. You might also need to connect a MIDI output from your interface as a return to this device, or as an input to a separate MIDI device, such as a synthesizer, for monitoring and playback purposes.

Example: *For basic recording in a home or project studio, you might con-nect a MIDI cable from the MIDI Out port on the back of a keyboard to the MIDI In port on an Mbox 2. For monitoring and playback purposes, you could also connect the MIDI Out port of the Mbox 2 to the MIDI In port on the keyboard (assuming onboard sound capabilities) or to the port on a sep-arate synthesizer unit.*

Enabling Input from the MIDI Device

To record from a MIDI controller in Pro Tools, the controller (input device) or MIDI interface must be enabled in the Input Devices dialog box.

To verify that the input device or MIDI interface is enabled, do the following:

1. Choose SETUP > MIDI > INPUT DEVICES. The MIDI Input Enable dialog box will open.

MIDI Input Enable dialog box

2. In the MIDI Input Enable dialog box, select the MIDI device or MIDI inter-face you will record from, if it is not already selected.

3. When you are finished, click **OK**.

 Devices do not need to be selected to receive MIDI data from Pro Tools. For example, a device used exclusively as a sound module does not need to be selected in the MIDI Input Enable dialog box.

Checking MIDI Inputs/Outputs

Next you will need to configure the inputs and outputs of your MIDI-compatible track(s) with the appropriate settings to route the MIDI signals into and out of the tracks.

MIDI Input

The MIDI Input selector in the Edit or Mix window for a MIDI-compatible track is the functional equivalent to the Audio Input Path selector for an audio track. This selector determines which incoming MIDI data gets recorded onto the track in Pro Tools.

On MIDI tracks, the MIDI Input selector is located in the track display (Edit window) or channel strip (Mix window), where the Audio Input Path selector would be on an audio track. On Instrument tracks, however, the MIDI Input selector appears in the Instrument MIDI Controls section. This section of the track display or channel strip is used only for Instrument tracks and needs to be displayed separately.

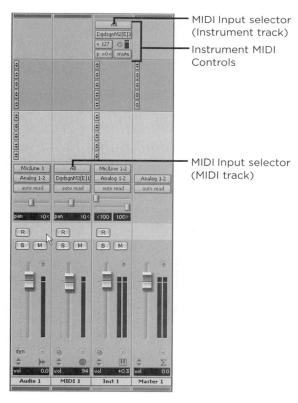

MIDI Input selector
(Instrument track)

Instrument MIDI
Controls

MIDI Input selector
(MIDI track)

The MIDI Input selector in the channel strip as it appears in a MIDI track and an Instrument track

To display the Instrument MIDI Controls, do one of the following:

- Choose VIEW > MIX WINDOW > INSTRUMENTS. The Instrument MIDI Controls will appear at the top of the channel strip.
- Choose VIEW > EDIT WINDOW > INSTRUMENTS. The Instrument MIDI Controls will appear at the head of the track display.

The MIDI Input selectors for MIDI-compatible tracks are set to All by default, such that the MIDI signals from all connected and enabled input devices are received in the track. If you prefer, you can set the MIDI Input to a specific device (port) and channel to more tightly control the routing of MIDI data.

To limit the MIDI input on a track to a specific device, do the following:

1. Click on the **MIDI INPUT SELECTOR** in the Edit or Mix window.
2. Select the MIDI device or interface and port that you want to route to the track.
3. Do one of the following:
   - Select ALL CHANNELS to route all channels from the selected device to the track.
   - Select a specific channel to route only the data being transmitted on that channel to the track.

MIDI Output

The MIDI Output selector for a MIDI-compatible track determines which device or port is used for monitoring and playing back MIDI data. Live MIDI signals can be routed to an audio sound source for monitoring purposes when MIDI Thru is enabled (see the "MIDI Thru" section later in this chapter). Similarly, recorded MIDI signals can be routed to an audio sound source for playback purposes. You use the MIDI Output selector to configure the device or port and the MIDI channel that the signal is routed to for both of these purposes. On MIDI tracks, the MIDI Output selector is located where the Audio Output Path selector would be on an Audio track; on Instrument tracks, it is located in the Instrument MIDI Controls section of the channel strip (Mix window) or track display (Edit window).

To set the MIDI Output, do the following:

1. Click on the **MIDI OUTPUT SELECTOR** in the Edit or Mix window.
2. Select the instrument or port and channel to use for MIDI playback.

Record-Enabling MIDI-Compatible Tracks

The process you use to enable recording on a Pro Tools MIDI track or Instrument track is the same as you use for an Audio track: Simply click the track's RECORD ENABLE button in either the Edit window or the Mix window. As with an Audio track, the Record Enable button flashes red when a MIDI-compatible track is record-ready.

Setting Record Options

Pro Tools provides various record options that are specific to working with MIDI data. You will need to set the MIDI Controls, quantizing, and MIDI Thru options as desired prior to beginning to record onto your MIDI tracks.

MIDI Transport Controls

As discussed in Chapter 2, the Pro Tools Transport window can be set to show MIDI Controls that you can use when recording MIDI data.

To display MIDI Controls in the Pro Tools Transport window, do the following:

1. Select WINDOW > TRANSPORT to display the Transport window, if it is not currently showing.

2. Select VIEW > TRANSPORT > MIDI CONTROLS to display the MIDI Controls, if they are not currently showing.

Before you begin recording MIDI data, take the following steps to set the MIDI Controls:

1. Enable WAIT FOR NOTE or COUNTOFF in the Transport window. Use Wait for Note to begin recording automatically when you begin playing; use Countoff to count off a specified number of measures before recording begins.

2. Enable the METRONOME CLICK, if desired, and specify the settings in the CLICK/COUNTOFF OPTIONS dialog box (SETUP > CLICK/COUNTOFF).

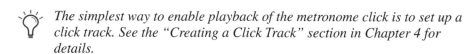

The simplest way to enable playback of the metronome click is to set up a click track. See the "Creating a Click Track" section in Chapter 4 for details.

3. Disable MIDI MERGE for initial recording. Once you have recorded a MIDI pass that you want to keep, you can enable this control to overdub the track.

4. Set the tempo for recording by doing one of the following:

- Engage the TEMPO RULER ENABLE button to follow the tempo map defined in the Tempo Ruler. See the "Setting the Default Tempo" section later in this chapter for more information.

- Disengage the TEMPO RULER ENABLE button to set the tempo using the Tempo field or the Manual Tempo Slider.

5. Set the meter as needed by double-clicking the CURRENT METER display in the Transport window. See the "Setting the Default Meter" section later in this chapter for more information.

The functions of each of the MIDI Controls are described in detail in the "Transport Window MIDI Controls" section in Chapter 2.

Input Quantize

When Input Quantize is enabled, all recorded MIDI notes are automatically aligned, or *quantized*, to a specified timing grid. This creates a style of recording similar to working with a hardware sequencer or drum machine. If you want to preserve the original "feel" of the performance, you might want to disable this option.

To enable Input Quantize, do the following:

1. Choose EVENT > EVENT OPERATIONS > INPUT QUANTIZE. The Event Operations window will open with Input Quantize selected in the Operation drop-down list.

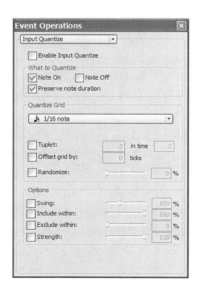

The Event Operations window

2. Select the ENABLE INPUT QUANTIZE option.

3. In the What to Quantize section of the window, choose the MIDI note attributes to quantize:

   • **Note On.** Aligns note start points to the nearest grid value.

   • **Note Off.** Aligns note end points to the nearest grid value.

   • **Preserve Note Duration.** Preserves note durations by moving end points in concert with start points. If this option is not selected, note start and end points can be moved independently, changing the duration of the note.

4. Set the quantize grid to the smallest note value that will be played. All notes in the performance will be aligned to the nearest value on this grid.

5. In the Options section of the Event Operations window, select any other desired options.

   • **Swing.** Shifts every other Grid boundary by the specified percentage value to achieve a "swing" feel. A Swing value of 0% yields no swing, while 100% yields a triplet feel.

   • **Include Within.** Quantizes attacks and releases only when located within the specified percentage of the Quantize Grid.

   • **Exclude Within.** Quantizes attacks and releases only when located outside the specified percentage of the Quantize Grid.

   • **Strength.** Moves notes by a percentage toward the Quantize Grid. Lower percentages preserve the original feel of the notes; higher percentages align the notes more tightly to the Grid.

MIDI Thru

To monitor MIDI-compatible tracks while recording, you need to enable MIDI Thru. When enabled, Pro Tools routes the MIDI signals it receives from your controllers out to the devices and channels assigned by the MIDI Output selectors for your MIDI-compatible tracks.

To enable MIDI Thru, select OPTIONS > MIDI THRU.

 When using MIDI Thru, you might need to disable Local Control on your MIDI keyboard controller. Otherwise, your keyboard could receive double MIDI notes, which can lead to stuck notes.

 You must enable MIDI Thru when using an Instrument track to record MIDI data; if MIDI Thru is not enabled, the track will not receive a MIDI signal.

Using Virtual Instruments

Virtual instruments are the software equivalents of outboard synthesizers or sound modules. A number of virtual instruments are available for Pro Tools in the form of real-time plug-ins. The popular Xpand! instrument plug-in and the newly available Structure Free sample player are two examples. Xpand! is distributed freely as a standard component of Pro Tools 7.1 and later, and it provides a robust library of sounds that can be combined and edited directly in Pro Tools. Structure Free is available as a free download from www.digidesign.com, bringing the world of Structure-compatible sample libraries to any Pro Tools system. Structure Free also comes with its own 600 MB sample library.

Virtual instrument plug-ins can be added to Auxiliary Input tracks or Instrument tracks and triggered by MIDI events routed through the respective tracks.

 Pro Tools 7.x users who do not already have Xpand! can install it using the installer included on the DVD provided with this book. After installing, check the support area of the Digidesign website for the latest updates. Visit www.digidesign.com and click Support.

 Users running Pro Tools 7.3 or later can install the Structure Free sample player using the installer included on the DVD provided with this book. After installing, check the support area of the Digidesign website for the latest updates.

For basic recording with a virtual instrument, you will want to create an Instrument track and connect a MIDI controller as described earlier in this chapter.

Placing a Virtual Instrument on an Instrument Track

A virtual instrument plug-in can be placed directly on an Instrument track, allowing the instrument to be triggered by the MIDI data on the track during playback or by MIDI data passing through the track for live input monitoring.

To add a virtual instrument such as Xpand! or Structure Free to an Instrument track in Pro Tools, do the following:

1. Display the track Inserts, if not already displayed, by choosing VIEW > MIX WINDOW or VIEW > EDIT WINDOW and selecting INSERTS.

2. Click an Insert on the Instrument track, choose PLUG-IN > INSTRUMENT, and select the virtual instrument to use on the track. The track's MIDI Output is automatically assigned to the virtual instrument plug-in, and the instrument's user interface opens.

 Stereo Instrument tracks provide two options for plug-ins: multi-channel plug-ins and multi-mono plug-ins. Choose multi-channel plug-ins for stereo virtual instruments; choose multi-mono plug-ins for mono virtual instruments.

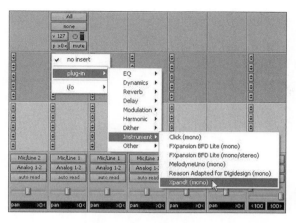

Selecting the Xpand! virtual instrument plug-in

3. Assign the appropriate hardware outputs, if not already selected, using the AUDIO OUTPUT PATH SELECTOR (for monitoring and playback purposes).

4. Set the track's VOLUME FADER to the desired output level.

5. Play notes on your MIDI controller. The meters on the Instrument track will register the instrument's audio output.

 The MIDI signal received on an Instrument track is displayed by the MIDI meter in the Instrument MIDI Controls section of the channel strip or track display. This meter will not register MIDI input until the track is record-enabled. To troubleshoot the signal flow through an Instrument track, you can record-enable the track to verify that the track is receiving a MIDI signal.

 If the MIDI meter on an Instrument track does not register a signal after you have record-enabled the track, verify that the MIDI output has been assigned with the MIDI Output selector.

Using the Xpand! Plug-In

Xpand! is a virtual instrument released by Digidesign's Advanced Instrument Research (A.I.R.) division. Designed to provide fast, efficient ways to access and manipulate high-quality sounds directly from within Pro Tools, Xpand! comes equipped with more than 1,000 preset patches and more than 500 combinable parts. The Xpand! sound library includes synth pads, leads, acoustic and electric pianos, organs, strings, vocals, brass and woodwinds, mallet percussion, ethnic instruments, loops, and more.

Xpand! uses a multi-synthesis engine to combine sampled instruments with synthesized tones, enabling you to create complex sounds with ease. Each Xpand! patch is composed of a blend of up to four individual parts (A, B, C, and D), which are layered together to produce a rich, dynamic texture.

To use the Xpand! plug-in, add the plug-in to an Instrument track as described in the "Placing a Virtual Instrument on an Instrument Track" section earlier in this chapter. The Xpand! user interface will open, displaying selectors for the four layer-able parts.

The Xpand! virtual instrument plug-in user interface

The plug-in initially opens to the <factory default> setting with the Soft Pads:Shimmer sound assigned for part A. Xpand! includes 28 folders of additional presets, with numerous patches to choose from in each.

To select a different patch preset, click either the LIBRARIAN MENU or the PLUGIN SETTINGS SELECT button in the plug-in window and navigate to the desired folder and patch. Each patch calls up a preset Xpand! configuration.

Clicking a selector in the plug-in window to change presets

Each of the four Xpand! sound parts in a preset can be turned on or off at any time by clicking on the blue indicator light next to the part letter. (When toggled off, the indicator turns black.) Sound parts can also be changed individually by clicking on the sound selector in the Xpand! user interface and selecting a different sound source from the pop-up list.

Clicking on an indicator light to turn off a sound part

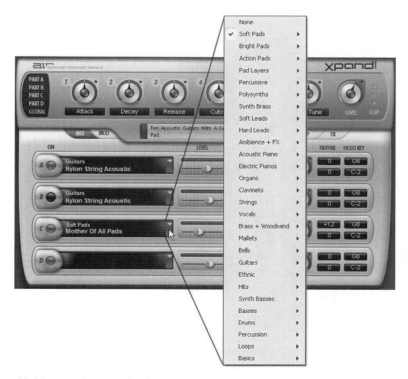

Clicking on the sound selector to change a sound part

The character of your Xpand! virtual instrument plug-in can be further customized by modifying the patch envelope settings and the mix, modulation, arpeggiation, and effects settings for each sound part. See the Xpand! Plug-In Guide for more information. Check www.digidesign.com for Xpand! updates.

Using the Structure Free Plug-In

Structure Free is the latest free virtual instrument released by Digidesign's A.I.R. division. Designed to provide full compatibility with all Structure versions (Structure, Structure LE), Structure Free comes equipped with 60 preset patches and a 64-voice multitimbral sound engine. The Structure Free sample library includes drum kits, drum loops, bass and guitar patches, leads, electric pianos, organs, pads, and more.

Structure Free loads a wide variety of sample libraries, including native Structure, SampleCell, SampleCell II, Kontakt, Kontakt 2, and EXS 24. The plug-in supports all common bit depths, sample rates, and surround formats, up to the capabilities of your Pro Tools system.

To use the Structure Free plug-in, add the plug-in to a stereo Instrument track as described in the "Placing a Virtual Instrument on an Instrument Track" section earlier in this chapter. The Structure Free user interface will open with the Sine Wave patch loaded.

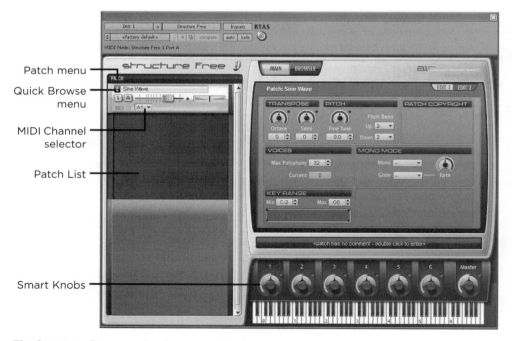

The Structure Free sample player user interface

To select a different patch preset, click the Quick Browse menu and navigate to the desired folder and patch. Each patch calls up a preset Structure Free configuration.

Selecting a patch from the Quick Browse menu

Additional patches can be added to the Structure Free Patch List using the Patch menu at the top of the Patch List. To add a patch, select Patch > Add Patch and navigate to the desired folder and patch. To configure a new patch to play back concurrent with existing patches, set its MIDI channel correspondingly (to MIDI Channel A1, for example).

Adding a patch from the Patch menu

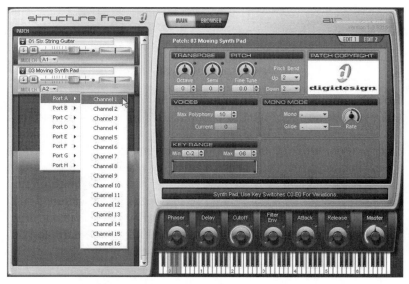

Selecting a MIDI channel from the MIDI Channel selector

Many of the Structure Free patches include *Key Switches*, special MIDI notes or keys that are assigned to change control values rather than trigger notes. Key Switches can toggle between different Smart Knob settings or mute certain parts within a patch. For example, a Key Switch can be assigned to Smart Knobs that control effect settings, allowing you to mix in effects by pressing the appropriate key in the onscreen keyboard or on your MIDI controller.

All available Key Switches appear blue on the screen keyboard. The currently activated Key Switch appears green.

The Structure Free patches can be further controlled and customized using the Smart Knobs and assigning them to MIDI Continuous Controllers, such as modulation wheels, pitch bend wheels, sustain pedals, and so on. See the Structure Free Plug-In Guide for more information.

Setting the Default Meter, Tempo, and Key Signature

Before you begin recording MIDI data, you will need to verify the meter and tempo settings for your session and make any necessary changes. You may also want to set the key signature for your session. The following sections describe how to set the meter, tempo, and key signature for your composition.

Setting the Default Meter

When you open a new session in Pro Tools, the meter defaults to 4/4. If you intend to record with the click and you are working with a different meter, make sure to set the default meter accordingly. Meter events, which can occur anywhere within a Pro Tools session, are registered and displayed using the Meter Ruler.

To set the default meter for a session, do the following:

1. With the Meter Ruler displayed in the Edit window, click on the **ADD METER CHANGE** button (or double-click on the **CURRENT METER** display in the Transport window). The Meter Change dialog box will open.

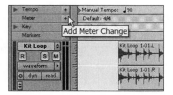

The Add Meter Change button on the Meter Ruler

The Meter Change dialog box

2. Enter the meter you will use for the session and enter 1|1|000 in the **LOCATION** field.
3. Choose a note value for the number of clicks to sound in each measure.
4. Click **OK** to insert the new meter event at the beginning of the session, replacing the default meter.

Setting the Default Tempo

When you open a new session in Pro Tools, the tempo defaults to 120 beats per minute (BPM). If you intend to record with the click and you are working with a different tempo, make sure to set the default tempo accordingly. If you know the tempo you will use for the session, you can insert a tempo event at the beginning of the session.

Tempo events, which can occur anywhere within a Pro Tools session, are registered and displayed using the Tempo Ruler.

To set the default tempo, do the following:

1. With the Tempo Ruler displayed and the Tempo Ruler Enable option selected (see the "Tempo Map Mode" section later in this chapter), click on the ADD TEMPO CHANGE button.

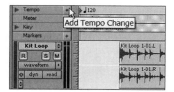

The Add Tempo Change button on the Tempo Ruler

2. Enter the BPM value you will use for the session and enter 1|1|000 in the LOCATION field.

The Tempo Change dialog box

3. To base the BPM value on something other than the default quarter note, select the desired note value.

4. Click OK to insert the new tempo event at the beginning of the session, replacing the default tempo.

Tempo Map Mode

When you create a new Pro Tools session, the session is configured by default to follow the tempo map defined in the Tempo Ruler. The tempo map can be toggled on and off as needed. To use the tempo map, ensure that the TEMPO RULER ENABLE (Conductor) button is activated in the Transport window.

Enabling the Tempo Ruler in the Transport window

Manual Tempo Mode

In Manual Tempo mode, Pro Tools will ignore the tempo events in the Tempo Ruler. In this mode, the tempo can be adjusted by moving the MANUAL TEMPO SLIDER or by typing a value directly into the CURRENT TEMPO field in the Transport window. The tempo can also be tapped in using the **T** key on your computer. Manually adjusting the tempo during playback will momentarily interrupt playback.

To put Pro Tools into Manual Tempo mode, click to deselect the TEMPO RULER ENABLE button in the Transport window.

Setting the Default Key Signature

When you open a new session in Pro Tools, the key signature defaults to C major. If you intend to use the key signature functionality in Pro Tools 7.3 and later, make sure to set the key signature for your session correctly. If you know the key you will use for the session, you can insert a Key Change event at the beginning of the session to change the default key of the session.

Key Change events, which can occur anywhere within a Pro Tools session, are registered and displayed using the Key Signature Ruler.

To set the default key signature, do the following:

1. With the Key Signature Ruler displayed, click on the **ADD KEY SIGNATURE** button.

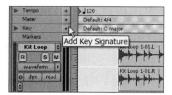

The Add Key Signature button on the Key Signature Ruler

2. Select the mode (major or minor) and key signature you will use for the session and enter 1|1|000 in the **FROM** field.

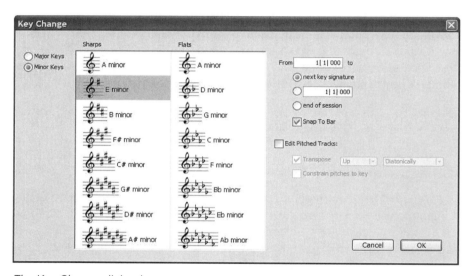

The Key Change dialog box

3. Click **OK** to insert the Key Change event at the beginning of the session.

Recording MIDI

With your MIDI controller connected to your Pro Tools system, the MIDI signal routed to a MIDI-compatible track, and the track record-enabled, you are ready to begin recording.

To record to a MIDI-compatible track, do the following:

1. Display the Transport window, if not already showing (**WINDOW >** **TRANSPORT**).

2. In the Transport window, click the **RETURN TO ZERO** button so the start and end times are cleared. This ensures that you'll start recording from the beginning of the track.

3. Verify that one or more tracks have been record-enabled (see the "Record-Enabling MIDI-Compatible Tracks" section earlier in this chapter).

4. Click the **RECORD** button in the Transport window to enter Record Ready mode. The button will turn red and begin to flash. If you are using Wait for Note, the Play and Wait for Note buttons will turn blue and also flash.

The Transport window in Record Ready mode

5. When ready, click **PLAY** in the Transport window, or if using Wait for Note, simply begin playing. Recording will begin.

> *If you are using Countoff, the Record and Play buttons will flash during the countoff, after which recording will begin.*

6. When you have finished recording, click **STOP**.

To play back the track through a connected virtual instrument or outboard device, do the following:

1. Click the **RECORD ENABLE** button on the Instrument track to disable recording.

2. In the Transport window, click the **RETURN TO ZERO** button.

3. Click **PLAY** in the Transport window to begin playback.

Viewing MIDI Data on MIDI-Compatible Tracks

After you've completed a recording, your MIDI data appears in the Edit window, arranged in a Track Playlist, against the same Timeline as audio. The MIDI information in the playlist can be viewed in a variety of ways, allowing you to perform editing tasks that affect different attributes of the data. This section introduces two of these views: the Notes view and the Regions view. You can quickly toggle between these two views by pressing START+– (Windows) or CTRL+– (Mac OS) whenever your insertion point is located in a MIDI-compatible track.

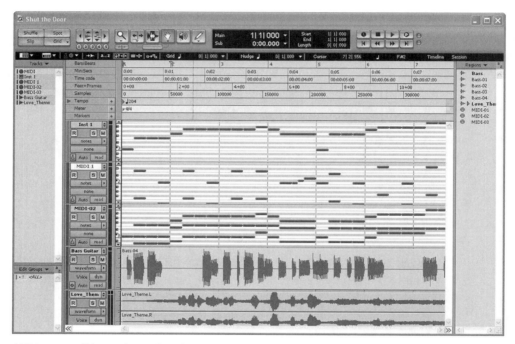

MIDI-compatible tracks and Audio tracks in the Edit window

MIDI Notes View

MIDI data is initially displayed in Notes view by default. This view shows individual MIDI notes in a piano-roll format, with pitch shown on the vertical axis and durations shown on the horizontal axis. The pitch range of MIDI notes displayed in a track depends on the track height and the current zoom value. A mini keyboard on the left side of the track allows you to scroll up or down to see all pitches in the track.

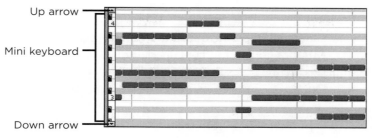

Up arrow

Mini keyboard

Down arrow

Mini keyboard with scroll arrows

When a track's notes do not fit within the track's current height, notes above or below the viewed area are shown as single-pixel lines at the very top and bottom of the track display.

 You can audition pitches on the mini keyboard by clicking on any key. The selected note is played through your connected virtual instrument or outboard device.

If a MIDI-compatible track has been set to a different view, you can easily change back to Notes view using the key command or the Track Display Format selector.

To switch to Notes view, do one of the following:

- Click anywhere in the track with the **SELECTOR** tool and press **START+-** (Windows) or **CTRL+-** (Mac OS) to toggle to Notes view.

- Click on the **TRACK VIEW SELECTOR** for the track and choose **NOTES** from the pop-up list.

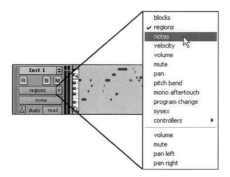

Selecting the Notes view from the Track View selector pop-up list

MIDI Regions View

The MIDI Regions view shows MIDI data grouped together as regions, similar to regions on Audio tracks. MIDI regions act as containers for the MIDI data that falls within the region boundaries. While notes are visible in Regions view, they cannot be individually edited in this view.

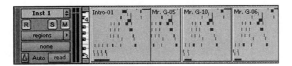

An Instrument track in Regions view

MIDI regions can be selected, copied, cut, and trimmed in the same way as audio regions, allowing you to quickly arrange song phrases or sections.

To switch to Regions view, do one of the following:

- Click anywhere in the track with the **SELECTOR** tool and press **START+−** (Windows) or **CTRL+−** (Mac OS) to toggle to Regions view. Depending on the currently selected view, you might have to toggle twice.
- Click on the **TRACK VIEW SELECTOR** for the track and choose **REGIONS** from the pop-up list.

 *If Zoom Toggle is active, pressing **START+−** (Windows) or **CTRL+−** (Mac OS) will toggle between Notes view and Velocity view.*

Chapter 7

Selecting and Navigating

This chapter covers various selection and navigation techniques that are available in Pro Tools. It includes descriptions of how to use Timeline and Edit selections, how to modify your session view (including setting track sizes and zoom displays), and how to use memory markers for quickly navigating to preset locations and views in your session.

Objectives

After you complete this chapter, you will be able to:

- Describe the difference between a Timeline selection and an Edit selection
- Mark and adjust selection in and out points
- Use the Tab key to navigate a Track Playlist
- Add and delete location markers

Notes

Introduction

Understanding selection and navigation techniques can dramatically improve your efficiency in working with Pro Tools. Whether you need to audition material you have just added to your session or edit a transition between regions, being able to quickly find and select the right material is of key importance. The sections in this chapter introduce you to various processes that you can use to streamline your work in all phases of your project.

Types of Selection

Pro Tools provides two types of selections: Timeline selections and Edit selections. Timeline selections can be made from any Timebase Ruler and are used to set a playback or record range. Edit selections can be made in any track, or in multiple tracks, and are used to set an edit range.

Timeline Selections

At any time while working in your Pro Tools session, you can create a Timeline selection. Timeline selections are frequently made by dragging with the SELECTOR tool and can also be created or adjusted using the TIMELINE SELECTION fields in the Transport window or the TIMELINE SELECTION MARKERS in the Main Timebase Ruler.

 With the Link Timeline and Edit Selection option enabled, a Timeline selection is also made whenever you select audio or MIDI data on a track. See the "Edit Selections" section later in this chapter.

Selecting with the Selector Tool

To make a Timeline selection with the Selector tool, do the following:

1. With any tool selected, move your pointer over a TIMEBASE RULER in the Edit window. The Selector tool will become active.

2. Click and drag with the SELECTOR tool in any Timebase Ruler to select the desired area of the timeline.

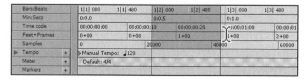

Making a Timeline selection with the Selector tool

The Timeline selection is indicated in the Main Timebase Ruler by blue Timeline Selection Markers (red if a track is record-enabled). The start, end, and length for the Timeline selection are also displayed in the Timeline Selection fields in the Transport window.

Timeline Selection Markers

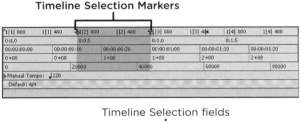

Timeline Selection fields

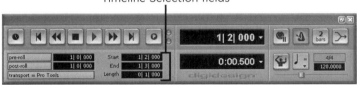

Timeline selection as indicated in Timebase Rulers and the Transport window

Selecting with the Timeline Selection Fields (Transport Window)

You can use the Timeline Selection fields in the Transport window to create a new selection or to adjust a selection numerically from the keyboard.

To create a new selection using the Timeline Selection fields:

1. Click on the first field in the **START** location box to activate it. The selected field will become highlighted.

Field selected in the Transport window

2. Enter the desired value or use the **UP** or **DOWN** arrow keys on the keyboard to increment or decrement the highlighted number one unit at a time.

3. Click on each successive field to select it (or use the **LEFT** and **RIGHT** arrow keys on the keyboard to cycle through the fields).

4. Enter the desired value in each field or select a value using the **UP** or **DOWN** arrow keys.

5. Press **RETURN** or **ENTER** to confirm your entry and move the insertion point to the location you have specified.

6. Do one of the following to complete the selection:

- Repeat this process for the fields in the End location box to specify the end point for the Timeline selection. The fields in the Length selection box will update accordingly.

- Repeat this process for the fields in the Length selection box to specify the length of the Timeline selection. The fields in the End location box will update accordingly.

 When you enter a value in a Timeline Selection field or an Edit Selection field (see the following "Edit Selections" section), Pro Tools will zero out all fields to the right of the changed field. To change a value without affecting the other fields (to move to a different bar but retain the beat and tick number, for example), select the value and press the UP or DOWN arrow key as needed.

 The plus (+) and minus (–) keys provide a calculator-like function allowing you to add or subtract a number from the currently highlighted field. To add or subtract a number from a field, press PLUS or MINUS in any field, followed by the desired number, and press RETURN or ENTER to display the new number or press ESCAPE to cancel.

Selecting with the Timeline Selection Markers

You can also use the Timeline Selection Markers on the Main Timebase Ruler to create a new selection or to adjust an existing selection. To set the Timeline selection by dragging the Timeline Selection Markers, do the following:

1. With any tool selected, move your pointer over a TIMELINE SELECTION MARKER in the Main Timebase Ruler. The TIME GRABBER tool will become active.

2. Drag the TIMELINE SELECTION END MARKER (up arrow) to set the end point.

3. Drag the TIMELINE SELECTION START MARKER (down arrow) to set the start point.

Dragging a Timeline Selection Marker

Edit Selections

When you are working with audio or MIDI data in your Pro Tools session, you can create an Edit selection to work with a portion of the material on a track. Edit selections are frequently made using the Grabber tool or the Selector tool. Edit selections can also be created or adjusted using the Edit Selection fields in the Edit window.

 With LINK TIMELINE AND EDIT SELECTION enabled, an Edit selection is also made whenever you select an area on a Timebase Ruler. See the "Timeline Selections" section earlier in this chapter.

Selecting with the Grabber Tool

The Grabber tool includes three modes: the Time Grabber, the Separation Grabber, and the Object Grabber. Throughout this chapter, the discussion of the Grabber tool refers to the Time Grabber, unless otherwise specified.

 Alternate tools, including the Separation Grabber and Object Grabber, are discussed in the Pro Tools 201 course.

You can use the Grabber tool to make an Edit selection on any region that exists on a Track Playlist. To select a region with the Grabber tool, click once on the region you want to select. The selected region will be highlighted. To select multiple regions, click on the first of the regions you want to select and then Shift-click on the last region. Both regions will be selected, along with all regions in between them.

Selected regions can be moved, copied, cut, or deleted (cleared) from the track.

 MIDI and Instrument tracks are set to Notes view by default. In this view, the Grabber tool is used to select an individual MIDI note (by clicking) or a range of notes (by click-dragging). To select MIDI regions, first set the track to Regions view (see the "MIDI Regions View" section in Chapter 6), then click on a region to select it.

Selecting with the Selector Tool

Using the Selector tool, you can select any portion of audio or MIDI data on your tracks for editing. To make an Edit selection with the Selector tool, do one of the following:

- Click and drag across the area on the track that you want to select.
- Click once to define a starting point for the selection, then Shift-click to define an ending point for the selection.

The selected area becomes highlighted, and the selection can be moved, copied, cut, or deleted (cleared) from the track.

 Double-clicking with the Selector tool will select an entire region; triple-clicking will select the entire Track Playlist.

Selecting with the Edit Selection Fields (Edit Window)

You can use the Edit Selection fields in the Edit window to create a new selection or to adjust a selection numerically from the keyboard.

The Edit Selection fields in the Edit window

To create a new selection using the Edit Selection fields:

1. Click on the first field in the START location box to activate it. The selected field will be highlighted.

2. Enter the desired value or use the UP or DOWN arrow key on the keyboard to increment or decrement the highlighted number one unit at a time.

3. Click on each successive field to select it (or use the LEFT and RIGHT arrow keys on the keyboard to cycle through the fields).

4. Enter the desired value in each field or select a value using the UP or DOWN arrow key.

5. Press RETURN or ENTER to confirm your entry and move the insertion point to the location you have specified.

 Use the slash key (/) to rotate between the Start, End, and Length boxes in the Edit Selection fields. This shortcut also works for the Timeline Selection fields (Transport window).

6. Do one of the following:
   • Repeat this process for the fields in the END location box to specify the end point for the Edit selection. The fields in the Length selection box will update accordingly.
   • Repeat this process for the fields in the LENGTH selection box to specify the length of the Edit selection. The fields in the End location box will update accordingly.

Working with Selections

Pro Tools provides various ways of making selections and adjusting the selection boundaries. The following sections describe some common selection techniques.

Creating Separate Timeline Selections and Edit Selections

The default setting in Pro Tools links Timeline selections and Edit selections together. This means that whenever you select an area on the Timeline, you simultaneously select the same area in each of your tracks. Conversely, whenever you select a region or area in any of your tracks, you simultaneously select the same area in the Timeline. This is often the easiest way to work because it allows you to easily play back areas as you adjust your selection and to easily re-record selected areas on a track.

However, in advanced workflows, you might encounter situations in which you want to unlink the Timeline selection from the Edit selection. You can link and unlink the Timeline selection and Edit selection using the LINK TIMELINE AND EDIT SELECTION toggle button in the Edit window. This toggle is outlined in blue when the Timeline and Edit selections are linked.

Using the toggle button to link the Timeline and Edit selections

For the purposes of this book, we assume that selections are made with the Timeline and Edit selections linked. Workflows that require unlinking the Timeline and Edit selections are introduced in later courses.

Making Selections on Multiple Tracks

Edit selections can be extended across multiple tracks in several different ways. The method you use will depend on the needs of the situation.

Selecting Material on Adjacent Tracks

When you create a selection with the Selector tool, you can drag vertically to select the same area on several adjacent tracks.

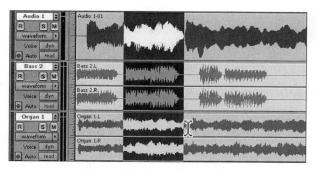

Making a selection across multiple tracks using the Selector tool

Selecting Material on Nonadjacent Tracks

After creating an initial selection on one or more tracks, you can also add the selection to additional tracks by Shift-clicking on those tracks. This technique allows you to make selections on nonadjacent tracks.

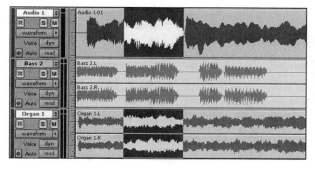

Making a selection across nonadjacent tracks using Shift-click

Selecting Material on Selected Tracks

The Link Track and Edit Selection setting in Pro Tools provides an option for sharing Edit selections among tracks by selecting or deselecting the desired tracks.

In normal operation, selecting a track in Pro Tools brings that track into focus for certain track-level operations, such as grouping, hiding, duplicating, making active/inactive, deleting, and so forth. To select a track, you simply click on the Track Nameplate in the Edit or Mix window. The Track Nameplate becomes highlighted to indicate that the track is selected.

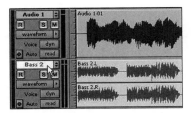

Selecting a track in the Edit window

By enabling the Link Track and Edit Selection setting (**OPTIONS > LINK TRACK AND EDIT SELECTION**), tracks that receive an Edit selection become selected automatically. Conversely, tracks that are selected after an Edit selection is made inherit the Edit selection. This option allows you to copy a selection to additional tracks, remove a selection from individual tracks, and move a selection among tracks by selecting or deselecting tracks, as needed.

The Edit selection can be linked or unlinked from selected tracks using the **LINK TRACK AND EDIT SELECTION** toggle button in the Edit window. This toggle is outlined in blue when the Edit selection is linked to selected tracks.

Using the toggle button to link the Edit selection to selected tracks

To copy an Edit selection to additional tracks with Link Track and Edit Selection enabled, do one of the following:

- To select a range of adjacent tracks, Shift-click on the nameplate of the last track in the range. All tracks in the range will be selected and will inherit the Edit selection.
- To select nonadjacent tracks, Ctrl-click (Windows) or Command-click (Mac OS) on the nameplates of the desired tracks. Each clicked tracked will be selected and will inherit the Edit selection.

To remove an Edit selection from a track while retaining it on others, Ctrl-click (Windows) or Command-click (Mac OS) on the nameplate of the unwanted track to deselect it. The Edit selection will be removed from that track.

To move a selection to a different track, click on the nameplate of the desired destination track to select it. The Edit selection will be removed from the previously selected track(s) and placed on the newly selected track.

Marking Selection In and Out Points during Playback

Another useful selection technique involves using the arrow keys to select a range of material on the fly during real-time playback. This technique can be a great time-saver, as you can make selections while auditioning your session, such as when playing back a record take. To make a selection during real-time playback, do the following:

1. Using the SELECTOR tool, place the cursor near the desired starting point of the track on which you want to make a selection.
2. Begin playback of the track.
3. Press the DOWN arrow key on the keyboard at the point where you want your selection to start. The cursor will mark your starting point on the screen for you during playback.
4. Press the UP arrow key to end your selection. The selected area will be highlighted.
5. Stop playback.

 Pressing an arrow key a second time during playback will update the starting/ending point and cancel the previously selected point.

 If you press the UP arrow key to mark the selection end point without having pressed the DOWN arrow key, the starting playback point will be used as the start of the selection.

Using the Tab Key

When working in a track or multiple tracks, you can use the Tab key to move the cursor based on region boundaries on the current track or on any track included in an Edit selection. To advance the cursor to the next adjacent region boundary to the right, press the TAB key. To withdraw the cursor to the previous adjacent region boundary to the left, press CTRL+TAB (Windows) or OPTION+TAB (Mac OS).

Using the Tab key to make selections can be quite useful when you want your selection to start or end exactly on a region boundary because it allows you to precisely locate the cursor to any region boundary.

- To select from the current cursor position or extend a selection to the next region boundary to the right, press SHIFT+TAB.
- To select from the current cursor position or extend a selection to the previous region boundary to the left, press CTRL+SHIFT+TAB (Windows) or OPTION+SHIFT+TAB (Mac OS).

Selection using Shift-Tab    Selection using Control-Shift-Tab

Extending a selection using the Tab key

 The Tab key is a repeater key; do not hold it down. Doing so will cause your selection to tab rapidly to successive region boundaries.

Tabbing to Transient Points

A variation on the Tab key is the Tab to Transients function. This function is extremely useful for finding the initial peak or modulation in an audio waveform, saving you time and trouble when locating the exact starting point of a sound or louder transition.

To use the Tab to Transients function, do the following:

1. Click on the TAB TO TRANSIENTS toggle button in the Edit window so that it becomes highlighted with a blue outline.

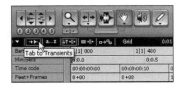

Enabling the Tab to Transients function

2. Press the **TAB** key to move the cursor forward to the next transient to the right. Press **CTRL+TAB** (Windows) or **OPTION+TAB** (Mac OS) to move the cursor backward to the previous transient to the left.

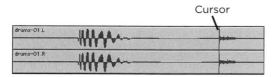

Using Tab to Transients to easily find the start of a drum hit

 The Tab to Transients threshold is set by Pro Tools and is not user-adjustable.

Using the Tab to Transients function is an easy way to make selections that start or end on a sound because it allows you to locate the cursor immediately before an audio peak.

- To select from the current cursor position or extend a selection to the next transient to the right, press **SHIFT+TAB**.
- To select from the current cursor position or extend a selection to the previous transient to the left, press **CTRL+SHIFT+TAB** (Windows) or **OPTION+SHIFT+TAB** (Mac OS).

To disable the Tab to Transients function (so that the Tab key again moves to region boundaries), click the **TAB TO TRANSIENTS** toggle button a second time so that it is no longer highlighted in blue.

 *Press **CTRL+ALT+TAB** (Windows) or **COMMAND+OPTION+TAB** (Mac OS) in Pro Tools 7.4 to toggle the Tab to Transients function on and off.*

Adjusting the Session View

Pro Tools enables you to adjust and customize many aspects of your session display. You can change the display size of individual tracks, change the order in which tracks are displayed, change the Zoom settings for the current view, and create Zoom presets to store and recall commonly used magnification settings.

Adjusting Track Size

Pro Tools allows you to change the size of the track display in the Edit window by adjusting the track height. Track height can be adjusted on a track-by-track basis, allowing each track to be displayed at any of the following heights:

- Micro (Pro Tools 7.3 and later)
- Mini
- Small
- Medium (default track size)
- Large
- Jumbo
- Extreme
- Fit to Window (Pro Tools 7.3 and later)

Larger track heights are particularly useful for precision editing because they show more detail. Smaller track heights are useful for conserving screen space in large sessions.

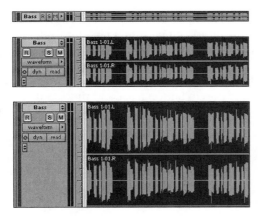

Tracks set to different heights (mini, medium, and large track sizes shown)

 Due to their small size, tracks using the micro or mini display options do not show Voice or Automation Mode selectors in the Edit window. These options remain available in the Mix window.

You can change the height for a track at any time by using the Track Height pop-up menu or by dragging the lower boundary of the track controls column.

To access the Track Height pop-up menu:

1. Click the mouse button anywhere within the amplitude scale area immediately to the right of the desired track meter or click directly on the **TRACK HEIGHT SELECTOR** button (right-pointing triangle to the right of the Track View selector).

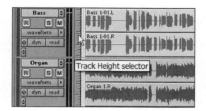 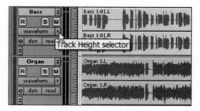

The amplitude scale area and the Track Height selector button

2. Choose the desired height from the pop-up menu.

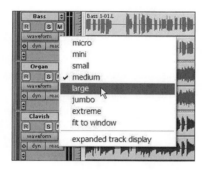

The Track Height pop-up menu

To incrementally resize the track height using the lower boundary of the track controls column:

1. Position your pointer over the lower boundary of any track controls column; the cursor will change into a double-headed arrow.

2. Click on the column boundary and drag up or down. The track height will change in continuous increments.

Press and hold **CTRL** *(Windows) or* **COMMAND** *(Mac OS) while adjusting track height for continuous, non-incremental adjustment.*

To set all tracks in the session to the same height, press the **ALT** *key (Windows) or* **OPTION** *key (Mac OS) and select the desired track height on any track.*

Changing the Track Order

Two common reasons exist for wanting to change the order of tracks in your session.

First, Pro Tools assigns priority to each track in a session based on the track's position: Tracks with higher positions (leftmost in the Mix window or topmost in the Edit window) have priority over tracks in lower positions. If the number of active audio tracks in the system exceeds the total number of voices available during playback, Pro Tools will give precedence to the tracks with the highest priority. Changing the position of a track could determine whether that track is represented during playback in a large session.

Second, arranging tracks in a logical order can simplify your navigation. This can be true even in relatively small sessions. Consider arranging the tracks in your session such that related tracks are displayed together, instruments are displayed in a logical order, or commonly used tracks are presented at the top. The order can be rearranged as needed as you work your way through the editing process.

To change the session's track order, do any of the following:

- In the Edit window, click on the Track Nameplate and drag the track above or below other tracks in the session.
- In the Mix window, click on the Track Nameplate and drag the track to the left or right of other tracks in the session.
- In the Track List, click on the track name and drag it to a higher or lower position in the list.

Clicking on a Track Nameplate and dragging the track to a new position (Mix window)

Track order after repositioning the track

Zoomer Tool

As discussed in Chapter 2, the Zoomer tool includes two modes: Normal Zoom and Single Zoom. Throughout this chapter, the discussion of the Zoomer tool refers to Normal Zoom mode, unless otherwise specified.

The Zoomer tool in Normal Zoom mode

The Zoomer tool can be used to examine a waveform up close for precision editing.

Zooming In and Out

To zoom in, centering on a certain point in a track, do the following:

1. If it is not already selected, click the ZOOMER tool. The pointer will turn into a miniature magnifying glass with a plus sign inside when positioned over a track.

2. Click once at the desired point within the track. The waveform will enlarge within the track display, with the zoom point centered horizontally in the Edit window.

3. To zoom in further, click multiple times. Each successive click zooms all tracks in by one additional level.

To zoom back out, **ALT-CLICK** (Windows) or **OPTION-CLICK** (Mac OS) with the **ZOOMER** tool. While you are pressing the **ALT** key (Windows) or **OPTION** key (Mac OS), the cursor will turn into a miniature magnifying glass with a minus sign inside when positioned over a track. Each successive click zooms all tracks out by one additional level, with the zoom point centered horizontally in the Edit window.

Zooming In on a Range

The Zoomer tool can also be used to zoom in on a particular range, enlarging the range to fill the visible area of the track. To zoom into a range, do the following:

1. If it is not already selected, click the **ZOOMER** tool to select it.

2. Click and drag with the magnifying glass over the horizontal portion of a track that you want to view up close. (To zoom horizontally and vertically, Ctrl-drag [Windows] or Command-drag [Mac OS].) As you drag, a dashed box will appear, indicating the range that you will be zooming in on.

3. Release the mouse. The display will fill the screen with the portion of the waveform you selected, zooming in horizontally to the same level on all tracks simultaneously.

 *Double-click on the **ZOOMER** tool to get a full track view that fills the screen with the longest track in the session.*

Horizontal and Vertical Zoom Buttons

The Edit window includes Zoom buttons in the toolbar area that allow you to adjust the track waveform or MIDI view without using the Zoomer tool. These buttons adjust the display around a cursor position or a selection's center point, keeping the display centered as it changes. Like the Zoomer tool, the Zoom buttons change only the display of the data and do not affect playback. Unlike the Zoomer tool, these buttons zoom in horizontal and vertical directions separately.

The Zoom buttons

From left to right, the Zoom buttons are as follows:

- **Horizontal Zoom Out button.** This button changes the time display of all tracks in the session by compressing the track timeline and audio waveform views inward, showing more time across the screen, with less detail. This adjustment is useful for obtaining a "big-picture" view of your waveform, showing more time on the screen at once.

- **Audio Zoom In and Out button.** This button changes the waveform amplitude display of all tracks in the session by expanding or compressing the track waveform views vertically, making the waveforms appear taller or shorter. Zooming in is useful in distinguishing low-amplitude audio waveforms because amplitude differences are viewed at a higher (taller) display resolution; zooming out is useful in distinguishing high-amplitude audio waveforms because amplitude differences are viewed at a smaller (shorter) display resolution.

- **MIDI Zoom In and Out button.** This button changes the display of MIDI data on all MIDI-compatible tracks in the session by expanding or compressing the note range shown in the track (represented by the track's mini-keyboard). Zooming in shows a narrower range of notes, with each MIDI note displayed larger (fatter); zooming out shows a broader range of notes, with each MIDI note displayed smaller (skinnier).

- **Horizontal Zoom In button.** This button changes the waveform time display of all tracks in the session by expanding the track waveform views outward, showing less time across the screen, with greater detail. This adjustment is useful for distinguishing precise edit points in the waveform because the interval of time shown across the Edit window can be magnified to a very high editing resolution, zooming all the way in to just a few samples.

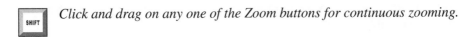

Click and drag on any one of the Zoom buttons for continuous zooming.

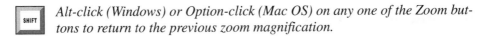

Alt-click (Windows) or Option-click (Mac OS) on any one of the Zoom buttons to return to the previous zoom magnification.

Zoom Presets

Directly beneath the Zoom buttons are five round buttons numbered 1 through 5. These are the Zoom Preset buttons, which are used to store and recall commonly used zoom magnifications. The Zoom Preset buttons are initially set up with factory default settings, giving you incrementally higher horizontal zoom magnifications from preset 1 through preset 5. Each of these presets can be updated to store a zoom setting of your choice. These custom presets are then saved with your session.

Zoom Preset buttons 1 through 5

To store a zoom setting as a zoom preset, do the following:

1. Using either the **ZOOM** buttons or the **ZOOMER** tool, set the screen to the desired zoom display.
2. While pressing the **CTRL** key (Windows) or **COMMAND** key (Mac OS), click one of the five **ZOOM PRESET** buttons, or click and hold a button and select **SAVE ZOOM PRESET** from the pop-up menu. Your zoom setting will be written into the corresponding zoom preset number.

To recall a zoom preset, click your mouse directly on the preset number you want to recall. The zoom setting will be instantly recalled.

*You can also recall Zoom Presets 1 through 5 by pressing the **START** key (Windows) or the **CONTROL** key (Mac OS) followed by a numeral key (1 through 5) on your computer's alpha keyboard.*

Adding Markers to Your Session

Markers can be used to bookmark locations in your session for quick recall. The following sections describe how to add and delete markers, how to use the Memory Locations window and other techniques to recall marker locations, and how to create selections using marker locations.

About Memory Locations

Pro Tools provides up to 999 memory locations, which can be used to store and recall a variety of commonly used display and edit settings. Like zoom presets, memory locations can store horizontal and vertical screen magnification settings. However, memory locations can also do much more.

Memory locations come in two main varieties: markers and selections. Markers are used to store locations on the timeline (playback locations), while selections are used to store Edit selections (edit locations). In this chapter, we will work only with markers.

In addition to storing a timeline location or Edit selection, a memory location can store any of the following optional information to associate with the marker or selection:

- A name for the location/selection
- A zoom setting (horizontal and vertical screen magnification)
- Pre- and post-roll times (covered in a later course)
- The track display settings (show/hide statuses)
- Track height settings
- Group enables (covered in a later course)
- Window configurations (covered in a later course)
- Comments

Any settings stored with a memory location are reestablished when the memory location is later recalled.

Creating a Marker

Markers can be added to a session at any time. Often you will be able to set markers at specified points when playback is stopped. Other times, you might find it useful to add markers on the fly during playback or recording.

Adding Markers at Specified Points

To create a marker at a specified point, do the following:

1. If it is not already displayed, choose VIEW > RULERS > MARKERS to display the Marker Ruler.
2. Place the cursor or make a selection at the desired location in the track, and configure any other display or edit settings that you want to store with the marker.
3. Click the ADD MARKER/MEMORY LOCATION button (plus sign) at the head of the Marker Ruler. The New Memory Location dialog box will appear, prompting you to choose the type of memory location and the parameters you want to store.

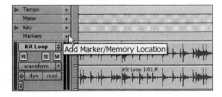

Adding a new marker using the Marker Ruler

4. In the Time Properties section of the dialog box, select **MARKER**.

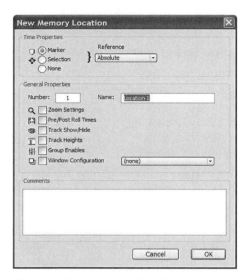

The New Memory Location dialog box

5. In the Reference pop-up menu, choose one of the following two options:
   - **Absolute.** This option sets the marker at a sample-based location on the timeline. The marker will remain at a fixed absolute location in time, regardless of session meter or timing changes.
   - **Bars/Beats.** This option sets the marker at a tick-based location on the timeline. The marker will maintain its relative location with respect to the bars and beats in the session, adjusting its absolute location as the session meter or timing is changed.

6. In the General Properties section of the dialog box, give the marker a descriptive name. This section of the dialog box also allows you to change the marker number, if desired, and select the optional information to associate with the marker. For basic marking, any or all of the optional selections can remain unchecked.

7. Click **OK**. A small yellow marker symbol corresponding to the memory location will appear in the Marker Ruler at the selected location.

Absolute marker symbol on the Marker Ruler

Adding Markers during Playback and Recording

Memory locations can be added during real-time playback and recording in much the same way as they are when playback is stopped. When used this way, a marker stores the cursor position at the time that the operation is initiated.

To create a marker during playback (or recording), do the following:

1. If it is not already displayed, choose VIEW > RULERS > MARKERS to display the Marker Ruler.
2. Start playback (or record) from the desired starting position.
3. Click the ADD MARKER/MEMORY LOCATION button (plus sign) at the head of the Marker Ruler. The New Memory Location dialog box will appear, prompting you to choose the type of memory location and the parameters you want to store.
4. Select the desired options (see steps 4 through 6 in the previous section) and click OK.

 You can also add markers on the fly by pressing ENTER on the numeric keypad during playback or recording.

The Memory Locations Window

The Memory Locations window can be used to view all markers and other memory locations that you have stored. To access the Memory Locations window, choose WINDOW > MEMORY LOCATIONS. The Memory Locations window will open.

The Memory Locations window

Recalling a Marker Location

To recall a marker location, do one of the following:

- In the Memory Locations window, click the entry for the desired marker location.
- On the numeric keypad, type a period, followed by the number that corresponds to the location (1 through 999), and another period.
- Click the corresponding marker symbol in the Marker Ruler.

The marker location will be instantly recalled, and the playback cursor will be positioned at this spot.

Automatically Naming Marker Locations

To save time, you can have Pro Tools automatically name the marker locations you store during playback (and recording) so that you are not prompted with the Memory Locations dialog box each time you initiate a marker. With this feature enabled, Pro Tools gives a default name to all markers based on their number.

To enable auto-naming of marker locations during playback, do the following:

1. If it is not already shown, choose WINDOW > MEMORY LOCATIONS to display the Memory Locations window.
2. Open the Memory Locations menu by clicking on the menu button in the upper-left corner of the dialog box.

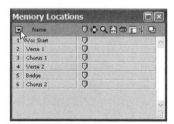

Accessing the Memory Locations menu

3. Select **Auto-Name Memory Location** from the Memory Locations pop-up menu.

Selecting the auto-name option

To disable the Auto-Name Memory Location option, deselect **Auto-Name Memory Location** from the Memory Locations menu.

 Markers can be edited and renamed at any time by double-clicking on the corresponding marker symbols in the Marker Ruler or the Memory Locations window.

Deleting Marker Locations

To delete a single marker that you no longer need, do the following:

1. If it is not already shown, choose **Window** > **Memory Locations** to display the Memory Locations window.
2. Click on the entry that you want to delete.

3. Open the Memory Locations menu by clicking on the menu button, and choose CLEAR "NAME" from the pop-up menu (where "Name" is the marker name). The selected marker will be deleted.

Removing the selected marker

SHIFT *ALT-CLICK (Windows) or OPTION-CLICK (Mac OS) on any entry in the Memory Locations window (or on a symbol in the Marker Ruler) to delete it.*

To delete multiple adjacent markers, select the markers by highlighting them on the Marker Ruler and press DELETE. Note that selections on the Marker Ruler must be made independently from Timeline or Edit selections.

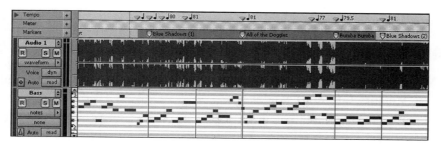

A selection on the Marker Ruler

To delete all markers (and any other memory locations in the session), do the following:

1. If it is not already shown, choose WINDOW > MEMORY LOCATIONS to display the Memory Locations window.
2. Open the Memory Locations menu by clicking on the menu button, and choose DELETE ALL from the pop-up menu. All memory locations will be cleared.

 ALT-SHIFT-CLICK (Windows) or OPTION-SHIFT-CLICK (Mac OS) on any entry in the Memory Locations window to clear all memory locations.

Creating a Selection Using Markers

You can easily select between two previously created markers. This can be handy for quickly selecting song sections that you have marked, such as a verse, chorus, bridge, or guitar solo, for example.

To make a selection between two marker locations, do the following:

1. Click the first marker to recall the stored location.
2. Press the SHIFT key and click the second marker. The area between the two markers will be selected.

Chapter 8

Basic Editing Techniques

This chapter covers the basics of editing audio and MIDI data in Pro Tools. It provides details on playback options, Edit modes, Edit commands, and moving and trimming operations. It also introduces techniques for creating fades and for undoing edit actions.

Objectives

After you complete this chapter, you will be able to:

- Describe the difference between Absolute Grid mode and Relative Grid mode
- Configure the Grid and Nudge values to appropriate intervals for your session and work preferences
- Use standard editing commands and Pro Tools–specific editing commands to modify your playlists
- Understand the effects of Edit modes on moving and trimming operations
- Create fade-in, fade-out, and crossfade effects on your tracks

Notes

Introduction

Any time you add audio or MIDI data to the tracks in your session, you are likely to need to do some editing. Whether you need to adjust timing, smooth out a transition, or improve a performance, editing techniques will play a big part in transforming a session from a basic recording to a polished final product. The processes described in the following sections will help you make that transformation, enabling your recordings and compositions to sound their best.

Selecting Playback Options

To simplify your navigation and workflow, Pro Tools provides various playback options that you can choose from while working on your sessions. Two common options you will likely want to adjust from time to time include the scrolling options and the Loop Playback option.

Scrolling

As discussed in Chapter 3, Pro Tools LE and M-Powered offer three scrolling options that determine how the contents of the Edit window are displayed during playback and recording. Two additional options that provide continuous scrolling are available on Pro Tools|HD systems only. Use the setting that matches your needs for a particular task:

- **No Scrolling.** This option prevents the screen from following the position of the Playback Cursor. Use this option to keep the display located on an area that you are editing while playing back an area that starts or ends off screen.
- **After Playback.** This option scrolls the screen to the point where playback ends, centering the end point on the screen. Use this option to locate an area that needs editing by auditioning your tracks. By stopping playback when you hear something amiss, your screen will automatically be scrolled to the area needing attention.
- **Page** or **Continuous Scrolling.** The Page option scrolls the screen one page, or screenful, at a time during playback, while the Continuous and Center Playhead options in Pro Tools HD scroll the contents of the screen continuously during playback. Use the Page option or one of the continuous scrolling options to view the contents of your tracks as they are played back. Scrolling places additional demands on your system resources, so deselect this option if your system is having difficulty keeping up with a large session.

Additional details on scrolling options are provided in Chapter 3.

Loop Playback

During editing, you will often want to listen to a selection repeatedly. Loop Playback allows you to repeat your selection continuously, looping from the end of the selection back to the start without interruption. This allows you to easily review the continuity of an edit or transition point.

To use Loop Playback, do the following:

1. Select the desired audio or MIDI data.
2. Choose OPTIONS > LOOP PLAYBACK. The Playback button in the Transport window will change to show a loop arrow.

Transport window with Loop Playback enabled

3. Click PLAY or press the SPACE BAR to start continuous looped playback.

You can adjust the start and end points of the loop during playback by modifying your selection, as discussed in Chapter 7. By dragging the corresponding start/end markers in the Timeline Rulers, for example, you can expand or contract your loop on either side. The loop will immediately play back from the start of the selection after you make an adjustment.

 Loop Playback requires a selection at least 0.5 seconds in length.

Drag to Adjust
Start of Loop

Drag to Adjust
End of Loop

Area selected for Loop Playback

Using the Edit Modes

As you learned in Chapter 2, Pro Tools provides four Edit modes: Shuffle, Spot, Slip, and Grid. The Edit modes affect the movement and placement of audio and MIDI regions, the results of commands such as Copy and Paste, and the functions of the Edit tools. You will use each Edit mode for different purposes while editing your sessions:

- **Shuffle.** This mode allows you to shuffle the order of regions without adding space between them or having them overlap. Use Shuffle mode to rearrange adjacent parts in your session.

- **Slip.** This mode allows you to place a region anywhere on a track without affecting the placement of other regions, leaving space between regions or overlapping regions as desired. Use Slip mode to move or arrange the parts of your session freely.

- **Spot.** This mode allows you to specify exact locations using numerical values when moving, placing, or trimming regions. Use Spot mode to move the parts of your session to specific known destinations.

- **Grid.** This mode allows you to snap regions and MIDI notes to the nearest time increment on a grid, based on the currently selected Time Scale. Use Grid mode to fine-tune timing by aligning parts using defined timing intervals.

The default Edit mode is Slip mode. You will use this mode for most of your editing tasks. You can activate a different mode at any time by clicking on the appropriate mode button in the toolbar area of the Edit window.

The Edit Mode buttons (Grid mode selected)

Shuffle, Slip, and Spot modes have only one option each and do not require any additional configuration before you use them. Grid mode provides two options to choose from, Absolute Grid and Relative Grid. The functions of both options are affected by the Grid configuration.

Shuffle Mode

In Shuffle mode, when you move or place regions on a track, their placement is constrained by other regions, and any edits you make to a region will affect the placement of subsequent regions on the track. Regions being moved or placed will automatically snap to the end of the preceding region, causing the two regions to butt up against each other. If a region is inserted between two existing regions, all subsequent regions on the track will move to the right to make space for the inserted region. Conversely, if a region is removed from between two existing regions, the subsequent regions on the track will move to the left to fill the void.

You can "shuffle" the order of regions in this mode, but you cannot separate them from each other to add space between regions, and you cannot make them overlap as in Slip mode. However, any space between existing regions is maintained when the regions move as a result of insertions, deletions, or edits made earlier in the track.

When using the Trim tool in Shuffle mode, changing a region's start or end point will automatically move the subsequent regions by the amount added to or trimmed from the edited region.

 The placement and insertion of individual MIDI notes is not affected by Shuffle mode.

To activate Shuffle mode, click on the Sʜᴜꜰꜰʟᴇ button in the Edit window or press function key **F1**.

Slip Mode

In Slip mode, when you move, trim, cut, or paste regions, their placement is unconstrained by other regions on the track. Editing a region has no effect on subsequent regions, unless the edit causes regions to overlap, in which case the underlying region is trimmed out to accommodate the added material.

To activate Slip mode, click on the Sʟɪᴘ button in the Edit window or press function key **F2**.

Spot Mode

In Spot mode, you can move or place regions within a track at precise locations by specifying the desired destination location. As in Slip mode, edit operations do not affect the placement of other regions on the track.

Spot mode allows you to specify a destination based on any time format. You can also use Spot mode to capture an incoming Time Code address or to spot a region using its time stamps as reference points. This can be particularly useful when you are performing post-production tasks involving SMPTE frame locations.

When Spot mode is enabled, Pro Tools prompts you with a dialog box whenever a region is dragged from the Region List or a DigiBase browser or whenever you click on a region with the Grabber or Trim tool. When placing or moving a region, you specify a destination location for the region's start, sync point, or end by entering a value in the Start, Sync Point, or End fields in the dialog box, respectively. When trimming a region, you specify the start or end points for the trim using the Start or End fields in the dialog box, respectively.

To activate Spot mode, click on the SPOT button in the Edit window or press function key F3.

Grid Mode

In Grid mode, you can make edits based on the timing interval defined by the Grid. (See the following "Configuring the Grid" section.) Selections and insertion points snap to Grid intervals, affecting cut, copy, and paste operations. Move and trim operations either align to the Grid or move in Grid increments relative to their origination point, depending on the option selected (Absolute or Relative).

- In Absolute Grid mode, moving any region snaps the region start to the Grid; trimming a region snaps the trimmed edge to the Grid. If a region's start point falls between beats and the Grid size is set to quarter notes, moving the region will snap its start time to the nearest quarter note; trimming it will align the trimmed edge to the nearest quarter note, causing the region to start or end on the beat, depending on which edge is trimmed.
- In Relative Grid mode, regions are moved and trimmed by Grid (or Nudge) units. If a region's start point falls between beats and the Grid is set to quarter notes, the region will move in quarter-note increments, preserving its relative position to the nearest beat. Likewise, the Trim tool will trim the region in quarter-note increments, preserving the starting point or ending point of the region relative to the beat.

To activate Grid mode using the last-used option, click the GRID button in the Edit window or press function key F4. To change the Grid mode from the last-used option, click and hold the GRID button and select the desired option from the pop-up selector.

 You can temporarily suspend Grid mode and switch to Slip mode by holding down the CTRL key (Windows) or COMMAND key (Mac OS).

Configuring the Grid

Pro Tools allows you to set up a timing grid, based on an interval of your choosing, to help maintain the timing of regions, notes, and events as you edit your session. The Grid settings affect edit operations in Grid mode. (See the preceding "Grid Mode" section.) In addition, the Grid sets the timing for the Region > Quantize to Grid command (discussed in a later course). The Grid can also be used for display only, allowing it to serve as a visual reference without affecting edit operations.

Grid boundaries, depending on the Main Time Scale, can be based on frames, bar and beat values, minutes or seconds, or a specified number of samples.

To configure the Grid, do the following:

1. Click the GRID VALUE pop-up selector in the toolbar area of the Edit window.

Grid Value pop-up selector

2. From the Grid Value pop-up menu, choose an appropriate TIME SCALE, or choose REGIONS/MARKERS, which causes regions and selections to snap to existing region boundaries and memory location markers whenever they are in close proximity. The menu will close after you make a selection.

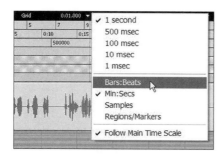

Selecting a Time Scale for the Grid

3. Click the GRID VALUE pop-up selector again to choose a corresponding Grid size; the options available will vary depending on the Time Scale selected in step 2.

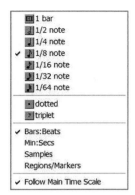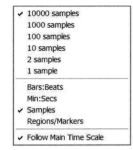

Grid-size options for each Time Scale

 The Follow Main Time Scale option at the bottom of the Grid Value pop-up menu always enables the grid to change automatically whenever the Main Time Scale is changed, using the Grid size last set for each Time Scale.

To use the Grid in a Time Scale that is different from your Main Time Scale, deselect this option.

Once you have set the Grid to an appropriate Time Scale and size, you have the option of displaying the Grid lines in the Edit window to serve as a visual reference. To display or hide Grid lines, click the currently selected TIMEBASE RULER name. The Grid lines will toggle on or off.

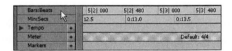

Click the current Timebase Ruler to toggle the Grid-line display

Editing Regions

Pro Tools offers a variety of standard editing commands, such as Copy, Cut, and Paste, as well as several application-specific commands, such as Capture Region, Separate Region, and Heal Separation, that affect regions.

As discussed in Chapter 4, Pro Tools uses two types of regions: whole-file regions and subset regions. The editing techniques described in this section apply to both types of regions, unless otherwise specified.

Standard Editing Commands

Like most Windows and Mac OS programs, Pro Tools offers standard Cut, Copy, Paste, and Clear (delete) commands. The Pro Tools Duplicate and Repeat commands also offer standard functionality similar to that found in other applications that use these commands. Pro Tools performs each of these editing functions nondestructively, meaning that the operations won't alter your audio files.

Each of these commands can be performed on a single track or on multiple tracks simultaneously, depending on the selection or the clipboard contents. Edits can apply to the following material:

- Part of a region or multiple parts of a region (selected with the Selector tool)
- A whole region or multiple whole regions (selected with the Grabber tool)

Selections made for Cut, Copy, and Clear commands can cross multiple region boundaries, can include whole regions or partial regions, and can even include silence, if desired.

The effects of Paste, Duplicate, and Repeat operations vary depending on the Edit mode being used:

- In Shuffle mode, all audio or MIDI data after the inserted selection is moved later in the track(s) by the length of the insertion.
- In Slip mode, all audio and MIDI data remains in place, so inserted material replaces any existing material for the length of the insertion.

When you use any of the standard editing commands on audio selections within a region or regions (excluding whole regions), Pro Tools creates byproduct regions and automatically adds them to the Region List.

The Cut Command

Using the Cut command, you can cut a selected range, region, or series of regions from its current position and place the audio or MIDI data on the clipboard for use elsewhere.

To cut a selection and place the material on the clipboard, do the following:

1. Make a selection of any length on a single track or multiple tracks.
2. Choose EDIT > CUT, or press CTRL+X (Windows) or COMMAND+X (Mac OS). The selected audio and/or MIDI data will be removed from the original location and copied to the clipboard.

When you cut or clear a selection in Shuffle mode, all audio to the right slides over by the amount of time removed so that no gap is added to the audio. In Slip, Grid, and Spot modes, a gap remains where the audio was removed.

The Copy Command

The Copy command is much like the Cut command, but instead of removing the selected range, it leaves the original and places a copy of it on the clipboard so that you can paste it elsewhere.

To copy a selection, do the following:

1. Make a selection of any length on a single track or multiple tracks.
2. Choose EDIT > COPY, or press CTRL+C (Windows) or COMMAND+C (Mac OS). The selected audio and/or MIDI data will be copied to the clipboard.

 When you place a selection on the computer's clipboard using a Cut or Copy command, you replace any material previously stored on the clipboard.

The Paste Command

Using the Paste command, you can insert the contents of the clipboard into a location that you have chosen with the Selector tool. You can paste data only after something has been cut or copied to the clipboard.

To use the Paste command, do the following:

1. Select the desired paste destination using one of the following methods:
   - Place the cursor (insertion point) on the desired destination track or tracks at the location where you want the start of the paste to occur.
   - Make a selection of any length on the desired destination track or tracks, with the beginning of the selection at the location where you want the start of the paste to occur.

 To paste on multiple tracks, you must make an insertion point or selection on each of the desired destination tracks.

2. Choose **EDIT > PASTE**, or press **CTRL+V** (Windows) or **COMMAND+V** (Mac OS). The material on the clipboard will be pasted in, beginning at the selected start point.

 If the clipboard contains material from multiple tracks, the data will be pasted in starting with the topmost track, and the selected destination tracks will be filled from top to bottom.

 *To paste data immediately after a region, use the **TAB** key (with the Tab to Transient function turned off) to place the cursor exactly at the region's end.*

The Clear Command

The Clear command allows you to remove any selected regions or any selected range of audio or MIDI data without placing the deleted audio on the clipboard.

To clear a selection, do the following:

1. Make a selection of any length on a single track or multiple tracks.
2. Choose **EDIT > CLEAR**, or press **CTRL+B** (Windows) or **COMMAND+B** (Mac OS). Note that this command has the same result as using the **DELETE** key on the keyboard.

The Duplicate Command

The Duplicate command copies a selection within a single region, a selection that crosses multiple region boundaries (including space), a whole-file region, multiple regions, or any combination of these and places the selected audio or MIDI data immediately after the end of the selection. This command provides a handy way of quickly repeating a selection to extend a sound or create a simple looping effect—it is faster and more convenient than copying and pasting data to achieve the same result.

 For advanced looping effects, use the region looping features in Pro Tools.

 Region looping is covered in the Pro Tools 110 course.

To duplicate audio or MIDI data, do the following:

1. Make a selection of any length. Your selection can be a selection within a region, a single region, a selection that crosses multiple region boundaries (including space), multiple regions, or any combination.

2. Play the selection using Loop Playback to ensure that it plays smoothly in succession, without glitches (optional). If the selection plays smoothly when it loops, you know that you can duplicate it without creating an audible edit point.

3. Adjust the selection as needed to eliminate any glitches noted in step 2 (optional). You might want to zoom in to position the start and end of the selection on a zero crossing (a point of no amplitude in a waveform).

4. After you are satisfied with the selection, choose EDIT > DUPLICATE, or press CTRL+D (Windows) or COMMAND+D (Mac OS). The selection will be duplicated and pasted onto the end of the selected area or region.

The Repeat Command

The Repeat command is similar to Duplicate, but it allows you to specify the number of times the selected material will be duplicated.

To repeat a selection of audio or MIDI data, do the following:

1. Make a selection of any length. Your selection can be a selection within a region, a single region, a selection that crosses multiple region boundaries (including space), multiple regions, or any combination.

2. Choose EDIT > REPEAT, or press ALT+R (Windows) or OPTION+R (Mac OS). The Repeat dialog box will open.

Repeat dialog box

3. Enter a number of times to repeat the selection and click **OK**. The selected material will be duplicated in succession immediately following the selection's end point, as specified in the Repeat dialog box.

Pro Tools–Specific Editing Commands

Pro Tools includes a number of editing commands that are specifically geared toward working with audio and MIDI regions. The following sections introduce commands for defining audio selections as regions, separating into two or more subset regions, and restoring regions that have been separated.

The Capture Region Command

The Capture Region command defines a selection as a new, independent region and adds it to the Region List without creating a separation in source location. You can then reuse the captured region by dragging it from the Region List onto any Track Playlist. Selections to be captured as an independent region must be totally contained within a single source region. You cannot capture a selection that crosses one or more region boundaries.

To create a new region using the Capture Region command, do the following:

1. Make a selection of any length within an existing whole-file region or subset region.
2. Choose REGION > CAPTURE or press CTRL+R (Windows) or COMMAND+R (Mac OS). The Name dialog box will open.

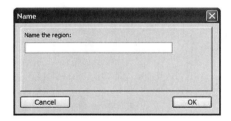

The Name dialog box

3. Enter a name for the new region and click **OK**. The new region will appear in the Region List on the right side of the Edit window.

 You can rename a region at any time by double-clicking on the region name in the Region List or by double-clicking on the region in a Track Playlist using the Grabber tool.

The Separate Region Command

Separating a region is the process of breaking a region in two or separating a section of an original region into a new region.

You can separate a region for one of several purposes:

- To split a region into two separate regions at the insertion point. Use this command to split the source region into two new regions in the track, adding both to the Region List.

- To separate a selection from a parent region or from the regions on either side in which the selection starts and ends. Use this process to separate a selection from its source region(s), creating new regions in the track and adding the newly created regions to the Region List.

- To create multiple new regions from a selection, dividing the selection at Grid intervals or at transients. Use this process to automatically create regions based on a defined timing or based on audio events on the track.

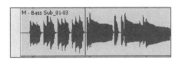 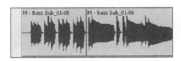

Separating a region at the insertion point (before and after)

 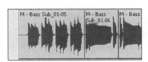

Separating a selection as a new region (before and after)

Separating a selection into new regions at Grid intervals (before and after)

When you separate regions, you create *byproduct* regions from the material remaining on either side of the selection. These new byproduct regions appear on the track and in the Region List with new edit numbers appended to the ends of their names.

To separate a region, do the following:

1. Make a selection of any length within a region or across multiple regions, or place the cursor (insertion point) at the location where you want a split to occur.

2. Do one of the following:

   - To create a separation at the insertion point or at the selection boundaries, choose EDIT > SEPARATE REGION > AT SELECTION or press CTRL+E (Windows) or COMMAND+E (Mac OS).

   - To create separations at each Grid boundary or at each transient, choose EDIT > SEPARATE REGION > ON GRID or EDIT > SEPARATE REGION > AT TRANSIENTS, respectively. The Pre-Separate Amount dialog box will open.

The Pre-Separate Amount dialog box

3. Enter the pre-separate amount in the dialog box, if needed, and click OK. This measurement will determine the amount of buffer time Pro Tools will include in the newly created regions before each Grid boundary or transient point.

Pro Tools creates new regions based on the selection start and end points. If the ON GRID or AT TRANSIENTS option was chosen, Pro Tools will create additional regions within the selection at each Grid line or transient point. Pro Tools automatically names all resulting new regions by appending the next available edit number to the end of the original region name.

 To have Pro Tools display the Name dialog box for new regions created from a continuous selection, deselect the AUTO-NAME SEPARATED REGIONS option in the Editing tab of the Pro Tools Preferences.

The Heal Separation Command

If you've separated a region and later decide to undo the separation, you can repair the separations and restore the original unedited material using the Heal Separation command. The Heal Separation command gives you a way to repair separated regions, provided that the regions are contiguous and their relative start and end points haven't changed since the separation.

To heal a separation between two or more contiguous regions, do the following:

1. Create a selection across the separation points of the regions to repair.

Selecting across separation points

2. Choose EDIT > HEAL SEPARATION or press CTRL+H (Windows) or COMMAND+H (Mac OS).

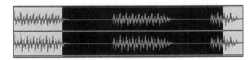

Selection after separations are healed

Moving and Trimming Regions

The following sections describe techniques for moving and trimming regions and discuss the effects of the Edit modes on these operations. The Nudge function is also introduced, along with the process for setting the Nudge value.

Using the Grabber Tool

The Grabber tool can be used to drag a region from the Region List or from an existing location on a Track Playlist. You can drag a region to a different location within the same track or to a different track.

The Grabber tool

Moving Regions in Slip Mode

In Slip mode, you can move regions freely within a track or onto other tracks using the Grabber tool. You can place regions so that they overlap or so that there is space between the regions on a track. When you play back the track, there will be silence in any open areas. Table 8.1 shows the results of moving regions in Slip mode.

Table 8.1 Rules for Moving Regions in Slip Mode

Slip Mode Action	Result
When regions partially overlap	The audio on top trims the audio underneath.
When a smaller region is completely covered by a larger region	The smaller region is cleared from the track with no warning, although this action can be undone.
When a smaller region is placed inside a larger one	The smaller region will trim out the audio it covers so that when it is dragged away, a hole (delete) results. The hole can be repaired using the Heal Separation command.

To move a region in Slip mode, do the following:

1. Select the GRABBER tool. The cursor will change into a hand.
2. Drag the region to the desired destination. The outline of the region appears on the track as you position it.
3. Release the mouse to position the region.

 As you drag regions, the Start, End, and Length Selection indicator boxes dynamically update to show you the result of the movement.

Moving Regions in Grid Mode

When using the Grabber tool in Grid mode, moving and dragging regions is constrained by the current Grid Value pop-up menu setting.

To move a region in Grid mode, do the following:

1. Verify that the Grid Time Scale and size have been set as desired. (See the "Configuring the Grid" section earlier in this chapter.)
2. Select the GRABBER tool. The cursor will change into a hand.
3. Drag the region to the desired destination. The outline of the region will appear on the track and will move incrementally as you position it, snapping to each successive Grid value.
4. Release the mouse to position the region.

Moving Regions in Shuffle Mode

In Shuffle mode, you can move regions within a track or onto another track, but their movement is constrained by other regions. When moved, regions automatically snap to each other like magnets. You can shuffle their order, but you cannot leave space between regions or overlap them.

To move a region in Shuffle mode, do the following:

1. Select the GRABBER tool. The cursor will change into a hand.

2. Drag a region to the desired destination. The insertion point will snap between the start and end points of existing regions on the track as you position the region.

3. Release the mouse to position the start of the region at the insertion point. Adjacent regions reposition themselves as needed to accommodate the region and to close up the space left at its point of origin.

Moving Regions in Spot Mode

Spotting is the process of placing regions at predetermined time locations within your tracks based on exact Time Scale units, such as Min:Secs, Bars:Beats, or SMPTE timecode.

To move and place a region in Spot mode, do the following:

1. Select the GRABBER tool. The cursor will change into a hand.

2. Click on the desired region or drag a region from the Region List. The Spot dialog box will appear.

The Spot dialog box

3. Choose the desired TIME SCALE from the Time Scale pop-up menu. (The menu selection defaults to the Main Time Scale of the session.)

4. Enter the new location in either the START or END field and click OK. (Other options for this dialog box are covered in later courses.) The region's start or end point will align to the location you specified.

Using the Trim Functions

Regions can be trimmed using either the Trim tool or the Trim command. The Trim functions allow you to shorten or lengthen regions as desired by trimming their heads or tails.

The Trim Tool

The Trim tool can be used to dynamically adjust the length of a region. By trimming the head or tail of a region, you can eliminate unwanted audio that precedes or follows any audio that you want to retain.

The Trim tool

To trim a region, do the following:

1. If needed, use the **Zoomer** tool to zoom in on the area you want to trim.
2. Click the **Trim** tool (Standard).
3. Move the cursor over the audio region you want to trim. The cursor will change to a left trim shape or right trim shape on either side of the region's midpoint.

Left Trim (from start)   Right Trim (from end)

Trim tool, as displayed on either side of the region midpoint

4. Click the cursor on the left side to trim the region head or on the right side to trim the region tail; drag toward the center to shorten the region or away from the center to extend the region. As you drag, the region outline will preview the trim effect.
5. Release the mouse button to accept the trim. The region will update to display the new length.

 *To reverse the direction of the Trim tool so that you can trim in either direction without having to trim past the midpoint, press **Alt** (Windows) or **Option** (Mac OS) before trimming a region.*

Trimming with the Edit Modes

The function of Trim tool is affected by the currently selected Edit mode. Slip, Shuffle, Spot, and Grid modes all affect trimming differently.

- **Trimming with Shuffle mode.** Trimming the head or tail of a region will cause all regions after the trim to move earlier or later, respectively, by the amount of the trim. Trimming the head of a region in this mode will cause the audio in the region to roll in or out to the right of the start point. (The head of the region remains stationary on the Timeline while the tail moves in or out.)

 Locked regions will not move, even if you trim audio before them in Shuffle mode.

- **Trimming with Slip mode.** In Slip mode, other regions in the track will not shift when a region is adjusted with the Trim tool. Any region that gets overlapped when a region is extended with the Trim tool is itself trimmed out in the area of the overlap.

 *Press and hold the **START** key (Windows) or **CONTROL** key (Mac OS) before you begin trimming in Slip mode to extend a region up to, but not beyond, the border of a neighboring region.*

- **Trimming with Grid mode.** In Grid mode, the Trim tool moves incrementally, snapping to Grid lines as the region is lengthened or shortened. Any region that gets overlapped when a region is extended with the Trim tool is itself trimmed out in the area of the overlap.

The Trim Region Command

The Trim Region command in the Edit menu allows you trim a region to the boundaries of a selection, to avoid having to trim the head and tail of the region separately, or to trim (clear) all audio within a region to the left or right of the insertion point. The Trim command cannot be used with selections that cross region boundaries.

To use the Trim Region command based on a selection within a region, do the following:

1. Select the portion of a region you want to retain.

Audio selected for trimming

2. Choose Edit > Trim Region > To Selection. The portion of the region outside of the selection will be deleted.

Selection after trimming

The Shuffle mode affects the Trim Region operation in the same way that it affects the operation of the Trim tool; the trimmed audio moves on the Timeline so that the region head retains its position, and any regions after the trimmed region move by the amount of the trim.

 You can also press Ctrl+T *(Windows) or* Command+T *(Mac OS) to trim a region to a selection.*

To use the Trim Region command to clear audio preceding or following the insertion point, do the following:

1. Position the insertion point within a region where you want the region to start or end.
2. Choose Edit > Trim Region > Start to Insertion or Edit >Trim Region > End to Insertion to trim all audio before the insertion point or after the insertion point, respectively.

Using the Nudge Function

Pro Tools allows you to set an increment for adjusting the placement of regions and selections in small, precise amounts using the keyboard. The increment amount, or *Nudge value*, is set much like the Grid size. Nudging a region is similar to moving a region in Grid mode, in that the region is moved incrementally by predefined units.

You can use the Nudge function in any of the four editing modes, although it's most commonly used in Slip, Shuffle, and Grid modes. Nudging will always move the selected region or regions without moving adjacent regions, regardless of Edit mode.

Configuring the Nudge Value

The Nudge value can be based on frames, bar and beat values, a time measurement (in milliseconds), or a specified number of samples, depending on the Time Scale selected.

To configure the Nudge value, do the following:

1. Click the **NUDGE VALUE** pop-up selector in the toolbar area of the Edit window.

Nudge value pop-up selector

2. From the **NUDGE VALUE** pop-up menu, choose the desired Time Scale. The menu will close after you make a selection.

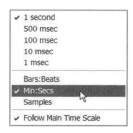

Selecting a Time Scale for the Nudge

3. Click the **NUDGE VALUE** pop-up selector again to choose a corresponding Nudge size; the options available will vary depending on the Time Scale selected in step 2.

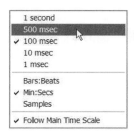

Selecting a Nudge size

 The Follow Main Time Scale option at the bottom of the Nudge value pop-up menu always enables the Nudge value to change automatically whenever the Main Time Scale is changed, adopting the last-used value for that Time Scale.

To use the Nudge in a Time Scale that is different from your Main Time Scale, deselect this option.

Nudging Regions

To nudge a single region or multiple regions, do the following:

1. Verify that the Nudge Time Scale and size have been set as desired. (See the preceding "Configuring the Nudge Value" section.)
2. With the GRABBER tool, select the region or regions you want to nudge.
3. On the numeric keypad, press the PLUS (+) key to move the region(s) later in the track or the MINUS (–) key to move the region(s) earlier in the track. The regions will move incrementally by the Nudge value.

 If you are using a laptop computer that does not have a numeric keypad, you can use the Function key (marked "Fn") and the corresponding +/– keys to nudge regions.

 You can manually enter a Nudge value by typing it directly into the Nudge display.

Nudging Selections

In addition to nudging regions, you can also nudge the start time and end time of a selection.

To nudge the start time of a selection, press ALT+SHIFT (Windows) or OPTION+SHIFT (Mac OS) and one of the following:

- The PLUS (+) key to nudge the selection start later using the current Nudge value
- The MINUS (–) key to nudge the selection start earlier using the current Nudge value

To nudge the end time of a selection, press CTRL+SHIFT (Windows) or COMMAND+SHIFT (Mac OS) and one of the following:

- The PLUS (+) key to nudge the selection end later using the current Nudge value
- The MINUS (–) key to nudge the selection end earlier using the current Nudge value

Creating Fade Effects

A *fade* is a steady volume ramp up or ramp down that Pro Tools can create on any region boundary you desire. Fades have many different applications, from smoothing out an edit, to creating seamless region overlaps, to building volume fade-ins and fade-outs for music and sound effects. This section covers the process of creating simple fade-ins, fades-outs, and crossfades for a variety of useful applications.

Fade-Ins and Fade-Outs

Fade-in and fade-out effects can be created at the beginning or ending of any audio region, respectively, using a selection that touches or crosses the region boundary.

Following are some basic guidelines for creating fades:

- Make your selection to match the desired fade; the length of the fade is determined by the selection length.

- Make a selection that touches or crosses an open region boundary (in other words, a boundary that is not adjacent to another region); boundaries between adjacent regions can be faded only with a crossfade (see the "Crossfades" section that follows).

- To create a fade-in, touch or cross the beginning region boundary; to create a fade-out, touch or cross an ending region boundary.

- Fade-ins always begin at the head boundary, and fade-outs always end at the tail boundary. Extending a selection into a blank area beyond a region's boundaries will not change the fade length.

- Fades are calculated in RAM prior to being rendered to disk as a file (stored in the Fades file folder of your session); for the best results, you should ensure that you have enough available RAM from the total allocation assigned to the Pro Tools application.

Keep these guidelines in mind as you prepare your selection for creating a fade.

To create a fade, do the following:

1. Select the beginning or ending of a region. (**SHIFT-CLICK** additional tracks to create fades on multiple tracks whose regions begin or end simultaneously.)

2. Choose EDIT > FADES > CREATE or press CTRL+F (Windows) or COMMAND+F (Mac OS). The corresponding Fade-In or Fade-Out dialog box will appear.

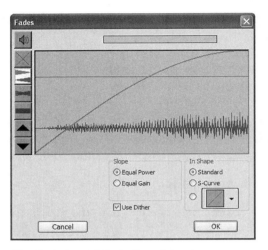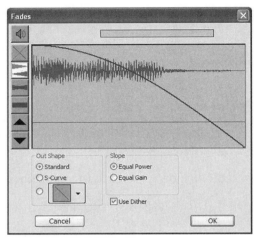

The Fade-In and Fade-Out dialog boxes

3. Choose the desired settings in the dialog box (see the "Fade Settings" section later in this chapter) and click **OK**. The fade will be generated and rendered in the Track Playlist as a separate region at the head or tail of the source region.

Fade-in at the head of a region

Crossfades

Pro Tools allows you to create crossfades between any two adjacent audio subset regions. *Crossfading* is essentially the process of overlapping two audio sources and fading out the first source while simultaneously fading in the second source. Pro Tools achieves this effect by overlapping the underlying audio on either side of the boundary between the adjacent regions.

To define an area for a crossfade, you must make a selection across the end of an outgoing region's file and the beginning of an incoming region's file, and both regions must have sufficient audio in their underlying audio files to extend across the length of the selection.

To create a crossfade between two adjacent regions, do the following:

1. Make a selection across the boundary between the regions.

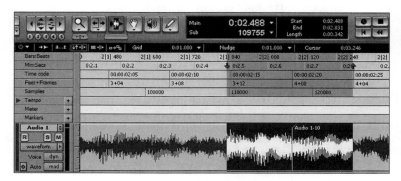

Area for crossfade selected in the Edit window

2. Choose **EDIT > FADES > CREATE** or press **CTRL+F** (Windows) or **COMMAND+F** (Mac OS). The Fades dialog box will open.

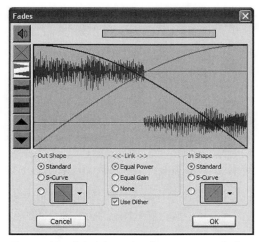

The Fades dialog box displaying a crossfade (mono track shown)

3. Choose the desired settings in the **FADES** dialog box (see the "Fade Settings" section that follows) and click **OK**. If sufficient underlying audio is available, the crossfade will be generated and rendered in the Track Playlist as a separate region between the source regions.

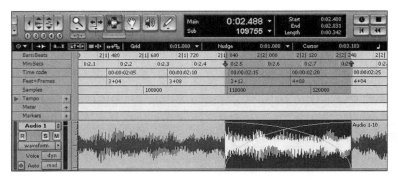

Crossfade rendered between regions

 You can audition and view the resulting crossfade before generating it by clicking the corresponding icons on the left edge of the Fades dialog box.

If either or both source regions lack sufficient underlying audio to generate a crossfade based on the selection boundaries, a warning will display after you click **OK** in the Fades dialog box to alert you that the attempted crossfade is invalid.

Invalid fade warning

Clicking the **ADJUST BOUNDS** button in this warning box will adjust the placement and length of the fade to fit the available audio from the incoming or outgoing region. If insufficient audio is available to overlap the regions at all, no fade will be created.

Fade Settings

The Fades dialog box displays the fade-in shape in red and the fade-out shape in blue. Either shape can be changed by choosing from the seven presets in the Shape drop-down selectors or by choosing one of the two editable fade shapes using the radio buttons. The shape of each curve determines how the amplitude of a region changes during the course of the fade.

The buttons arranged vertically along the left side of the Fades dialog box can be used to preview the fade in different ways.

- Click the AUDITION button to hear the results of the current fade settings.
- Click the FADE CURVES ONLY button to display the fade curves without showing the actual audio waveforms.
- Click the FADE CURVES AND SEPARATE WAVEFORMS button to display the fade curves along with separate views of the fade-in and fade-out waveforms.
- Click the FADE CURVES AND SUPERIMPOSED WAVEFORMS button to display the fade curves along with superimposed views of the fade-in and fade-out waveforms.
- Click the FADE CURVES AND SUMMED WAVEFORM button to display the fade curves along with a single waveform representing the summation of the crossfaded audio.
- Click the ZOOM IN or ZOOM OUT button to scale the view of the waveform's amplitude upward or downward, respectively.

Undoing Your Work

Often your editing tasks will involve performing a series of related steps to achieve a desired effect. Along the way, you might find that you want to go back to an earlier point, either to start over or to do a before-and-after comparison of the composition. Fortunately, Pro Tools provides rich undo options that give you the flexibility you need to work without worry.

Using Multi-Level Undo

Multi-level undo operations make it possible to revert to earlier stages of work during the editing process. This in turn enables you to experiment more freely, with the confidence of knowing you can return to an earlier point if you are not satisfied with the results.

Pro Tools provides up to 32 levels of edit undo. All commands that are undoable are stored sequentially in a queue for undo/redo purposes. However, certain commands cause changes that are not undoable, and any of these events will clear the undo queue.

Some common actions that *cannot* be undone include the following:

- Deleting tracks
- Closing a session and/or quitting Pro Tools
- Clearing audio from the Region List
- Destructive recording

The Pro Tools default settings provide the maximum of 32 levels of undo operation. If available memory for your system is running low, you can lower this setting to free up memory used by the undo queue. (Large undo queues require more RAM and can affect system performance if you have insufficient RAM.)

To change the number of levels of undo, follow these steps:

1. Choose **SETUP > PREFERENCES**, and then click the **EDITING** tab.
2. At the bottom of the dialog box, enter the desired undo setting between 1 and 32 and click **OK**.

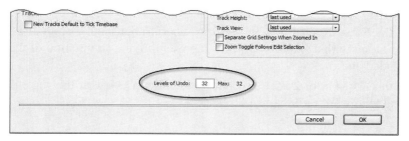

Levels of undo, as set in the Editing Preferences tab

Undoable actions are stored sequentially in the queue, with the most recent action at the front of the queue. Actions must be undone in reverse order; you cannot undo an individual action out of sequence.

To access the Undo command, choose **EDIT > UNDO** or press **CTRL+Z** (Windows) or **COMMAND+Z** (Mac OS). The Undo command in the Edit menu lists the action to be undone along with the command name.

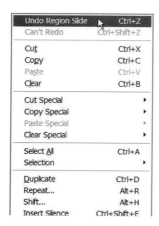

The Undo command, showing the action that will be undone

To perform multiple undo operations, repeat the above process as needed, up to the limit set on the Editing Preferences page.

If you undo an action that you want to keep, you can reinstate the action using the Redo command. To access the Redo command, choose EDIT > REDO or press CTRL+SHIFT+Z (Windows) or COMMAND+SHIFT+Z (Mac OS). Like the Undo command, the Redo command lists the action that it will affect.

Undo History

The Undo History window displays the undo queue, showing up to the last 32 actions that can be undone. You can use this window to view the recent actions taken and the sequence of those actions, as well as any actions recently undone. The Undo History window allows you to instantly return to any previous state from the actions listed. The Undo History can also show the creation time of each action, enabling you to revert to the state a session held at a particular time.

To show the Undo History window, choose WINDOW > UNDO HISTORY. The Undo History window shows undoable operations that have been performed in bold and operations that have already been undone in italics.

The Undo History window

The following actions can be performed using the Undo History window:

- **Multiple simultaneous undos.** To undo multiple operations in the Undo History window, click on the last bold operation that you want to undo in the list. The selected operation and all operations performed after it will be undone; the undone operations will display in italics.

- **Multiple simultaneous redos.** To redo multiple operations in the Undo History window, click the latest italicized operation that you want to redo in the list. The selected operation and all operations that precede it will be redone; the redone operations will display in bold.

- **Undo all.** To undo all the operations in the undo queue, click the OPTIONS pop-up menu and choose UNDO ALL.

- **Redo all.** To redo all the operations in the redo queue, click the OPTIONS pop-up menu and choose REDO ALL.

- **Clear the queue.** To clear the undo queue, click the OPTIONS pop-up menu and choose CLEAR UNDO QUEUE. When you select this option, a dialog box opens verifying the action; click YES to complete the command.

When the number of operations in the Undo History exceeds 32 or the limit set in the Edit Preferences, the operations at the top of the list are removed. The operation next in line to be pushed out of the queue is shown in red.

Revert to Saved

If you need to undo changes that are not available in the Undo Queue, you can use the Revert to Saved command to restore the last saved version of your session. Reverting to the last saved version has the same effect as closing the session without saving changes, and then re-opening it.

To revert to the last saved version of your session, do the following:

1. Choose FILE > REVERT TO SAVED. A dialog box will prompt you to verify that you want to revert the session.

2. Click REVERT to continue.

Chapter 9

Basic Mixing Techniques

This chapter covers basic mixing techniques and processes as they are performed in a Pro Tools environment. It includes discussions of mixer terminology, Mix window configuration (including configuring inserts, sends, and returns), basic automation, and real-time plug-ins.

Objectives

After you complete this chapter, you will be able to:

- Configure Inserts and Sends to add external signal processing to your tracks
- Configure the Sends view in the Mix window to display a single send across all tracks
- Record and edit basic automation for your mix
- Add plug-ins to your tracks for internal effects processing and sound shaping

Notes

Introduction

In this chapter, we focus on using Pro Tools' mix functions to route signals, set levels, and add effects when creating a session mix and preparing for mixdown. For the purposes of this course, we will limit our focus to standard stereo mixing. Other mixing options, such as mixing for surround sound, are covered in advanced courses.

Basic Mixer Terminology

The fundamental job of any audio mixer is to route incoming and outgoing audio via the mixer's inputs and outputs. Additional signal routing and processing can be achieved using the mixer's inserts and send and return functions. These terms are defined in the following sections, as they apply to general audio mixing; specific Pro Tools applications of these concepts are described in "The Pro Tools Mix Window" section later in this chapter.

Inputs

The term *input* refers to an audio signal traveling into an audio hardware device, such as a mixer or an audio interface.

The inputs available from within the Mix window of the Pro Tools software vary depending on the Pro Tools system and hardware interfaces you are using.

Outputs

The term *output* refers to an audio signal traveling out of an audio hardware device, such as a mixer or an audio interface.

The outputs available from within the Mix window of the Pro Tools software vary depending on the Pro Tools system and hardware interfaces you are using.

Inserts

Most mixers have a feature known as a *channel insert*. A channel insert is an audio patch point that allows either a plug-in insert or a hardware signal processor to be inserted directly into the signal path of an audio channel.

Sends and Returns

The term *send* is used for a mix output of one or more audio tracks sent to another receiving device, such as an external reverb or digital delay. A send can be *pre-fader*, meaning the send level is independent of the channel's fader level, or *post-fader*, meaning the send level is affected by the channel's fader level. Pro Tools allows you to set sends to pre- or post-fader, as needed.

Once the sent signal is received on the input of the desired audio device, usually some type of effect is added to the signal, and then the signal is returned to the original sending device.

The input used to return the signal to the sending device is called an *auxiliary input* or *auxiliary return*. These mono or stereo return inputs also have output assignments, with level and pan controls, allowing precise control over how the reintroduced signal combines with other audio in the system. The final result can then be rerouted to another output destination.

The Pro Tools Mix Window

Many of Pro Tools' mixing operations and functions are performed using the Mix window. The Mix window in Pro Tools is very similar to a standard mixing console. If you are acquainted with mixing console functions, the Pro Tools Mix window will be familiar territory. This window offers a variety of display options, many of which can also be customized.

The Mix window can be displayed or hidden as needed. To toggle the Mix window display on or off, choose WINDOW > MIX. If the Mix window is already open but is inactive (such as when it is hidden behind another window), this command will make it active, bringing it to the front of the display.

 Press CTRL+= *(Windows) or* COMMAND+= *(Mac OS) to toggle between the Mix and Edit windows.*

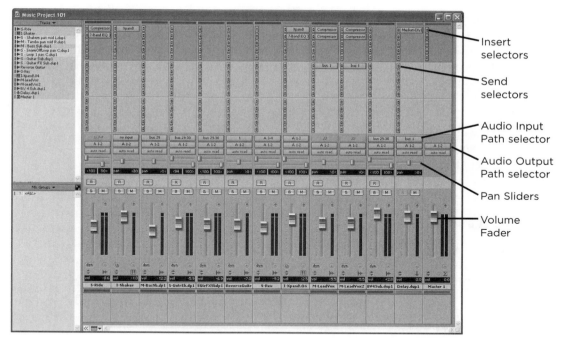

Insert
selectors

Send
selectors

Audio Input
Path selector

Audio Output
Path selector

Pan Sliders

Volume
Fader

Mix window controls

Configuring the Mix Window

The Mix window includes several component parts, a number of which can be selectively turned on and off as needed. Among the parts of the Mix window that you will use to create a session mix are Track Volume Faders, Pan Sliders, I/O selectors, and Insert and Send selectors.

 The Input and Output selectors (I/O selectors) include Audio Input Path selectors and Audio Output Path selectors as well as MIDI Input selectors and MIDI Output selectors (MIDI and Instrument tracks only).

To create a session mix, you will set the Volume Faders and Pan Sliders for each track to achieve an appropriate blend of audio levels and the desired positioning of sounds within the stereo field. You can make adjustments in real-time during playback/mixdown either by manually adjusting the controls or by using automation. (See the "Basic Automation" section later in this chapter.)

To route signals during your mix, you will use the Input selectors and Output selectors. Often these selectors will already be set as needed, based on the routing you used during recording and editing operations. However, your mix might call for new or different input and output settings for certain tracks; use these selectors to configure your I/O as needed. See the following "Input and Output Selectors" section for more detail.

Mixing also often involves using Inserts and Sends to add various types of signal processing to the audio on a session's tracks. Use the Insert and Send selectors in the Mix window to achieve these operations. See the "Inserts and Sends Views" section later in this chapter for more detail.

Input and Output Selectors

The Mix window always displays the Input and Output selectors for each track in the session (with the exception of the MIDI Input and MIDI Output selectors for Instrument tracks, displayed via the Instruments view). Though much of your signal routing might have been set up during the recording and editing stages of your project, it is always a good idea to double-check the I/O settings when you begin mixing.

When modifying or setting up tracks for mixing, pay particular attention to the Audio Input Path selector settings for the following types of tracks:

- Auxiliary Input tracks
- Instrument tracks
- Audio tracks used for internal mixing

For Auxiliary Input tracks and Instrument tracks, the Audio Input Path selector is often used to route audio from an available input source connection on the system. For internal mixing on Audio tracks, the Input selector is often used to route audio from a bus path. (See Chapter 10, "Finishing Your Work," for more information on setting up an internal mix.)

The following diagram shows how the Audio Input Path selector for an Auxiliary Input track corresponds to the input connectors of a Digi 002.

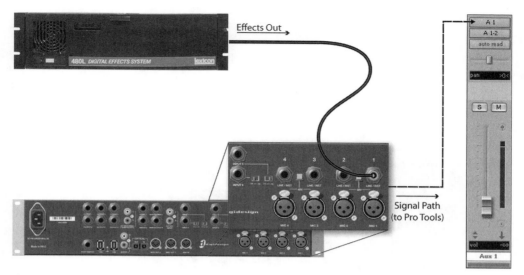

Effects Out

Signal Path
(to Pro Tools)

Common signal flow using an Auxiliary Input track (Digi 002 shown)

Pro Tools gives you the flexibility to route the output of each track to any output channel or bus. For the purposes of creating a stereo mix, however, you will generally select the stereo outputs of your audio interface.

To set up your mix, verify that the Audio Output Path selectors for the tracks in your session are set to the stereo outputs of your audio interface, as appropriate, so that the audio from each track is included in the stereo mix. Exceptions would include the following:

- Tracks that you don't want to include in the mix
- MIDI tracks feeding an outboard device
- Tracks sent to a bus to create a sub-mix

If needed, use the Audio Output Path selector to remove a track from the stereo mix and/or to select any of the other available outputs. The following diagram shows how the Audio Output Path selector on an Audio track corresponds to the output connectors of a Digi 002.

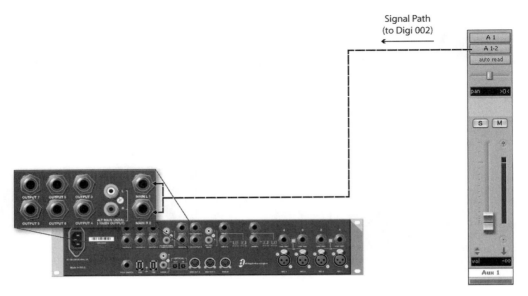

Signal flow from an Audio track to stereo (left and right) outputs (Digi 002 shown)

Inserts and Sends Views

The Mix window has independent view areas for the track inserts and the track sends. These view areas can each be toggled on or off in the Mix window.

- **Inserts view.** The Inserts view area, shown in dark gray, allows you to access and view the five track Insert selectors.

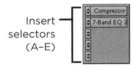

Insert selectors (A–E)

Inserts view area

- **Sends view.** The two Sends view areas (Sends A–E and Sends F–J), shown in light gray, allow you to access and view the 10 track Send selectors. (Five are displayed in each view area.)

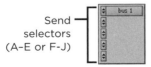

Send selectors (A–E or F–J)

Sends view area

To toggle the display of the Inserts or Sends view areas in the Mix window, choose VIEW > MIX WINDOW and click an option in the submenu to select or deselect it.

Toggling the Inserts view area from the Mix Window submenu

The two Sends view areas can be further customized to display their Sends in one of two ways.

- **Assignments.** Shows the status of all five track Send selectors simultaneously. Each Send that has been assigned will display the Send Assignment.

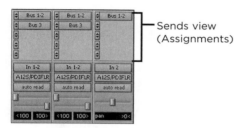

Sends view in Assignments display mode

- **Single Send.** Shows only one Send selector at a time across all tracks. On any tracks that have that Send assigned, the Send view will display the Send Assignment and additional Send level controls. In Single Send display mode, each Sends view area can be set to display any one of its five Send selectors.

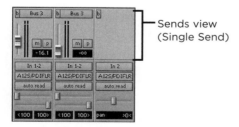

Sends view in Single Send display mode (Send B displayed)

To toggle between the Send Assignments and the Single Send display modes, choose VIEW > SENDS A–E or VIEW > SENDS F–J and select the desired display mode from the submenu. The corresponding Sends view will be displayed using the chosen mode.

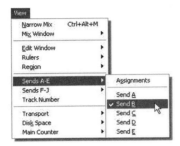

Selecting a Single Send display mode for Send B

 You can also access the Send Assignments and Single Send display options by Ctrl-clicking (Windows) or Command-clicking (Mac OS) on a Send selector.

 The Inserts and Sends view areas are available in both the Mix and Edit windows and can be displayed differently in each window.

Configuring Inserts

With the Inserts view area displayed in the Mix window, you can add an insert to any track. To add an insert, click on the Insert selector and choose a plug-in option or an I/O option from the pop-up menu. Plug-ins provide software-based signal processing, while I/O routing lets you use an external hardware device.

Plug-In Insert

Plug-in inserts can route audio through a software add-on from within the channel strip in the Mix window.

Choose a plug-in insert to add a software signal processor, such as the 1-band EQ III plug-in, directly into the signal path of the channel.

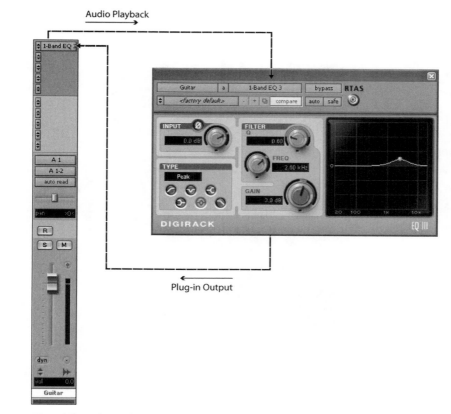

Audio Playback

Plug-in Output

Signal flow through a plug-in insert (EQ III shown)

Hardware I/O Insert

Hardware I/O inserts can route audio through an external device connected to parallel inputs and outputs of an audio interface.

Choose an I/O assignment to add a hardware device, such as an external graphic equalizer, directly into the signal path of the channel using an output and input on the connected audio interface.

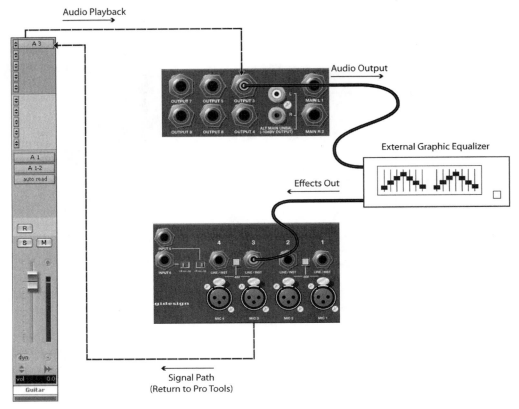

Signal flow through a hardware insert using a Digi 002 audio interface

Configuring Sends and Returns

Sends are used to route a track's signal to a secondary path for parallel processing (internal or external) without interrupting the signal flow through the originating track. To add the processed signal back into the mix, it is usually returned via an Auxiliary Input.

To route a send to an external device, choose INTERFACE from the Send selector and select the appropriate output(s) on your audio interface. Connect these outputs to the external device and return the processed the signal from the device to available inputs on your audio interface. This signal is the return, which then must be routed to the Audio Input of an Auxiliary Input track.

To route a send to an internal processor, such as a plug-in on an Auxiliary Input, choose BUS from the Send selector and select the appropriate bus for routing the signal. Buses can also be used to create submixes that are returned via an Auxiliary Input.

Example: *Suppose you have a sound-effects track named SFX1 that you want to route through a Lexicon 480L reverb. You might route it as a Send on output A4 and return it after the reverb effect is added using input A4 on an Auxiliary Input track named 480L Ret. Finally, you send the "wet" 480L Ret signal to outputs A1–2 to add it to the stereo mix.*

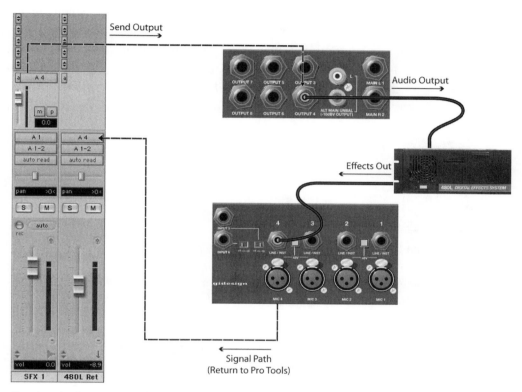

Send and return arrangement using a Digi 002

Basic Automation

For a very simple mix, you might be able to set your Track Volume Faders, Pan Sliders, and other controls and leave them unchanged from the start of a piece to the end. Most mixes are more complex, though, and require dynamic changes during the course of playback. Pro Tools allows you to record and edit these changes, automating various controls on your tracks. The automatable controls can include volume, pan, mute, and real-time plug-in controls, depending on the track type.

Pro Tools tracks use automation modes to determine how automation is used on the track. You can set the automation mode for each track independently using a pop-up menu. The following sections discuss three of these modes, Write, Read, and Off, to illustrate the basic automation functions that Pro Tools offers.

Recording Automation (Write Mode)

By setting automation on a track to Write mode, you can record the changes you make to the controls on the track in real time. The basic steps for recording automation on a track are as follows:

1. Enable the automation type that you want to record, such as volume or pan, as follows:

   a. Choose **WINDOW > AUTOMATION**. The Automation window will open.

   b. Verify that the automation type is write-enabled (armed) for the session. Automatable controls are generally armed by default.

   c. Click on an automation type to toggle its state (armed versus suspended).

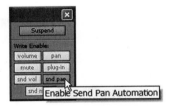

Toggling an automation type in the Automation Enable window

 The Automation Enable window shows armed automation types as selections with a white background; suspended automation types are indicated by a gray background.

2. Put the track in automation writing mode by choosing **WRITE** from the Automation Mode selector.

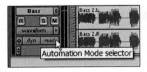  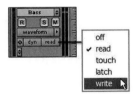

Selecting Write mode from the Automation Mode selector pop-up menu

Automation Mode Selector in the Edit window and Mix window

3. Begin playback to start automation recording, and adjust controls as needed. Pro Tools will record all adjustments performed on enabled controls.

If you are not satisfied with the automation, you can repeat these steps to write new automation over the previous data.

Viewing and Editing Automation

Each Pro Tools track contains a single automation playlist for each automatable parameter. The automation playlist can be displayed in the Edit window, providing a convenient way to view the recorded automation changes over time. While visible, the automation playlist can also be edited and refined using Edit tools, such as the Grabber.

To display the automation playlist, do the following:

1. Click on the TRACK VIEW SELECTOR in the Edit window.

Track View selector

2. Select the automation playlist that you want to display from the TRACK VIEW pop-up menu. The automation graph line will be displayed, superimposed on the track audio or MIDI data.

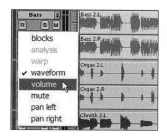

Track View pop-up menu

You can edit an automation playlist by adding, moving, or deleting breakpoints using the Grabber tool. To edit a playlist with the Grabber tool, do any of the following:

- Click on the automation graph line to add a breakpoint.
- Click and drag an existing breakpoint to adjust its position.
- **ALT-CLICK** (Windows) or **OPTION-CLICK** (Mac OS) on an existing breakpoint to remove it.

Editing the Volume Playlist using the Grabber tool

Automation playlists can also be edited using other Edit tools. Additional details on using and editing automation are covered in advanced courses.

Playing Back Automation (Read Mode)

The default mode for a track is Read mode. In this mode, the automation playlist is used to play the automation data that has been recorded or written for a track. Automation is not recorded in Read mode, but the Automation Playlist can be edited with the Edit tools.

To return to Read mode when a different mode has been activated, click the **AUTOMATON MODE SELECTOR** and choose **READ**.

 Use Read mode to play back automation without running the risk of recording over any of it.

Turning Automation Off

The Off mode turns off automation for all automatable parameters on the track, such as the following:

- Volume
- Pan
- Mute
- Send volume, pan, and mute
- Plug-in controls
- MIDI volume, pan, and mute

In Off mode, automation is not recorded during playback, and automation data for all parameters is ignored. To turn automation off, click the AUTOMATION MODE SELECTOR and choose OFF.

Real-Time Plug-Ins

As you learned in earlier chapters, plug-ins can be used to add functionality to a Pro Tools session, such as a Click track or a virtual instrument. Plug-ins are external software programs that function as add-ons to Pro Tools. Plug-ins exist for a multitude of sound-processing applications—from synthesis to effects processing to sonic modeling of hardware processors, amplifiers, and microphones.

Pro Tools provides two main categories of plug-ins:

- Real-time processing
- File-based processing (non-real-time)

The following sections explain the basic concepts behind real-time plug-ins.

Real-Time Plug-In Features

Real-time plug-ins are available as track inserts in Pro Tools. When you add a real-time plug-in to a track, it processes the audio or MIDI data non-destructively and in real time—you instantly hear its effect on the track while playing back audio.

Pro Tools supports two formats of real-time plug-ins: *TDM* and *RTAS*. The difference between the formats lies in how your system provides processing power for the plug-in. Both types of plug-ins function as track inserts, are applied to audio during playback, and process audio non-destructively in real time.

TDM Plug-Ins (Pro Tools|HD Systems Only)

TDM plug-ins are designed for use on TDM-based Pro Tools|HD systems and rely on the processing power of Digidesign DSP cards.

RTAS Plug-Ins (All Pro Tools Systems)

Real-Time AudioSuite, or RTAS, plug-ins rely on, and are limited by, the processing power of the host computer. The more powerful your computer, the greater the number and variety of RTAS plug-ins that you can use simultaneously. You can increase the number of RTAS plug-ins your system can support by increasing the Hardware Buffer Size and CPU Usage Limit. See Chapter 2 for details on adjusting these parameters.

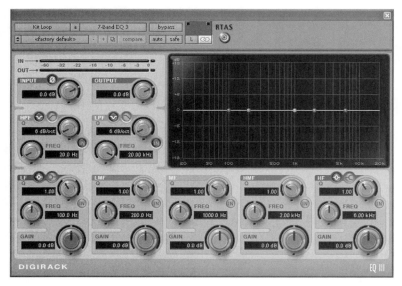

DigiRack EQ III 7-band equalizer plug-in

Real-Time Plug-In Formats

Plug-ins can be used in mono, multi-mono, or multi-channel formats. (For the purposes of this book, discussion of multi-channel formats will be limited to stereo configurations.) The plug-in format(s) available depend on the plug-in selected and the format of the track (mono or stereo). You should generally use multi-channel plug-ins for stereo tracks, if possible; if no multi-channel version is available, use a multi-mono version.

- **Mono plug-ins.** Plug-ins in this format are used on mono tracks. Some mono plug-ins can generate stereo output from a mono channel.
- **Multi-mono plug-ins.** Plug-ins in this format are used on stereo or multi-channel surround tracks when a multi-channel version of the plug-in is not available. Multi-mono plug-ins can analyze and process each channel independently. Controls for all channels are linked by default so that adjustments are made to all channels in tandem. The controls can be unlinked for specialized purposes, allowing you to adjust channels independently.
- **Multi-channel plug-ins.** Plug-ins in this format are used on stereo or multi-channel surround tracks. Controls for all channels are always linked together in multi-channel plug-ins.

Plug-Ins Provided with Pro Tools

Pro Tools comes bundled with a variety of additional software packages that extend its functionality. Among the extras bundled with Pro Tools 7.4 are the DigiRack EQ III plug-in and the DigiRack Dynamics III plug-in, which support both TDM and RTAS formats for real-time, non-destructive processing.

DigiRack EQ III

The DigiRack EQ III is a high-resolution, 48-bit equalizer plug-in for adjusting the frequency spectrum of audio material in Pro Tools. This plug-in can be added to a track in a 1-band, 4-band, or 7-band configuration. The plug-in is designed as a parametric EQ and includes selectable shelving filters and settings as well as separate high-pass, low-pass, and variable Q notch filters.

EQ III supports all Pro Tools session sample rates and operates as a mono or multi-mono plug-in. (Stereo and multi-channel tracks are supported through multi-mono operation.)

To add the EQ III plug-in to a Pro Tools track, do one of the following:

- For a mono track, click on an **INSERT SELECTOR** and choose **PLUG-IN > EQ > 1-BAND EQ 3 (MONO)** (or choose the 4- or 7-Band EQ 3, as appropriate). The DigiRack EQ III plug-in window will open.

- For a stereo or multi-channel track, click on an **INSERT SELECTOR** and choose **MULTI-MONO PLUG-IN > EQ > 1-BAND EQ 3 (MONO)** (or choose the 4- or 7-Band EQ 3, as appropriate). The multi-mono DigiRack EQ III plug-in window will open.

The DigiRack EQ III plug-in window (mono shown)

DigiRack Dynamics III

The Dynamics III plug-in provides a high-resolution suite of dynamics processing plug-ins, including a Compressor/Limiter, an Expander/Gate, and a De-Esser. The Compressor/Limiter and Expander/Gate plug-ins feature a side-chain section with two adjustable side-chain filters. Dynamics III also includes an interactive dynamics display graph for ease of use, speed, and accuracy.

Dynamics III supports all Pro Tools session sample rates. The Compressor/Limiter and Expander/Gate plug-ins are available in mono, stereo, and multi-channel surround formats; the De-Esser plug-in is available in mono and stereo formats only.

The Compressor/Limiter plug-in can be used to control dynamic levels, from attack, release, threshold, and ratio to the "knee" compression rate. The Expander/Gate plug-in can be added to a track to eliminate unwanted background noise by fine-tuning the ratio, attack, hold, release, and range. The De-Esser can be used to reduce sibilants with the frequency and range controls.

To add a Dynamics III plug-in to a Pro Tools track, do one of the following:

- For a mono track, click on an INSERT SELECTOR and choose PLUG-IN > DYNAMICS > COMPRESSOR/LIMITER DYN 3 (MONO) (or choose the De-Esser or Expander/Gate Dyn 3, as appropriate). The selected DigiRack Dynamics III plug-in window will open.

- For a stereo track, click on an INSERT SELECTOR and choose PLUG-IN > MULTI-CHANNEL PLUG-IN > DYNAMICS > COMPRESSOR/LIMITER DYN 3 (STEREO) (or choose the De-Esser or Expander/Gate Dyn 3, as appropriate). The selected DigiRack Dynamics III plug-in window will open.

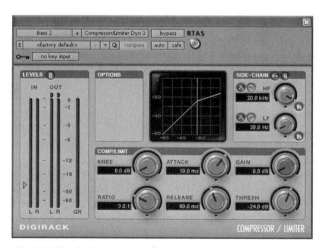

The DigiRack Compressor/Limiter Dynamics III plug-in window (stereo shown)

Chapter 10

Finishing Your Work

This chapter covers processes that you can use to create copies of your work in various formats. It describes how to create a session backup, how to mix down tracks for use within or outside of Pro Tools, and how to create an audio CD of your completed mix.

Objectives

After you complete this chapter, you will be able to:

- Describe the purpose of the Save Copy In command and recognize situations in which you should use it
- Create a copy of your session for use on a different Pro Tools system
- Create a mixdown of tracks in your session by bouncing to tracks or bouncing to disk
- Select appropriate options for your bounced files when bouncing to disk
- Create an audio CD of your bounced files to share your results with others

Notes

Introduction

After completing any significant recording, editing, or mixing work, it is wise to safeguard your work by creating a backup copy. You might also need to convert your session for subsequent work on another system or bounce your tracks to share your results as a completed mix. The sections in this chapter provide details on the processes you can use to create a finished copy of your work at any milestone point in your project's lifecycle.

Backing Up Your Session

Creating backups of your sessions is critical for archival and disaster recovery purposes. Because Pro Tools sessions are stored electronically, you typically will have no physical media housing your work other than a hard drive. As a result, it is possible to lose your work by accidentally deleting or overwriting files, having a file become corrupt, contracting a virus, or having a drive fail.

To protect yourself against these problems, it is a good idea to create regular session backups. Some of the best protection measures include creating multiple copies of your files, using a separate drive for backup copies, and storing backup copies offsite to protect against a local disaster, such as a fire or flood. Obviously, the more valuable your sessions, the more robust your backup plans should be. At a minimum, you should create a backup session upon completing work that would be difficult to recreate or any time you have worked on a session that has significant value or importance to you or your clients.

Saving a Session Copy

To create a session backup, you can save a copy of your session and all related files using the Save Copy In command. Unlike the Save As command, which creates a copy of the Pro Tools session file only, the Save Copy In command can be used to save all files used in the session, allowing you to create a self-contained duplicate session folder in a separate location, such as on another drive.

The Save Copy In command saves a copy of your current session without closing the original session, meaning that as you continue to work, any subsequent changes are saved in the original and do not affect the copy.

When using the Save Copy In command, you have a number of options available that allow you to convert and consolidate session information as you are saving. Some of the more useful applications of the Save Copy In command are as follows:

- It allows you to back up an entire Pro Tools session and all of its associated files without leaving the original session.

- It allows multiple versions of a session to be saved at various stages of a project. Later, these multiple versions can be used as a basis of comparison or to easily revert to an earlier stage of the project.

- It allows sessions to be saved using a different resolution (16-bit or 24-bit), sample rate (up to the maximum rate supported by your system), and/or file format (SD II, AIFF, or WAV) from the original. This allows complete flexibility and compatibility with other Pro Tools systems.

- It allows all session audio files, fade files, video files, and plug-in settings to be copied into one single folder.

- It allows a current Pro Tools session to be saved as an earlier version so that it can be opened on older Pro Tools systems.

To use this saving option, do the following:

1. Choose FILE > SAVE COPY IN. A special Save dialog box will open, allowing you to specify format options for the session copy.

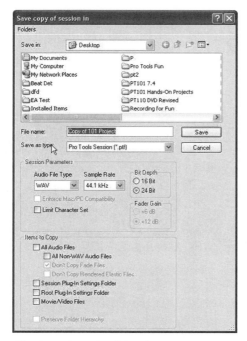

The Save Copy In dialog box

2. Type the new session name and set the save directory path as desired.

3. In the SAVE AS TYPE drop-down menu, choose from among the available format options, as needed, to maintain compatibility with an earlier Pro Tools version.

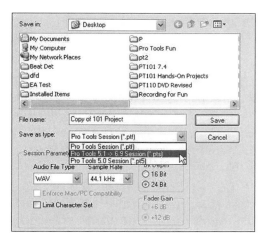

Selecting an earlier Pro Tools version

4. In the BIT DEPTH and SAMPLE RATE sections of the dialog box, choose a desired bit depth and sample rate. The bit depth and sample rate settings default to the settings of your current session and can be changed as needed.

5. In the AUDIO FILE TYPE drop-down menu, choose the desired file format: SDII (Mac OS only), AIFF, or WAV.

 If you choose the Pro Tools 5.1 -> 6.9 Session option in step 3 and either the AIFF or WAV file format in step 5, the Enforce PC/Mac Compatibility check box will become available. Enabling this option ensures that the session and its associated files will be compatible with supported Mac OS and Windows Pro Tools systems.

6. To limit the character set to a single language, select the LIMIT CHARACTER SET option. A pop-up menu will appear, allowing you to select the desired language encoding.

7. In the ITEMS TO COPY section of the dialog box, enable additional options as desired:

   • **All Audio Files.** If you are changing the original sample rate, bit depth, or file format of the session, this option will be selected automatically; otherwise, you can choose whether to copy all associated audio files for the session using this option.

Optional items that can be copied with the session

- **All Non-WAV Audio Files.** If your session contains two or more different file types, you can choose to copy only non-native files in the session. For example, if your session file format is set to WAV files, but your session also includes some imported SD II files, you can choose to copy the SD II files by checking the box. If All Audio Files is selected, this check box will be selected and the option will be grayed out.

- **Don't Copy Fade Files.** Fade files will not be copied if no audio files are copied (the check box will be selected and the option will be grayed out); if All Audio Files is selected, fade files can be excluded by selecting this check box.

- **Don't Copy Rendered Elastic Files.** Rendered elastic audio files will not be copied if no audio files are copied. (The option will be grayed out.) If All Audio Files is selected, rendered elastic audio files can be excluded by selecting this check box.

- **Session Plug-In Settings Folder.** This option copies the session's Plug-In Settings folder, if present, to the new session location.

- **Root Plug-In Settings Folder.** This option copies the contents of the root-level Plug-In Settings folder to a folder in the new session named "Place in Root Settings Folder." These files will need to be moved to the root-level Plug-In Settings folder on the destination system.

 The location options for plug-in settings files are discussed in the Pro Tools 201 book.

- **Movie/Video Files.** This option copies the movie or video files (if present in the session) to the new session location.

8. Click **SAVE** when you are finished selecting all of the options you want. The new session and optional files will be saved into the directory location you selected.

Sharing a Session between Systems

After completing your editing work on a session, you might want to save and convert your session data for use on a different Pro Tools system. The Save Copy In command can be used to ensure the compatibility of your session. See the preceding "Saving a Session Copy" section.

Creating a Stereo Mixdown

Mixing down is the process of recording the output from multiple tracks to a stereo or multi-channel format. This process is also often referred to as *bouncing*, which traditionally has been done to combine several tracks together to free up resources or reduce track count. Mixdown is often the last phase of music production, but in Pro Tools, mixdown can be done any time you want to bounce tracks or create a completed mix for use outside of your session.

The most common mixdown technique in Pro Tools is to mix down to a stereo file (or left and right mono files). You can record your mix to Audio tracks within your session or create an external recording using the Bounce to Disk command. Once you have created a stereo mix, you can play back the results outside of Pro Tools and share your composition with others by burning the file onto a CD.

 Pro Tools HD also provides multi-channel mixdown and bouncing options for use in surround-sound applications. Multi-channel mixing is covered in advanced Pro Tools courses.

Considerations for Bouncing Audio

Most digital audio workstations provide functions for mixing down or bouncing tracks; however, not all systems approach the process the same way. For example, some non–Pro Tools systems include only internal hard disk tracks when bouncing to disk and do not include any live or virtual tracks being brought into the system. Likewise, some systems will not capture automation when bouncing to disk. Pro Tools, however, performs real-time bounces, capturing all audible information in your mix just as you hear it during playback.

Here are some specific details about how Pro Tools processes a bounce. These principles apply both when bouncing to tracks and when bouncing to disk, unless otherwise noted.

- **Pro Tools bounces all audible tracks in real time.** When you play back your session, all tracks that you hear are included in the bounce. Any tracks that are muted will not appear in the bounce. If you have soloed any tracks or regions, only those soloed elements will appear in the bounce.
- **Pro Tools bounces tracks based on the output path.** All source tracks for the bounce must be assigned to the same output path. Any audio not assigned to that common output path will not appear in the bounce file.
- **Pro Tools does not require extra voices to bounce to disk.** You can use all available voices in your system when using the Bounce to Disk command, without requiring extra voiced tracks for recording the bounced file.
- **The bounced file will be a "flattened" version of your session.** Inserts, sends, and external effects are applied permanently to the bounced tracks, so make sure that you set levels carefully before bouncing tracks. Listen closely to ensure that everything sounds as it should. Pay close attention to levels, being sure to avoid clipping.
- **Pro Tools bounces tracks based on timeline selections.** If you have made a selection on the timeline (or on a track with timeline and edit selections linked), Pro Tools will bounce all audible tracks for the length of the selection only. If no selection is present in any track, Pro Tools will bounce the audible tracks in your session from the start of the session or from the playback cursor position to the end of the longest track in the session.
- **Bounced material is automatically time-stamped.** You can drag a bounced file into a track and place it at the same location as the original material using Spot mode.

Bouncing to Tracks

To create a stereo mixdown (or submix) within Pro Tools, you can record any or all of your session tracks to an available stereo Audio track. This technique lets you add live input to the mix, adjusting volume, pan, mute, and other controls in real time during the mixdown process. Recording to tracks requires that you have an available voiced track for each channel that you will be recording. For a stereo mix using Pro Tools M-Powered 7.x or Pro Tools LE 7.x, this simply means that you will need a stereo Audio track or two mono Audio tracks available.

Bouncing tracks in a large session using Pro Tools HD might require that you consider voice allocation. Voicing considerations are covered in advanced courses.

The typical process for creating a stereo mixdown within a session is to combine the audio output of selected tracks using an internal bus and to record the resulting mix onto a separate stereo Audio track.

To create a stereo mixdown using this method, do the following:

1. Create a stereo mix from the source tracks as described in Chapter 9, using appropriate settings for volume, panning, inserts, sends, plug-ins, and automation.

2. Set the output for each track you want to include to the same unused stereo bus. These tracks will be the source playback tracks for the bus bounce.

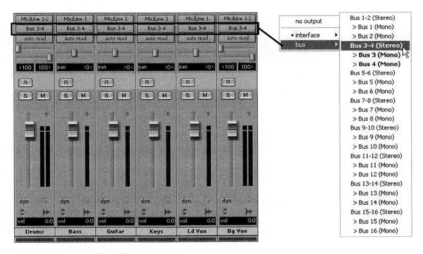

Outputs set to Bus 3–4 (stereo)

3. Create a stereo Audio track and record-enable the track. This track will be the destination track for the bus bounce.

4. Set the inputs for the stereo track to correspond to the stereo output bus you selected in step 2, and set the output for the track to your main output path (typically analog outputs 1–2).

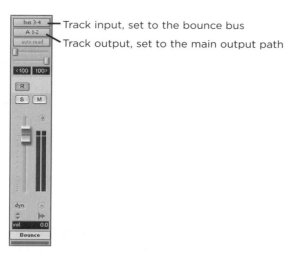

Track input, set to the bounce bus
Track output, set to the main output path

Stereo Audio track set up for an internal bounce

5. Do one of the following:

 • Make a selection (to manually set the start and end times for the bounce).

 • Place the playback cursor at the beginning of the session or at the desired start point.

6. In the Transport window, click the **RECORD** button followed by the **PLAY** button to begin recording the bounce.

7. During recording, perform any desired "live" mixing, such as Volume Fader adjustments and panning changes.

8. Allow recording to continue until playback stops automatically (if recording from a selection) or until you reach the desired end point. To stop the recording manually, press the **STOP** button in the Transport window or press the **SPACE BAR**.

After the recording is complete, you should see the waveform for your combined source tracks on the destination tracks. If no waveform is present, check the settings for your source outputs and record inputs and verify that the faders are set to an audible level.

9. Disarm the record-enabled track and rename the recorded region if desired.

Once you have combined multiple tracks into a single stereo track, you can continue with more recording or editing, using the stereo track in place of any original tracks to free up resources. You can also use the stereo track as part of a Bounce to Disk operation to create a completed audio mix.

Bouncing to Disk

The Bounce to Disk command allows you to mix your entire session directly to a hard drive in the same way a mixdown would occur with a traditional studio setup. This can be useful when you want to work with the mixed recording outside of Pro Tools, such as when you are posting song files to the Internet or burning them to CD. The Bounce to Disk function also provides more robust control than you have when bouncing to tracks, enabling you to set the bit depth, file format, and sample rate for the resulting bounced file.

The Bounce to Disk command combines the outputs of all currently audible tracks routed to a common output or output pair to create a new audio file on a selected hard drive or other supported volume. The newly bounced file can be automatically imported into the session at the completion of the bounce, if desired.

To bounce all currently audible tracks, do the following:

1. Adjust track output levels and finalize an automated mix. Any inserts or effects settings that are active on your tracks will be permanently written to the bounced audio files.
2. Make sure that all of the tracks you want to include in the bounce are audible (not muted). If you want to create a submix of tracks, solo only those tracks. Conversely, if you want to mix down all tracks in your session, make sure no tracks are soloed.
3. Assign the output of each track you want to include in your bounce to the same output pair by clicking the Audio Output Path selector and choosing the corresponding output from the pop-up menu.

Selecting an output pair

4. Choose FILE > BOUNCE TO > DISK. The Bounce dialog box will appear.

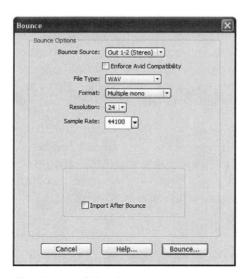

The Bounce dialog box

5. Select the output pair that you used in step 3 from the BOUNCE SOURCE drop-down list.

6. Choose the desired file type for your bounce file from the FILE TYPE pop-up menu. Available options include the following:

- **WAV.** This is the default file format for Windows and Mac OS–based Pro Tools systems and is supported by many other Windows and Mac OS applications.

- **AIFF.** This file format is primarily used on Mac OS systems. The AIFF format is useful if you plan to use bounced audio in other Mac OS applications.

- **MP3.** This is a popular file format for audio use on the Internet, personal computers, and portable devices. When you choose this format, the Resolution and Sample Rate pop-up menus are unavailable because they are set by the encoder. Use this file format when you want to use bounced files with MP3-compatible applications and devices.

 Bouncing to MP3 requires the purchase of an MP3 software option (included with the Music Production Toolkit).

- **QuickTime.** This is a file format for multimedia developed by Apple Computer. Pro Tools does not directly support this file type for audio in its sessions. Use the QuickTime format if you plan to use your audio in multimedia applications that support QuickTime, such as Adobe Premiere, Final Cut Pro, or Macromedia Director.
- **Windows Media (Windows systems only).** Microsoft's Windows Media Audio-9 file format is used for creating high-quality digital media files for streaming and download-and-play applications on PCs, set-top boxes, and portable devices. The WMA-9 file format supports 16- and 24-bit audio files, sample rates up to 96 kHz, multi-channel audio from stereo through 7.1 surround, lossless encoding, and file sizes that are roughly one-half the size of an equivalent MP3 file.
- **MXF (Pro Tools with DigiTranslator only).** MXF (*Material Exchange Format*) is a media file format that includes both video and audio files and is designed for the interchange of audio-visual material with associated data and metadata. This option will be grayed out on systems without DigiTranslator.

 The SD II and Sound Resource formats are also available (Mac OS only). Use these formats only if you have a specific need for them in the Mac OS.

7. Choose the MULTIPLE MONO or STEREO INTERLEAVED file format for your stereo bounce from the FORMAT pop-up menu.
   - **Multiple mono.** This option creates split stereo files from the stereo bus path. Two mono files will be created, one for the left channel and one for the right channel, with .L and .R suffixes appended to the file name of each, respectively. Use this file format if you want to import the bounced audio back into a Pro Tools session without conversion. This option is not available for use with MP3 or Windows Media file types.
   - **Stereo Interleaved.** Choose this option to create a single interleaved stereo file from the stereo bus path. This file format is directly compatible with most applications that process stereo files for commercial use, including all Apple software applications and Roxio's Toast software application.

Selecting a format for the bounced file

The Mono (summed) format provides a single audio file that is a summed mono mix of the bus path. Choose this option only if you need to create a composite monophonic mix of tracks, such as to reduce track count. All panning information will be disregarded.

 The Multiple mono format can also be used to preserve multi-channel mixes, using a separate mono file for each channel. Multi-channel mixdown is covered in advanced courses.

 To bounce compatible stereo files for use in any Avid system or DAE-compatible sequencer program, use the Multiple mono file option.

8. Choose the desired bit depth for the bounced file(s) from the RESOLUTION pop-up menu. You can choose 8-, 16-, or 24-bit resolution.

   - **8-bit.** Use this option to minimize file size for recordings that do not require rich dynamic resolution. Eight-bit files are often used in multimedia applications.

     If the audio you are working with is relatively simple, such as a voice-over, you can use the Pro Tools Squeezer feature to optimize results when you convert to 8-bit. Squeezer improves dynamics by preprocessing the audio before converting it. However, Squeezer does not work well with all material and should be tested on your audio before you convert an entire session with it.

   - **16-bit.** This is the standard resolution for compact discs. Use this option if you plan to burn your bounce to CD without further processing.

   - **24-bit.** This setting provides the highest dynamic resolution. Use this option when you want to create a bounce that retains full resolution, such as a final mix that is ready to master.

9. Choose the desired sample rate for the bounce files from the SAMPLE RATE pop-up menu. Higher sampling rates will provide better audio fidelity but will also increase the size of the resulting file(s).

 The standard sample rate for compact discs is 44.1 kHz; the standard rate for professional and DVD video is 48 kHz. Selecting a multiple of the standard sample rate for the destination media will simplify the final sample rate conversion (44.1, 88.2, or 176.4 kHz for CD audio; 48, 96, or 192 kHz for DVD audio).

 If you plan to burn your bounced audio directly to CD without further processing, choose 44.1 kHz as the sample rate for the bounce.

10. If the sample rate for your bounce differs from your session's sample rate, the Conversion Quality pop-up list will become available. Select from the five choices on the list, based on the project needs. Note that higher Conversion Quality settings require longer rendering times. The default choice (Good) is adequate for general-purpose bounces.

The Conversion Quality pop-up list

11. Choose from the two conversion options, if applicable.
    • **Convert During Bounce.** This option converts file type, sample rate, and bit depth during the bounce process. This option generally takes less time than Convert After Bounce, but it might not maintain plug-in automation accuracy. This option is best for bounces that do not involve plug-in automation.
    • **Convert After Bounce.** This option converts file type, sample rate, and bit depth after bouncing is complete. This option is more time-consuming than Convert During Bounce, but it offers the highest level of plug-in automation accuracy possible.
12. To automatically import the newly bounced files into the Region List of your session, select the IMPORT AFTER BOUNCE option.

 The Import After Bounce option is available only if the target bit depth and sample rate for the bounce file match the bit depth and sample rate of your session.

13. After confirming your settings, click the BOUNCE button. A Save dialog box will prompt you to name the new audio file and navigate to the desired location to store the file.

The Save Bounce As dialog box

14. Select a destination for the new audio file, enter a name, and click **SAVE**. You will hear the audio play back as Pro Tools processes your bounce, and a countdown window will appear, displaying the time remaining for your bounce to complete.

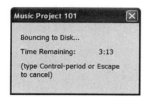

 You will not hear the bounce file play back in real time if you are not monitoring the bounce source.

 If you did not select the Import After Bounce option, you can import the bounced files to your session later using the Import Audio command.

Burning Songs to CD

Both Windows XP and Mac OS X enable you to create audio CDs from your bounced mix using software included with your computer or software purchased from a third-party developer. You can copy one or more bounced files to create tracks on either compact disc-recordable (CD-R) or compact disc-rewritable (CD-RW) media.

This section provides an overview of the typical processes of burning audio CDs on Windows XP and Mac OS X operating systems. The exact steps may vary, depending on the operating system and software you use.

 CD-R disks provide a universal format that can be played on most CD players; CD-RW discs can typically be played only by using a CD-ROM drive.

 When creating an audio CD using CD-R or CD-RW media, you must copy all tracks at the same time. You cannot add subsequent tracks after you have burned the disc. (CD-RW discs allow you erase the disc and start over, however.)

Creating a CD Using Windows Media Player

On Windows XP systems, you can create (burn) an audio CD using Windows Media Player. The Player converts tracks into CDA files to copy them to the compact disc and burns the audio CD according to the Red Book audio format.

To create a CD, you must have a CD recorder (burner) installed or attached to your computer and a blank CD to which you can copy tracks.

Supported File Types

Windows Media Player can use any of the following file types to create an audio CD:

- WMA (Windows Media Audio) files
- MP3 files
- WAV files

During the CD creation process, Windows Media Player automatically converts the files to CDA format for use on the CD.

Burning a CD

To burn your bounced audio to CD on a Windows XP system, do the following:

1. Insert a blank CD-R or CD-RW in your CD-ROM drive. A dialog box will open, prompting you for the action you want to take.

2. Choose SELECT MEDIA TO COPY TO CD USING WINDOWS MEDIA PLAYER. Windows Media Player will open.

3. If it is not already selected, click on COPY TO CD OR DEVICE in the Taskbar on the left side of the user interface.

4. Open Windows Explorer and resize/reposition the window as needed, such that Explorer and Windows Media Player are both visible on screen.

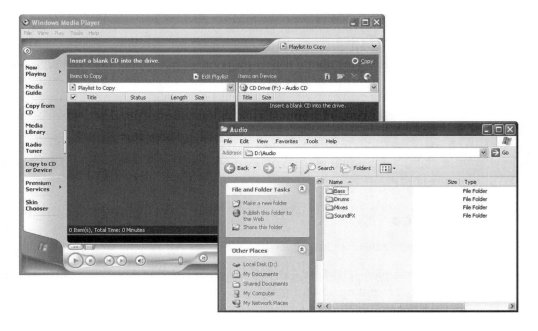

5. In the Explorer window, navigate to the location of your bounced audio files.

6. Select the files you want to include on the CD and drag them to the ITEMS TO COPY pane in Windows Media Player (left side pane). The number of selected items and the total play time of the tracks will be displayed at the bottom of the Items to Copy pane.

7. In the ITEMS ON DEVICE pane, click on the drop-down list and select AUDIO CD, if it is not already selected.

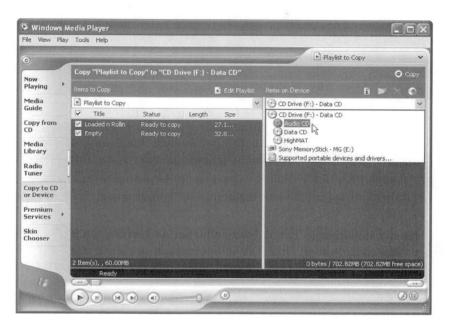

 The Audio CD option is available only on computers running Windows XP Home Edition or Windows XP Professional. Older systems running under Windows 98 Second Edition, Windows Millennium Edition (Me), or Windows 2000 have a Roxio CD burning option.

8. Click COPY. The selected tracks will be converted and burned to the disk.

Creating a CD on Mac OS X

Mac OS X allows you to create audio CDs using iTunes. To create an audio CD from a Mac system, your computer must have a Combo drive, a CD-R/CD-RW drive, or a SuperDrive connected or installed.

By default, Mac OS X burns CDs in a format that can also be used on non-Macintosh computers.

To burn an audio CD of your bounced files on a Mac, do the following:

1. Insert a blank CD into the optical drive of your computer. A dialog box will open, prompting you for the action you want to take.

2. Select **OPEN ITUNES** from the drop-down list and click **OK**. A second dialog box will open, providing directions for burning items on the CD.

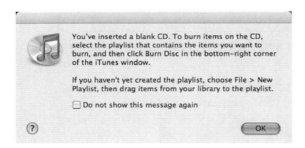

3. Review the directions and click **OK**.

4. If your files are not already in iTunes, choose **FILE > IMPORT**. Navigate to and select the files you wish to import, selecting them one at a time and clicking **CHOOSE**. The selected files will be added to your iTunes Music library.

5. Repeat as needed to add each of the files you want to include on your CD.

6. If needed, create a new playlist and drag the imported files from the Music library into the playlist. Name the playlist; this name will be used as the title for your CD.

7. When you are ready, select the playlist and click the **Burn Disk** button in the bottom-right corner of the iTunes window. The files in the playlist will be burned to the disc.

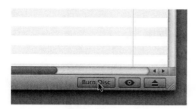

The Burn Disk button in iTunes

When burning is complete, the CD will be displayed in the left pane of the iTunes window, under Devices. Click the **Eject** button next to the CD name to remove the disc from your computer. You can now share your recordings with friends, band-mates, and more!

 The exact process can vary depending on the version of iTunes you are using. See the iTunes documentation for further details.

PART III

Hands-On Projects

Components

Overview

Part III of this course includes two projects that allow you to work with pre-recorded sessions to experiment with Audio, MIDI, and Video files. Throughout this part, you will apply many of the concepts that you learned in Parts I and II of this book. The goal of the projects is to illustrate the concepts discussed earlier in the book using straight-forward, practical workflows. The projects also include examples of more advanced functionality to broaden your understanding of Pro Tools in the music and post-production environments.

Overview | Project Introduction and Setup

The following pages describe the two hands-on projects included in this course and provide setup instructions for the work you will be doing. Included are instructions for installing the media files from the DVD and for installing the plug-ins used in the projects.

Notes

Getting to Know the Projects

The projects that you will complete are real-world sessions provided in incomplete form. This part of the coursework includes two projects, one from a music production workflow and one from a video post-production workflow. While these projects remain focused on the core set of Pro Tools functions described in the first two parts of the book, you will find that the workflows occasionally introduce concepts that have not been covered. (These concepts are discussed in later courses.)

Completing the Projects

Project 1, the Music Hands-On Project, is a three-minute song by Smack called "Waiting Here," consisting of 18 tracks in rough form. To complete this project, you will add Audio and Instrument tracks, add drums using the Xpand! plug-in, record an overdub using the Structure Free plug-in, import lead vocals and other audio, and add loops and effects processing to polish the mix.

Project 2, the Post Hands-On Project, is a 45-second commercial spot for Lotto Denmark called "Red Dragon," consisting of 21 tracks in rough form. To complete this project, you will create a new track and record a voice-over, import the QuickTime movie containing the video footage, import additional music and sound effects files, place sound effects and build fade-in and fade-out effects, replace the music bed, improve the quality of specific audio regions, and add effects processing to polish the mix.

Project Credits

The session files for the projects are provided courtesy of the following:

Project 1: "Waiting Here"

WRITTEN BY: Sean Householder and Anthony Mazza
PERFORMED AND PRODUCED BY: Smack, ©2005

Project 2: "Red Dragon"

PRODUCTION COMPANY: Social Club, Stockholm
PRODUCER: Markus Ahlm
DIRECTOR: Axel Laubscher
AGENCY PRODUCER: Lars Sundin Lowe, Copenhagen
CLIENT: Lotto Denmark

Pro Tools System Requirements

To complete these projects, you will need a qualified Pro Tools interface and compatible Pro Tools software installed. The projects are designed for Pro Tools 7.4. Most parts of the projects can be completed using Pro Tools 7.1 or later software with slight modifications in various steps; however, the projects cannot be completed in their entirety without current software.

Installing Free Plug-Ins

The DVD includes two plug-ins for Pro Tools 7.x that you can install and use free of charge. The Xpand! and Structure Free plug-ins provide powerful virtual instruments from Digidesign's Advanced Instrument Research (A.I.R.) division:

- **Xpand!** A popular virtual instrument, Xpand! provides fast, efficient access to high-quality sounds from within Pro Tools, including more than 1,000 preset patches and more than 500 combinable parts. The Xpand! sound library includes synth pads, leads, acoustic and electric pianos, organs, strings, vocals, brass and woodwinds, mallet percussion, ethnic instruments, loops, and more.
- **Structure Free.** The latest free virtual instrument released by Digidesign's A.I.R. division, Structure Free provides sample playback, full compatibility with all Structure versions, 60 preset patches, and a 64-voice multitimbral sound engine. The Structure Free sample library includes drum kits, drum loops, bass and guitar patches, leads, electric pianos, organs, pads, and more. This plug-in requires Pro Tools 7.3 or later.

System Requirements for Plug-Ins

Each plug-in has specific system requirements. For details on a particular plug-in, see the plug-in guide for that component included on the DVD. To install and use the plug-ins required to complete the two projects in this section, you will need the following:

- A computer running Windows XP or Mac OS X operating system
- Pro Tools HD 7.x, Pro Tools LE 7.x, or Pro Tools M-Powered 7.x software and a qualified interface (Pro Tools 7.3 or later required for Structure Free)
- Approximately 1.65 GB available disk space on the system drive

Plug-In Installation Instructions

To install the plug-ins, run the installers on the DVD:

1. Insert the DVD and open it to view the included files and folders.
2. Open the INSTALLERS folder.
3. For each plug-in, open the associated folder (XPAND! or STRUCTURE).
4. Open the appropriate folder for your operating system (marked with "PC" for Windows XP installers or "MAC" for Mac OS X installers).
5. Double-click the .EXE file (Windows) or .DMG file (Mac OS) to begin the installation.
6. Double-click the installer icon when it appears on screen (Mac OS only).
7. Follow the on-screen instructions to complete the installation.

Complete this process for each of the plug-in packs. For additional information on installing any of the plug-ins, see the associated plug-in guide included on the DVD.

Installing Project Session Files

Before you begin work on the projects, you will need to install the session files onto an available hard drive. The session files are included on the DVD along with the additional audio, MIDI, and other media files that you will need to complete the projects.

System Requirements for Project Sessions

The projects are designed to be completed using Pro Tools M-Powered 7.4, Pro Tools LE 7.4, or Pro Tools HD 7.4 software with a qualified audio interface. See Chapter 1 for a description of qualified interfaces or check the Digidesign website for the latest qualified products (www.digidesign.com).

Users with earlier Pro Tools versions (7.1 through 7.3) can complete the projects using alternate methods for features that are not available in their software. (Alternate methods are typically noted in the text.) However, certain menu commands, preference options, dialog boxes, and user interface features may vary on older systems.

You will need space available on your destination drive to copy the session files and related media. If possible, select a hard drive that is separate from your system drive to use as the destination for the session files.

The recommended disk space for completing both projects is 892 MB:

- 465 MB for the Music project session files
- 127 MB for the Post project session files
- 300 MB+ available for recording

To check the available space on your selected drive, do the following:

- In Windows, double-click on MY COMPUTER to display information about the available drives.
- In Mac OS, click on the selected drive icon from the desktop and choose FILE > GET INFO to display the Information window for the drive.

Installation Instructions for Session Files

To install the project session files and related media, copy the materials from the DVD to your selected hard drive:

1. Insert the DVD and open it to view the included files and folders.
2. Open the HANDS-ON PROJECTS folder.
3. Copy the MUSIC PROJECT and the POST PROJECT folders from the DVD to your selected hard drive.
4. Close the DVD window when finished copying.
5. For Mac OS only, do the following:

   a. Click on each project folder on your hard drive individually and choose FILE > GET INFO (or press COMMAND+I). The Information window for the folder will open.

   b. At the bottom of the window, change the OWNERSHIP & PERMISSIONS setting to READ & WRITE.

   c. Click the disclosure triangle next to DETAILS to display additional options.

   d. Click APPLY TO ENCLOSED ITEMS to enable read and write permissions for all subfolders. Click OK when prompted by the verification dialog box.

Project 1

Music Hands-On Project

In this project, you will work with a three-minute song consisting of 18 tracks in rough form. To complete this project, you will add Audio and Instrument tracks, add drums using the Xpand! plug-in, add an overdub using the Structure Free plug-in, import lead vocals and other audio, and add loops and effects processing to polish the mix.

The media files for this project are provided courtesy of Sean Householder of Smack:

- WRITTEN BY: Sean Householder and Anthony Mazza
- PERFORMED AND PRODUCED BY: Smack, ©2005

 The audio files provided for this project are to be used only to complete the exercises contained herein. No rights are granted to use the files or any portion thereof in any commercial or non-commercial production or performance.

Notes

Powering Up

To get started on this project, you will need to power up your system. It is important to power up your system *properly*, because improper power-up procedures can lead to various problems and can possibly damage your equipment.

When using audio equipment, you should power up components in the order that the audio signal flows through them. The general process for powering up a Pro Tools M-Powered or LE system is as follows (see your system documentation for powering up a Pro Tools|HD system):

1. Power up external hard drives.
2. Verify connections and power up audio/MIDI interfaces.
3. Start your computer.
4. Power up your monitoring system, if applicable.
5. Launch Pro Tools.

Refer to Chapter 2 for more details on powering up your system.

Opening the Music Project

In this section of the hands-on project, you will open the Music project and prepare your session windows for the work you will be performing in this project.

The session that you will use for this project was last saved using a Pro Tools LE system with an Mbox 2 interface. When you first open a project session created on a different system, you are often prompted by several dialog boxes notifying you of setup differences. This is normal behavior; simply select the default options to close the dialog boxes and continue working.

Locate the Session Using the Workspace Browser

Pro Tools provides a number of ways to open a session. For instance, you can always use the **OPEN** command in the File menu. For the purposes of this project, however, you will locate and open the session file from the Workspace browser. The Workspace browser is a one-stop shop for all of your opening and importing needs, and it includes a handy search function (should you forget were you placed some of those elusive audio files).

Locate and open the Music session from the Workspace browser:

1. With no session open in Pro Tools, choose **WINDOW > WORKSPACE** to open the Workspace browser.

 *You can also press **ALT+;** (Windows) or **OPTION+;** (Mac OS) to toggle the Workspace browser open and closed.*

2. Click the **FIND** icon (magnifying glass) in the Workspace window.
3. Type **Music Hands-On Project** in the **NAME** field.
4. Select **SESSION FILE** from the **KIND** drop-down menu.

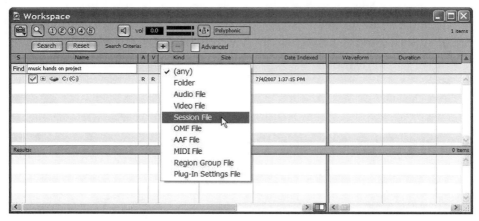

Selecting a file type to search for from the Kind drop-down menu

5. Click the **SEARCH** button. After a few moments the session will display in the lower (green and white) area of the Workspace browser.
6. Double-click on the session to open it.

 Make sure to open the session copy from your hard drive and not the original file on the DVD.

Refer to Chapter 3 for additional information on locating and opening sessions.

Dismiss warnings:

As the session opens for the first time, you could be prompted by two dialog boxes notifying you of changes in the system setup. Dismiss each of these by selecting the default options:

- **Playback engine not available.** Choose **OK** to continue with the current playback engine.

Example of the playback engine notification dialog box

- **Disk allocation and I/O setup change.** Choose **No** to continue without saving a report.

Example of the disk allocation and I/O setup notification dialog box

Orient the Session Windows

When the session opens, you will see the Edit window displayed on your screen. (If you have closed the Edit window, choose **WINDOW > EDIT** to reactivate it.) You will use the Edit window for much of the recording and editing you do in this project. You will also be using the Mix window and the Transport window throughout the project. Before getting started, you should open each of these windows and orient them on your screen. In Pro Tools 7.3 and later, you can do this using a Window Configuration that has been saved with this session:

1. Choose **WINDOW > CONFIGURATIONS > WINDOW CONFIGURATION LIST**. The Window Configurations List will open.

2. Click on the Window Configuration named "Main Windows." The Mix, Edit, and Transport windows will open on screen.

3. Reposition/resize the windows as desired to maximize the use of your screen.

The 18 tracks in the session are displayed horizontally (left to right) as channel strips in the Mix window and vertically (top to bottom) as Track Playlists in the Edit window—you might need to scroll each window to view all of the tracks.

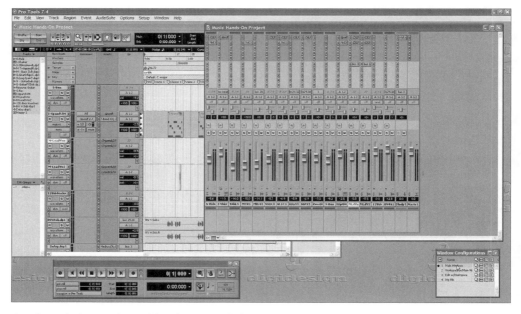

Session windows oriented for the start of the project

Set the Preferences

This project requires certain preference settings. Before continuing, you will need to verify the preference settings for your session.

 In Pro Tools 7.3 and earlier, some of the Preference options will be slightly different; users on older systems should use those settings that are applicable.

Check preferences settings:

1. Choose Setup > Preferences. The Preferences window will open.
2. Click on the Operation tab.
   - Verify that Timeline Insertion/Play Start Marker Follows Playback is not selected (unchecked).
   - Verify that Edit Insertion Follows Scrub/Shuttle is selected (checked).
   - Leave all other settings unchanged.

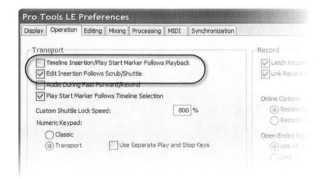

Preference settings under the Operation tab

3. Click on the Editing tab.
   - Verify that Edit Selection Follows Region List Selection is checked.
4. In the Zoom Toggle section of the Editing tab, select the following settings:
   - Set both Vertical MIDI Zoom and Horizontal Zoom to Selection.
   - Verify that Remove Range Selection After Zooming In is unchecked.
   - Set Track Height to Jumbo.
   - Set Track View to Waveform/Notes.
   - Verify that Zoom Toggle Follows Edit Selection is unchecked.
   - Leave other settings unchanged.

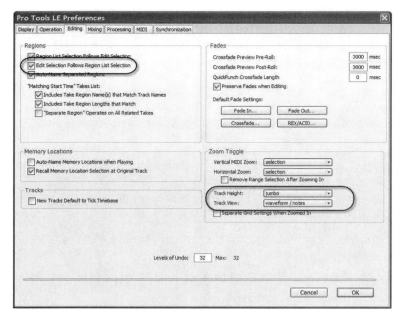

Preference settings under the Editing tab

5. Click on the **PROCESSING** tab.
   - In the **IMPORT** section, verify that **IMPORT REX FILES AS REGION GROUPS** is unchecked.

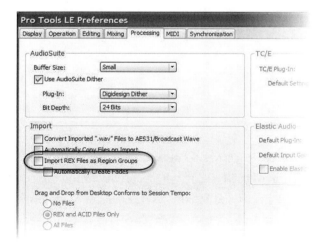

Preference settings under the Processing tab

6. Click **OK** to close the Preferences window.

Connect Input and Monitoring Devices

For this project, you will be recording MIDI performance data. If you have an available MIDI controller, you should connect it to your audio interface now. To do so, run a MIDI cable from the MIDI Out port on your keyboard or other MIDI device to the MIDI In port on your Mbox 2 or other qualified interface.

If you do not have an available MIDI device, you can skip this step and follow the alternative procedures provided during the project.

If you have a monitoring system connected to the left and right outputs of your audio interface, you will use that to listen to the session playback. If you do not have a monitoring system, you can listen to the session playback using headphones on compatible audio interfaces. If your interface has an available headphone jack, plug in your headphones and test the playback level.

Creating New Tracks

In this section of the project, you will create the new tracks needed for the session. The information in this section is based primarily on the material in Chapter 3.

Create and Name Tracks

You will need to create three new tracks for the session, one to record and play back MIDI information using a virtual instrument, a second to record the output of the virtual instrument track, and a third to use as a click track. When creating tracks, you will select the track type and format, based on how each track will be used. In this case, the first track will be used for a stereo virtual instrument, so you will create a stereo Instrument track for this. The second will be used to record the audio output of the virtual instrument, so you will create a stereo Audio track. The third track will be used to generate a click; for this you will use the Create Click Track command (requires Pro Tools 7.3 or later).

Create the new Audio and Instrument tracks:

1. If needed, activate the Edit window by clicking on it or choosing **WINDOW > EDIT**.
2. Scroll to the top of the window so that the S-Ride track displays at the top.
3. Click on the **S-RIDE** Track Nameplate to select the track so that your new tracks will appear directly below this track.

 Pro Tools always places new tracks below the lowest selected track in the session. If no tracks are selected, Pro Tools places the new tracks at the bottom of the session.

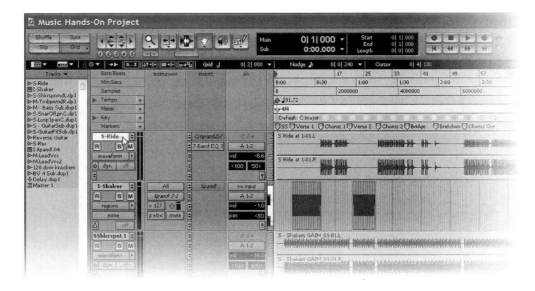

Selecting the S-Ride track

4. Choose **TRACK > NEW**. The New Tracks dialog box will open, displaying Mono, Audio Track, and Samples as default selections from left to right.

5. Click on the **TRACK FORMAT** pop-up menu and choose **STEREO**.

6. Click on the **TRACK TYPE** pop-up menu and choose **INSTRUMENT TRACK**.

7. Click the **ADD ROW** button (plus sign) to the right of the pop-up selectors. A second entry will appear in the dialog box.

8. Choose **STEREO** and **AUDIO TRACK** as the track format and type for the second track.

9. Click **CREATE**. Two new tracks will be added to the session, beneath the S-Ride track.

Creating the new tracks for your session

Create the click track:

1. Choose TRACK > CREATE CLICK TRACK. A new click track will be added to the session, beneath the new Instrument and Audio tracks.

 The CREATE CLICK TRACK command is available only in Pro Tools 7.3 and later. Users with older systems should skip this step.

Next, you will give the tracks meaningful names. You can rename your tracks at any time as needed.

Name your new tracks:

1. Double-click on the nameplate of the Instrument track (Inst 1) to open the Track Name dialog box.
2. Type **I-Xpand! Drums** in the Name the Track field.
3. Add comments to help identify the track function, such as "Instrument - Xpand! Drums."
4. Click the NEXT button. You will see Audio 1 displayed.

Naming tracks and adding comments

5. Type **S-Drums** in the Name the Track field, and add comments, such as "Stereo - Drums."
6. Click OK. The tracks will display with their new names.

Save Your Session

After making any significant changes to a session, it is a good idea to save. That way, if something should disrupt your progress (such as a power outage) you will not have to redo any of your work. To preserve the original session for future use, use the SAVE AS command at this point.

Save a copy of your session, adding your initials to the session name:

1. Choose FILE > SAVE AS. The Save As dialog box will open with the session name highlighted.
2. Click in the FILE NAME field after the session name and type a dash followed by your initials.
3. Click SAVE.

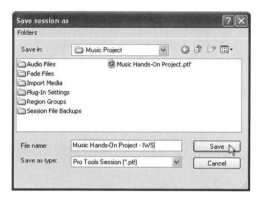

Saving the session with your initials after the session name

Now you have saved a copy of the session file with a different name. This new session continues to reference the original audio, video, and fade files. For more information on Save options, see Chapters 3 and 10.

Recording MIDI

For this section of the project, you will add the Xpand! virtual instrument plug-in to your Instrument track, route (and verify) MIDI to the instrument from your MIDI controller, route (and verify) audio from the Xpand! plug-in, set up the click track, record MIDI data from your controller onto your Instrument track, and add a MIDI region from the Region List onto your Instrument track. You will also make a quick overdub on the I-Structure track using the Structure Free sampler plug-in.

Some parts of this section require the use of a MIDI keyboard/controller. If you do not have an available MIDI controller, you can skip over these portions or use the alternate procedure noted.

The information in this section is based primarily on the concepts discussed in Chapter 5.

Add a Virtual Instrument

In the last section, you created an Instrument track and named it "I-Xpand! Drums." Now, you will add a virtual instrument to this track using the Xpand! plug-in. This will allow the Instrument track to play back audio based on recorded or live MIDI data.

Insert Xpand! onto the I-Xpand! Drums track:

1. In the Edit window, click on INSERT SELECTOR A on the I-Xpand! Drums track.

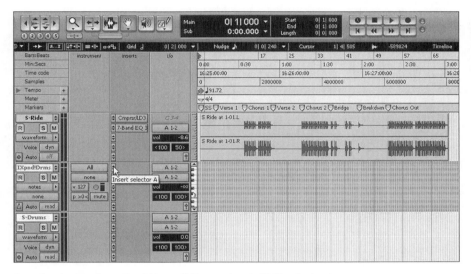

Insert selector A on the I-Xpand! Drums track (Edit window)

2. Choose MULTI-CHANNEL PLUG-IN > INSTRUMENT > XPAND! (STEREO) from the pop-up list. The Xpand! plug-in window will appear on screen.

3. Click on the LIBRARIAN MENU, and choose 26 DRUMS > 07 ROCK KIT.

4. Click on the **Close** button in the upper-right corner (Windows) or upper-left corner (Mac OS) of the Xpand! window to close the plug-in window.

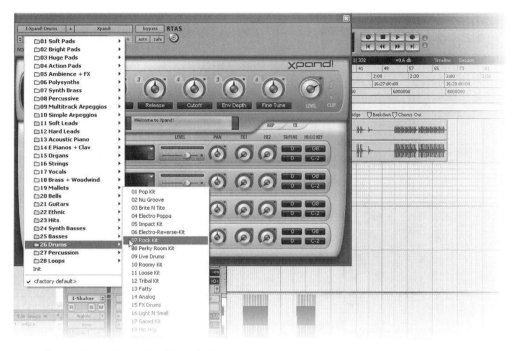

Selecting a drum kit for the Xpand! plug-in

Verify the Routing

When you add a virtual instrument to an Instrument track, Pro Tools intelligently routes all of the MIDI and audio connections automatically. While this is convenient, at times you might want to customize the routing or do some troubleshooting.

At this point in your project, you will need to verify that all of the routing is correct and make any changes necessary.

Verify the MIDI signal routing:

1. In the Edit window, click on the **Track Record Enable** button (labeled "R") under the track name of the I-Xpand! Drums track to enable it to register MIDI data being sent from your MIDI controller.

2. Check that the **MIDI INPUT SELECTOR** on the I-Xpand! Drums Instrument track is set to **ALL**. If it isn't, click on the **MIDI INPUT SELECTOR** and choose **ALL** from the pop-up menu.

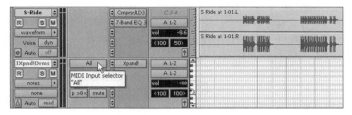

MIDI Input selector on the I-Xpand! Drums track

 If you use multiple virtual instruments in your session, it is possible to have your Instrument track triggering the wrong instrument. If you are getting unexpected results, verify that the MIDI Output selector of your Instrument track matches the MIDI Node displayed in the instrument plug-in window.

3. Play some notes on your MIDI controller and check the level on the Instrument track's MIDI meter. The level is not important at this point; you are just using the level meter to verify that MIDI data is being received.

   (Alternate) If you don't have a MIDI controller connected, click a key on the mini keyboard on the Track Height selector (available on Instrument and MIDI tracks) to trigger MIDI notes.

4. Verify that the MIDI signal is registering on the MIDI meter. If no signal registers, verify your MIDI controller settings and connections and double-check the settings in steps 1 and 2 of this section.

Signal registering on the MIDI meter

Once you have verified that the MIDI signal is being received, you will need to ensure that the audio generated by the virtual instrument is routed properly.

Verify the audio signal routing:

1. Toggle to the Mix window by pressing **CTRL+=** (Windows) or **COMMAND+=** (Mac OS) to make the channel strips visible.

2. If needed, **ALT-CLICK** (Windows) or **OPTION-CLICK** (Mac OS) on the **VOLUME FADER** of the I-Xpand! Drums Instrument track to set the level to 0.0 (unity gain).

3. Play some notes on your MIDI controller.

   (Alternate) If you don't have a MIDI controller connected, press CTRL+= (Windows) or COMMAND+= (Mac OS) to toggle to the Edit window. Click on the mini keyboard to trigger MIDI notes.

4. Verify the audio signal. You should hear a variety of drum sounds and see a signal register on the track's level meters.

Set Up the Click

When recording in Pro Tools, it is often helpful to record to a click. That way, the recording will match the tempo and grid defined in your session, allowing you to edit and arrange session parts more easily. In this section, you are going to verify that your click track is active. (Users with systems prior to Pro Tools 7.3 can skip this section.)

Enable the Click plug-in:

1. Press CTRL+= (Windows) or COMMAND+= (Mac OS) to toggle to the Mix window, if it is not already active.

2. If it is not already visible, press CTRL+[1] (keypad) (Windows) or COMMAND+[1] (keypad) (Mac OS) to activate the Transport window.

3. Click the METRONOME CLICK button in the Transport window to activate the click. The button will turn blue when active.

4. Solo the Click track by clicking on the SOLO button (labeled with an "S") above the track Volume Fader (Mix window).

5. Press the SPACE BAR to audition the click.

6. Click the SOLO button again to take the track out of Solo mode.

7. Press the SPACE BAR a second time to stop playback.

For more information on creating and configuring a click track, see Chapter 4.

Make a Recording

Next you will record a MIDI drum beat in real time to the click. The data that you record will ultimately be replaced by a prerecorded MIDI region, so you don't have to be a virtuoso performer (or even a competent performer) to complete this part of the project. You simply need to be able to use your MIDI controller to trigger record-able MIDI events.

If you do not have a MIDI controller or you don't want to record, you can skip this section and move directly to the "Drag in a MIDI Region" section.

 You will need a MIDI keyboard or other MIDI controller connected to your system to complete the recording. You cannot record from the mini keyboard on screen.

Locate the starting point for the recording:

1. Press **CTRL+=** (Windows) or **COMMAND+=** (Mac OS) to toggle to the Edit window.
2. With the **SELECTOR** tool, click anywhere on the I-Xpand! Drums track.
3. Choose **WINDOW > MEMORY LOCATIONS** to open the Memory Locations window.
4. Click the memory location labeled "Song Start." The insertion point will automatically move to the proper location.
5. Close the Memory Locations window to reduce the on-screen clutter.

Record a MIDI drumbeat:

1. Solo the I-Xpand! Drums track by clicking on the track's **SOLO** button (labeled "S") in the Edit window under the track name. The Solo button will turn solid yellow.

The Click track is Solo-Safe–enabled, so it will continue to play when other tracks are soloed.

2. If necessary, record-enable the I-Xpand! Drums track by clicking on the **TRACK RECORD ENABLE** button (labeled "R") under the track name. The button will flash red.
3. Check that countoff has been enabled using the **COUNTOFF** button in the Transport window with the default of two bars. The button should be blue.

Click the Countoff button to enable countoff; double-click to change the countoff value.

4. Click the **RECORD ENABLE** button in the Transport window. The **RECORD ENABLE** button will flash red, showing that Pro Tools is armed and ready to record.

5. Press the SPACE BAR to start the countoff. The Record Enable button on the track will turn solid red, and you will hear the countoff begin. After two bars, the play line will begin to move down the track, indicating that it is recording MIDI data.

6. Play in a few bars of a drum beat using your MIDI controller, keeping time with the click.

7. When you are finished, press the SPACE BAR again to stop recording.

 If you want to retry the recording, you can choose EDIT > UNDO to undo the recording and repeat steps 4 through 7. You might have to reposition the insertion point by clicking on the SONG START memory location.

8. Take the I-Xpand! Drums track out of Solo mode by clicking on the track's SOLO button a second time.

9. Click on the TRACK RECORD ENABLE button on the I-Xpand! Drums track to take the track out of Record Enable mode.

10. To listen to your recording in context, press the SPACE BAR to begin playback. Press the SPACE BAR a second time to stop playback.

Drag in a MIDI Region

The session's Region List includes a MIDI region containing a previously recorded MIDI drum performance for this song. You will now bring it onto the I-Xpand! Drums track, replacing any data on the track that you have recorded.

Drag the Xpand! Drums MIDI region onto the I-Xpand! Drums track:

1. Verify that the I-Xpand! Drums track is not record-enabled. If necessary, click on the TRACK RECORD ENABLE button to take the track out of Record Enable mode.

2. Click on the TRACK VIEW SELECTOR of the I-Xpand! Drums track, and choose REGIONS from the pop-up menu.

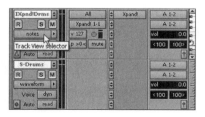 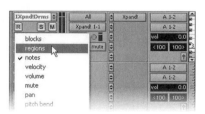

Click the Track View selector to switch to Regions view

3. Solo the I-Xpand! Drums track by clicking on the track's **SOLO** button (labeled "S") in the Edit window under the track name.

4. With the **GRABBER** tool, select the Xpand! Drums MIDI region in the Region List.

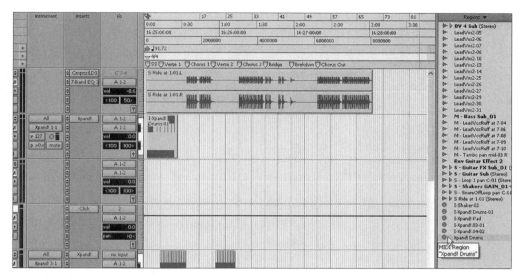

Selecting the Xpand! Drums region in the Region List

5. Drag the Xpand! Drums region from the Region List onto the I-Xpand! Drums track. Position the region to start at the beginning of the session (0|1|000).

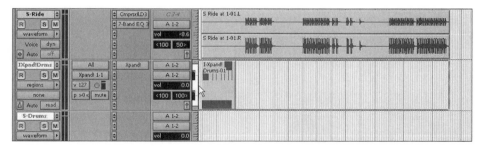

Placing the prerecorded drum region onto the virtual Instrument track

6. Press the **SPACE BAR** to audition the MIDI drums with the click. Press the **SPACE BAR** a second time to stop playback.

7. If necessary, adjust the region placement to ensure that it begins at 0|1|000 to match the click timing.

8. When you are satisfied with the drum timing, unsolo the I-Xpand! Drums track.

Recording an Overdub

In the steps that follow, you will record an overdub on the I-Structure track using MIDI Merge Mode. This Instrument track uses the Structure Free sample playback plug-in to produce an acoustic guitar sound and includes two previously recorded MIDI regions. Using the key switches defined for this patch, you will record MIDI notes that set the effects levels for these regions.

If you do not have a MIDI controller, you can skip the recording steps in this section; you might want to complete the non-recording steps, however, to gain a better understanding of the key switch function in Structure Free.

 The Structure Free plug-in requires Pro Tools 7.3 or later. Users with older systems can skip this section.

Locate the area for the recording:

1. Scroll the Edit window down to locate the I-Structure track.

2. With the **SELECTOR** tool, click anywhere on the I-Structure track.

3. Choose **WINDOW > MEMORY LOCATIONS** to open the Memory Locations window.

4. Click the memory location labeled "Verse 2." The insertion point will move to the start of the second verse.

5. While holding the Shift key, click on the **CHORUS 2** memory location. The area between the two memory locations will be selected on the track.

6. Close the Memory Locations window to reduce the on-screen clutter.

Prepare for recording:

1. Click on the Structure Free plug-in on Insert A of the I-Structure track to open the Structure Free plug-in window.

Clicking on the Structure Free plug-in

2. Using the on-screen keyboard, play some notes in Structure Free. Note that the C0 and D0 keys are shaded blue, indicating that these are available key switches.

3. Click on each key switch and note the change in the Reverb Mix and Reverb Time Smart Knobs. These key switches enable you to boost and cut the reverb effect as part of a performance.

4. In the Transport window, enable **MIDI MERGE MODE**, if not already active, and disable countoff.

5. Record-enable the I-Structure track by clicking on the **TRACK RECORD ENABLE** button (labeled "R") under the track name. The button will flash red.

6. Click the **RECORD ENABLE** button in the Transport window. The **RECORD ENABLE** button will flash red, showing that Pro Tools is armed and ready to record.

Record the overdub:

1. Close the Structure Free plug-in window.

2. Press the SPACE BAR to start recording. The Record Enable button on the track will turn solid red, and the play line will begin to move down the track, indicating that it is recording MIDI data.

3. At any point before playback reaches the first region on the track, press the **C0** key on your MIDI controller to cut the reverb. (This will ensure that the reverb is reset to its default state each time the track is played back.) Allow recording to continue though the existing region.

4. At any point after the first region and before the second region, press the **D0** key on your MIDI controller to boost the reverb.

5. When finished, press the SPACE BAR to stop recording or allow it to stop automatically when it reaches the end of the selection.

6. Click on the **TRACK RECORD ENABLE** button on the I-Structure track to take the track out of Record Enable mode.

Save Work in Progress

Earlier, you created a copy of the session using the Save As command under the File menu. As you complete each main portion of the project, you should save your work in progress. To do this, you will use the **SAVE** command from the File menu. This will not create a copy of your session; rather, it will save your changes to the existing session that is currently open.

Save your work:

1. Choose **FILE > SAVE** to save your progress up to this point.

Recording Audio

In the next section of the project, you will use the concepts discussed in Chapter 4 to record audio. For the purposes of this project, you will be recording the audio output of a virtual instrument. Although the recording process described here is generally the same as you would use when recording from a microphone or an external instrument, the exact steps and setup will vary in each situation depending on the type of audio interface you are using and the specific sound source you are recording. Refer to Chapter 4 in this book and the Getting Started guide that came with your audio interface for more information.

The general workflow for preparing to make a recording is as follows:

1. Check disk space.
2. Route the signal.
3. Record-enable the track.
4. Set the input level.

In the sections that follow, you will work through each of these steps to create a recording.

Check Disk Space

Because the audio signal is recorded directly to disk, your total available recording time will depend on the amount of free disk space that you have. Refer to Table 3.1 in Chapter 3 to determine the amount of disk space required for a project. If you have limited space on your hard drive, it is a good idea to check just how much free disk space you have before you start recording. Fortunately, you can access this information very easily from within Pro Tools, using the Disk Space window.

For this project, you will only be recording a few minutes' worth of material, so you can get by with as little as 50 MB or so. However, we recommend starting with a minimum of 300 MB of disk space available.

Verify that you have adequate free disk space:

1. Choose WINDOW > DISK SPACE. A small window will open, indicating the available space on each of your drives.
2. Verify that you have adequate space available on the drive that you are using for the project.
3. If the available space is less than 300 MB, consider freeing up additional space on the drive or switching to another drive before continuing.
4. Close the Disk Space window when finished to minimize on-screen clutter.

Full multi-track recording sessions can easily consume several gigabytes of disk space, especially at higher bit depths and sample rates. Be sure to calculate your storage needs for a project in advance, taking into account the probability of multiple takes on each track.

Route the Signal

To record onto a track, you need to properly route the signal to the track. Often this is done by connecting a microphone, instrument, or other external sound source to an appropriate input on your audio interface. For the purpose of this project, however, you will route the audio output of your virtual Instrument track to a bus.

Send the I-Xpand! Drums output to bus 1–2:

1. Press CTRL+= (Windows) or COMMAND+= (Mac OS) to toggle to the Mix window.
2. Click on the AUDIO OUTPUT PATH SELECTOR for the I-Xpand! Drums track and choose BUS > BUS 1-2 (STEREO).

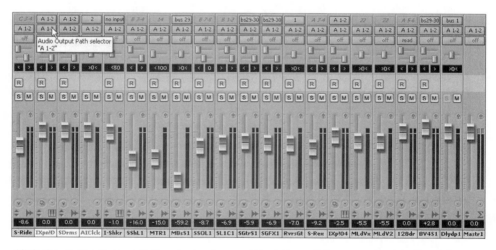

Click the Audio Output Path selector to send the I-Xpand! Drums output to Bus 1–2.

Enable an Audio Track for Recording

Next you need to set the input on the track you will be recording to so that it receives the incoming signal. Often this is done by selecting the input on your audio interface that your external sound source is plugged in to. For the purpose of this project, however, you will select the bus that is carrying the output from your virtual Instrument track.

Set the S-Drums track's input to bus 1–2:

1. Locate the S-Drums track in the Mix window.

2. Click on the AUDIO INPUT PATH SELECTOR for the track and choose BUS > BUS 1–2 (STEREO).

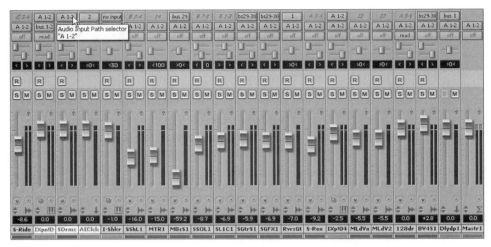

Click the Audio Input Path selector to receive the Bus 1–2 signal on the S-Drums track.

You will now use the S-Drums track to record the output of the Instrument track as live audio. Pro Tools will allow you to record onto one or more tracks while playing back from others. To do so, you will need to record-enable the track.

Record-enable the S-Drums track:

1. Click on the RECORD ENABLE button (labeled "R" above the track Volume Fader) for the S-Drums track. The Record Enable button will begin to flash red.

Set Recording Level

With the input of the track assigned and the track record-enabled, you will next need to set the record level such that the track receives an adequate signal without clipping. The level meter indicator should fluctuate in the top half of the meter, averaging about two-thirds up. The red portion of the meter should never light up. If the signal is either too weak or too hot, you will need to adjust the volume or signal level of your sound source. For this project, that means adjusting the playback volume of your virtual instrument.

Set the record level for the S-Drums track:

1. Press the SPACE BAR to begin playback.
2. While viewing the level meter for the S-Drums track, adjust the Volume Fader for the I-Xpand! Drums track. Note the change in the record level of the S-Drums track.

 If you do not see any level on the S-Drums track, activate Input Only mode by choosing TRACK > INPUT ONLY MONITORING. This allows Pro Tools to monitor audio input only, regardless of the track's punch-in/out selection or state.

3. Set the Volume Fader for the I-Xpand! Drums track such that the S-Drums track is receiving a steady, strong signal without clipping.
4. Press the SPACE BAR a second time to stop playback.

 Adjusting the Volume Fader on a record-enabled track has no effect on the record level for that track; the record level is determined by the strength of the signal coming into the track.

 When you record with a microphone, the level must be adjusted at the mic preamp. If a microphone is plugged directly into a Digidesign Pro Tools LE interface, the level can be adjusted using the gain knob on the interface for that input.

Record a Track

At this point in your project, you should be ready to begin your actual recording. To do so, you will position the insertion point at the starting point for the recording, arm Pro Tools to record, and proceed with the recording pass.

Place the insertion cursor at the starting point for the recording:

1. Press CTRL+= (Windows) or COMMAND+= (Mac OS) to toggle to the Edit window.
2. Choose WINDOW > MEMORY LOCATIONS to open the Memory Locations window.
3. Click the memory location labeled "Song Start." This will automatically move the insertion point to the proper location.
4. Close the MEMORY LOCATIONS window to reduce on-screen clutter.

Arm Pro Tools and record the S-Drums track:

1. Click the RECORD button in the Transport window. The Record button will flash red, showing that Pro Tools is armed and ready to record.
2. Press the SPACE BAR to start recording. The Record Enable button on the track will turn solid red. After two measures of countoff, recording will start, and you will see a red waveform being written on the S-Drums track. (You might need to scroll up to see the track.)
3. After the song has finished, press the SPACE BAR again to stop the recording.
4. Click the RECORD ENABLE button (Mix or Edit window) on the S-Drums track to disable recording on the track.

 If you need to redo the recording, you can choose EDIT > UNDO after step 3 to undo the recording and repeat the process.

Rename Audio Files and Regions

You might notice that the audio file/region you have recorded has a similar name to the track on which it was recorded. This is one of the reasons for giving your tracks meaningful names before you start recording. However, you might find that at times you would like the audio file or region name to be different from the track name. For this project, you will rename the audio file and region using the name of the virtual instrument that was recorded.

Rename the S-Drums audio file and region:

1. In the Edit window, select the GRABBER tool.
2. Double-click with the GRABBER tool on the region you recorded on the S-Drums track. A Name dialog box will appear.
3. In the NAME THE REGION field, type **Xpand! Drum Audio**. Since this region represents the entire audio file (or whole-file region), the Name dialog gives you the option to either name the region only or rename both the region and the audio file.
4. Choose NAME REGION AND DISK FILE using the radio button.
5. Click **OK**. The region will display in the Edit window and the Region List with the new name.

You have now successfully recorded the output of your virtual instrument and renamed both the audio file and the region. At this point, you no longer need to use the Instrument track, meaning that you can free up the resources it uses for other purposes. The easiest way to do this is to make the Instrument track inactive. Inactive tracks don't consume any of your computer's processing power, but they can still be accessed in the session if needed at a later point. For instance, if you later decide that you want to change the sound of the drums, you can reactivate the I-Xpand! Drums track, make the changes, re-record the audio output, and deactivate the track again.

Make the I-Xpand! Drums track inactive:

1. ALT-CLICK (Windows) or OPTION-CLICK (Mac OS) on the nameplate of any selected track to deselect all tracks.
2. Click on the I-XPAND! DRUMS Track Nameplate to select just that track.
3. Choose TRACK > MAKE INACTIVE. The track will become grayed out, showing that it is now inactive.

Save Work in Progress

Now that you have completed another main portion of work on the project, you should again save your work in progress.

Save your work:

1. Choose FILE > SAVE to save your progress up to this point.

Importing Media

Not all of the audio that is used in a Pro Tools session needs to be recorded directly into the session. For instance, you might have recordings that you made in other sessions that you would like to use or prerecorded loops (such as ACID and REX files) that you want to include in your current session. In these cases, you will want to import the existing audio from your hard drive into the current session.

Pro Tools provides many ways to import audio into your session. (Refer to Chapter 5 for detailed information regarding importing media.) For this project, you will import audio using the Import command and using the Workspace browser.

Import REX Files to the Region List

For this part of the project, you will need to import some additional REX files into your session. When importing audio, you can choose to place it either into the Region List or directly onto a track. In this case, you will import to the Region List because the imported material won't be starting at the beginning of the song. You can import these particular files from the Import Media folder.

Some steps in this section require Pro Tools 7.3 or 7.4 software. Users with older systems can skip such steps or use workarounds where provided.

Import the REX files into the Region List:

1. In the Window Configurations List, click on the Window Configuration named "Workspace w/Main Windows" to open the Workspace browser (or choose WINDOW > WORKSPACE). Position the Workspace browser such that the Region List remains visible in the Edit window.

2. If needed, click the RESET button in the Workspace browser to clear the previous search.

3. Click the FIND button (magnifying glass), if not already active, to reveal the search fields.

4. Type **084** in the Name field and select AUDIO FILE from the Kind pop-up menu. Make sure that there is a check next to the disk volume that contains the Music Project folder.

5. Click SEARCH. After a moment, one or more files will appear in the lower pane of the Workspace browser.

6. Click on the TOOLBOX button next to the magnifying glass to activate the Browser menu, and verify that the Audio Files Conform To Session Tempo option is enabled (checked). (This step requires Pro Tools 7.4.)

7. Click on the **084** MACHINE GRASP.RX2 file to select it and drag it to the Region List in the Edit window. The file will convert to the session format, and two new regions will appear at the top of the Region List: a sample-based whole-file region and a duplicate tick-based copy (Pro Tools 7.4 only).

8. Begin a new search in the Workspace browser by typing **128** in the Name field and clicking SEARCH.

9. After the files appear in the lower pane, click on the **128** DOOR KNOCKERS.RX2 file to select it and drag it to the Region List in the Edit window. This file will also convert to the session format, creating a new sample-based whole-file region and a duplicate tick-based copy in the Region List (Pro Tools 7.4 only).

10. Close the Workspace browser to reduce on-screen clutter.

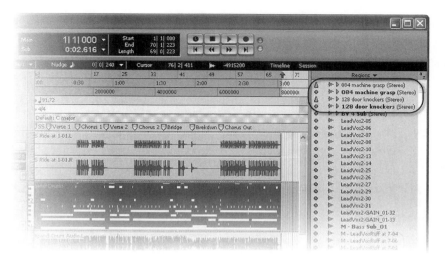

The imported files as they appear in the Region List.

 On Pro Tools 7.3 and older systems, imported REX files will appear in the Region List as region groups, along with all of the slices that make up the REX files.

Import a Region Group to a Track

As you've already seen, the Workspace browser is a great resource for locating, opening, and importing all sorts of media files. For this part of the project, you will use the Workspace browser to import a region group containing lead vocals for the song. A region group can be thought of as simply a collection of regions grouped together to look and act as a single region.

 Region groups are covered in greater detail in the Pro Tools 110 course.

For this project, all of the lead vocals have been recorded, edited, and spotted to the song outside of the current session. You will need to drag the region group from the Workspace browser onto a stereo Audio track; the region group (along with all associated regions and audio files) will be automatically imported into your session.

Locate the Lead Vocal Group region group with the Workspace browser:

1. Using the scroll bar, scroll the Edit window down until you can see the M-LeadVox track in the middle of your display.

2. In the Window Configurations List, click on the Window Configuration named "Edit w/Workspace" to resize the Edit window and open the Workspace browser (or choose WINDOW > WORKSPACE).

3. Click the FIND button (magnifying glass), if not already active, to reveal the search fields or click RESET to clear the previous search.

4. Type **Lead Vocal Group** in the Name field.

5. Select REGION GROUP FILE from the Kind pop-up menu. Make sure that there is a check next to the disk volume that contains the Music Project folder.

6. Click SEARCH. After a moment, the Lead Vocal Group file will appear in the lower pane of the Workspace browser.

Drag the region group to the M-LeadVox stereo Audio track:

1. Reposition the Workspace browser, if necessary, so you can see both the M-LeadVox track in the Edit window and the Lead Vocal Group file in the Workspace browser.

2. Drag the LEAD VOCAL GROUP file from the Workspace browser onto the M-LeadVox track in the Edit window.

3. If necessary, use the GRABBER tool to drag Lead Vocal Group to the very start of the session.

4. Close the Workspace browser to reduce on-screen clutter.

Save Work in Progress

You have now imported the additional audio files needed for the session, including REX files you will use later to create loops and all Lead Vocal regions. You should take this opportunity to save your work.

Save your work:

1. Choose FILE > SAVE to save your progress up to this point.

Editing in Pro Tools

With all of the media recorded and imported, it is now time to do some editing on your project. So far, you have used the Selector and Grabber tools. In addition to these, you will use the rest of the Edit tools (Zoomer, Trim, Scrubber, and Pencil) to modify the project so that it sounds more complete.

Add Guitar Effects

In this section, you will use some the editing techniques you learned in Chapter 6 to enhance this project.

The first element that you will be adding is a reversed guitar effect. A region has already been created for this effect and placed in the Region List, so you will simply need to place it at the right location on the right track. Often, regions are aligned to the music based on the region start time. However, at times you will want to base a region's alignment on a point within the region. This particular region has a long attack, and the downbeat that needs to sync with the music is about halfway though. This effect already has a Sync Point to identify the downbeat. You will use Pro Tools' Spot mode to align the region's Sync Point to a specific beat.

 Check out the "Add Sound Effects" section in the Post Project to learn how to place a Sync Point in a region.

 Sync Points are covered in more detail in the Pro Tools 210M and 210P courses.

Place the Rev Guitar Effect 2 region on the Reverse Guitar track and spot it to the proper location:

1. If necessary, scroll the EDIT window until you can see the Reverse Guitar track on the screen.
2. Drag the REV GUITAR EFFECT 2 region from the Region List to any open space on the Reverse Guitar track.
3. Click the SPOT button in the Edit window to activate Spot mode.
4. With the GRABBER tool, click on the region you just placed on the Reverse Guitar track. The Spot dialog box will open.
5. Set the Timescale to BARS:BEATS.
6. In the Sync Point field, type **3|1|000** and click **OK**. The region will appear near bar 3, with its Sync Point aligned at the first beat.

Because this part of the song repeats after the first chorus, you will need to copy this effect to repeat there as well.

Place a copy of the Rev Guitar Effect 2 region near bar 22:

1. With the GRABBER tool, ALT-CLICK (Windows) or OPTION-CLICK (Mac OS) on the Rev Guitar Effect 2 region to duplicate it. The Spot dialog box will appear on the screen.
2. In the Sync Point field, type **22|1|000** and click **OK**. A copy of the region will appear near bar 22, with its Sync Point aligned at the first beat.

Add REX Loops

Now you are going to drag the regions corresponding to the REX files that you imported earlier onto the S-Rex track. In Pro Tools 7.4, tick-based regions imported from REX files will automatically conform to the session tempo when placed on a track.

By way of example, the 128 Door Knockers REX file was originally recorded at a tempo of 128 BPM (hence the "128" in the file name). Because this file was imported with the option for Audio Files Conform To Session Tempo enabled in the Workspace browser, the resulting tick-based region will automatically match the session tempo (91.72 BPM) when placed on a track.

For this project, you will add the 084 Machine Grasp tick-based region to the breakdown section of the song and add the 128 Door Knockers tick-based region to each of the choruses.

 Users with Pro Tools 7.3 and older should use the 084 Machine Grasp region group and the 128 Door Knockers region group to complete the following sections.

Drag the 084 Machine Grasp region onto the S-Rex track and spot it to the proper location:

1. Click the SPOT button in the Edit window to place Pro Tools into Spot mode, if it is not already active.
2. Drag the tick-based 084 MACHINE GRASP region from the Region List to any point on the S-Rex track. (The tick-based region is the one that is not bold and has a metronome icon next to it in the Region List.) The Spot dialog box will appear on screen.
3. In the Start field of the Spot dialog box, type **44|4|480** and click **OK**. The region will appear at bar 44, midway through beat 4 (tick 480), on the S-Rex track.

The end of this region is slightly too long. You will need to trim the region to end at the start of bar 52.

Trim the end of the 084 Machine Grasp region:

1. Click the GRID button to place Pro Tools into Grid mode.
2. With the 084 Machine Grasp region selected, press **E** on your keyboard to activate Zoom Toggle. The selected region will expand to fill the available space in the window.

3. Set the Grid value by clicking on the **GRID VALUE** pop-up arrow in the Edit window and selecting 1 bar, if it is not already selected.

Click the Grid value pop-up arrow to select the Grid size.

 For details on setting the Grid value, see Chapter 8.

4. Using the **TRIM** tool, drag the end of the **084 MACHINE GRASP** region so that it snaps to 52|1|000. The region will now end at the start of bar 52.

While trimming, you can refer to the Edit Selection End time to verify that you are at the proper location before releasing the mouse button.

Trim the region to end at 52|1|000.

5. Press **E** on your keyboard to return the session to the previous view.

Add the 128 Door Knockers region to the S-Rex track:

1. If needed, select **WINDOW > MEMORY LOCATIONS** to open the Memory Locations window.
2. Click the **CHORUS 1** memory location. The insertion point will move to the start of the first chorus.

3. While holding the **START** key (Windows) or the **CONTROL** key (Mac OS), drag the tick-based **128 DOOR KNOCKERS** region from the Region List to the S-Rex track. (Be sure to use the non-bold tick-based region.) The region will snap to the insertion point.

Place a copy of the region at each chorus:

1. In the Memory Locations window, click the **CHORUS 2** memory location. The insertion point will move to the start of the second chorus.
2. Using the **GRABBER** tool, **ALT-START-CLICK** (Windows) or **OPTION-CONTROL-CLICK** (Mac OS) on the 128 Door Knockers region. A copy of the region will be placed at the second chorus.

 When used in conjunction with the Grabber tool, the Alt key (Windows) or the Option key (Mac OS) will always make a copy of a region.

3. Repeat steps 1 and 2 to duplicate the 128 Door Knockers region and place it at the Chorus Out memory location.
4. Close the Memory Locations window to reduce on-screen clutter.

Next you will need to change how this region accents the beat by nudging the region 1/16 note earlier at each chorus.

Nudge the 128 Door Knockers region:

1. Set the Nudge value to 1/16 note, if not already selected, by clicking on the **NUDGE VALUE** pop-up arrow in the Edit window.

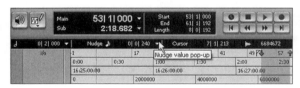

Click the Nudge value pop-up arrow to select the Nudge size.

 For details on setting the Nudge value, see Chapter 8.

2. Using the **GRABBER** tool, click on the first 128 Door Knockers region.
3. Press the **– (MINUS)** key on the numeric keypad to nudge the region 1/16 note earlier.

On a laptop computer that does not have a numeric keypad, press **FN+;**. *(The semicolon key corresponds to the minus key on a numeric keypad when used with the Fn key.)*

4. Repeat steps 2 and 3 for each of the other 128 Door Knockers regions on the track.

Loop a Region

The final 128 Door Knockers region isn't quite long enough to span the ending chorus. In this section you will turn that region into a looped region, allowing it to repeat until the end of the song.

Loop the final 128 Door Knockers region to the song end:

1. With the GRABBER tool, click on the last region on the S-Rex track.
2. Choose REGION > LOOP. The Region Looping dialog box will appear on screen.
3. Select the LOOP LENGTH option, and type **15|0|000** in the corresponding field to extend the loop to 15 bars.
4. Click **OK**.

The region now displays a looped arrow at the bottom, signifying that it is a looped region. It has also been extended out to 15 bars in length.

Edit MIDI Performance

Next you need to edit the MIDI shaker track to help it stand out more. To do this, you will edit the velocities of the MIDI events on the I-Shaker track to accent the off-beats. Because this track contains a single region repeated over and over, you can use a Pro Tools feature called *mirrored MIDI editing* to make the change. Any changes made to one MIDI region will be reflected in all of the others that are part of the repeating region.

View the MIDI velocity stalks on the I-Shaker track:

1. Scroll the Edit window as needed so that the I-Shaker track is visible on screen (toward the top).
2. Ctrl-Start-click (Windows) or Command-Control-click (Mac OS) on the Xpand! plug-in (Insert A) on the I-Shaker track to make it active.

Inactive plug-in on the I-Shaker track

3. Click on the **I-Shaker-02** MIDI region in the Region List (toward the bottom). The first instance of the region will become selected on the I-Shaker track.

4. Hold down the **Shift** key and press **Tab** three times to extend the selection across the next three region boundaries. A total of four regions will become selected on the I-Shaker track.

5. Press **E** on your keyboard to activate Zoom Toggle. The selection will expand, filling the available space in the window, and the track will change to Notes view. Notice that each region contains four MIDI notes.

6. Click on the **Track View selector** of the I-Shaker track and choose **Velocity** from the pop-up menu.

The Velocity view displays a velocity stalk associated with each MIDI note, representing the velocity value for that note (the longer the stalk, the higher the velocity value).

Audition the selection:

1. Click the **Solo** (S) button on the I-Shaker track to solo it.

2. Press the **space bar**. The track will play back, stopping at the end of the selection.

3. Choose **Window > Memory Locations** to open the Memory Locations window.

4. Click **Verse 1** to place the insertion point at the beginning of the MIDI region.

Edit the velocities for the first region:

1. Click the **Mirrored MIDI Editing** button at the top of the Edit window to enable mirrored MIDI editing. The button will be outlined in blue when active.

Click the Mirrored MIDI Editing button to enable it.

2. With the GRABBER tool, click and drag on the top of the velocity stalk for the second MIDI note, raising it close to the top of the track. The second velocity stalk in each instance of the MIDI region will update to reflect your edit.

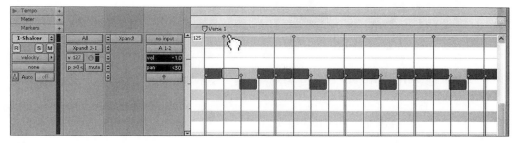

Raising the velocity stalk with the Grabber tool

3. Drag the velocity stalk for the third note to be 3/4 of the distance to the top of the track.

4. Drag the velocity stalk for the fourth note to be close to the top of the track.

5. Press the SPACE BAR to begin playback and hear the effect of the changes you've made. Press the SPACE BAR a second time when finished to stop playback.

6. Click the SOLO (S) button to unsolo the track.

7. Close the Memory Locations window.

8. Press **E** on your keyboard to return the session to its previous view, and click the MIRRORED MIDI EDITING button a second time to disable mirrored MIDI editing.

Remove a Section

This song currently contains an eight-bar breakdown section. In this part of the project, you need to cut this section down to half of its length, making it only four bars.

Select the time to remove from the breakdown section:

1. In the Edit Selection Start field at the top of the Edit window, type **48|1|000** to begin the selection at bar 48:

   a. Click on the first field to activate it and type **48**.

   b. Click on the second field and type **1**.

   c. Click on the third field and type **000**.

   d. Press ENTER (Windows) or RETURN (Mac OS) to confirm the entry.

2. In the Edit Selection Length field, type **4|0|000**, using the same process, to create a four-bar selection spanning from bar 48 to bar 52.

Enter the values for the Edit Selection start and length to create a four-bar selection.

Use the Cut Time operation to remove the selected time:

1. Choose EVENT > TIME OPERATIONS > CUT TIME. The Time Operations window will appear on screen.
2. Verify that the Start, End, and Length times are correct. The values should be the following:
   - START: 48|1|000
   - END: 52|1|000
   - LENGTH: 4|0|000
3. Click APPLY. Four bars will be removed from the session.
4. Close the Time Operations window.

Listen to the edit:

1. Choose WINDOW > MEMORY LOCATIONS to open the Memory Locations window.
2. Click BREAKDOWN to move the insertion point to the start of the breakdown section.
3. Press the SPACE BAR to begin playback.
4. Press the SPACE BAR a second time after the next chorus begins.
5. Close the Memory Locations window to reduce on-screen clutter.

You might have noticed a slight problem with the vocals: The vocal line at the end doesn't make sense in context with the edit you just performed. To fix the problem, you will now edit the M-LeadVox track.

Edit the M-LeadVox track:

1. If necessary, scroll the Edit window so that the M-LeadVox track is visible on screen.
2. In the Region List, click on the LEAD VOCAL GROUP-04 region group (toward the bottom) to select the region on the Track Playlist. You might need to scroll the Region List to make the region group visible.

3. Press **E** on your keyboard. The selected region will expand to fill the available space in the window.

4. Choose REGION > UNGROUP. The regions that comprised the Lead Vocal Group-04 will be displayed individually.

5. Click on the LEADVOX2-GAIN_01-33 region in the Region List to select the region in the Track Playlist.

6. Choose REGION > MUTE/UNMUTE to mute the region.

7. Press **E** on your keyboard to return to the previous view.

Muting the region will prevent it from playing back, without requiring you to delete it from the track. You can later unmute the region to have Pro Tools begin playing it again, if desired.

Confirm the edit:

1. Choose WINDOW > MEMORY LOCATIONS to open the Memory Locations window.

2. Click BREAKDOWN to move the insertion point to the start of the breakdown section.

3. Press the SPACE BAR to begin playback.

4. Press the SPACE BAR a second time when the chorus begins.

5. Close the Memory Locations window to reduce on-screen clutter.

You should now hear silence preceding the last chorus.

Save Work in Progress

You have now completed the editing tasks for your project. You should take this opportunity to save your work.

Save your work:

1. Choose FILE > SAVE to save your progress up to this point.

Mixing in Pro Tools

Now that all of the editing is complete, you will use some of the mixing features in Pro Tools to add real-time processing to the project and blend the sound elements together. Before getting started, you will activate and resize the Mix window using a preset Window Configuration.

Activate the "Big Mix" Window Configuration:

1. In the Window Configurations List, click on the Window Configuration named "Big Mix." The Mix window will become active and will expand to fill the screen, and the Memory Locations window will open. (This step requires Pro Tools 7.3 or later.)

In this configuration, the Narrow Mix option is disabled in the Mix window (VIEW > NARROW MIX), so each channel strip displays at full width.

Add EQ

The S-Rex track is a bit too bright, making it difficult to blend the track with the rest of the session. To fix the problem, you will need to use the DigiRack EQ III plug-in to roll off some of the high end.

Insert the 1-Band EQ III plug-in on the S-Rex track:

1. Click on the INSERT SELECTOR A of the S-Rex track and choose MULTI-MONO PLUG-IN > EQ > 1-BAND EQ 3 (MONO) from the pop-up menu. The 1-band EQ III plug-in window will appear.
2. In the 1-Band EQ III plug-in window, select the LOW-PASS filter type.

Selecting the Low-Pass filter in the EQ III plug-in window

Adjust the EQ to roll off the high end:

1. Solo the S-Rex track by clicking on the SOLO (S) button just above the Volume Fader in the Mix window.
2. Click on CHORUS 1 in the Memory Locations window to place the insertion point at the beginning of the first chorus.
3. Press the SPACE BAR to initiate playback.

4. In the 1-Band EQ III plug-in window, drag the gray ball to the left or right until you hear the desired reduction in high frequencies when playing back the 128 Door Knockers region (try around 2.25 kHz).

5. Unsolo the S-Rex track and press the SPACE BAR to stop playback.

6. Close the EQ III plug-in window and the Memory Locations window to reduce on-screen clutter.

Add Delay

Next, you will add some effects to the M-LeadVox track to help fit it into the rest of the mix. This project includes an Auxiliary track that was previously set up with its input assigned to Bus 3 and a Medium Delay II plug-in configured. Additionally, Send A on the M-LeadVox track has been assigned to Bus 3. Therefore, all you will need to do is increase the level of the send on the M-LeadVox track to add delay to the mix.

Increase the Send A level on the M-LeadVox track:

1. Click on SEND ASSIGNMENT A on the M-LeadVox track. The Send A window will appear.

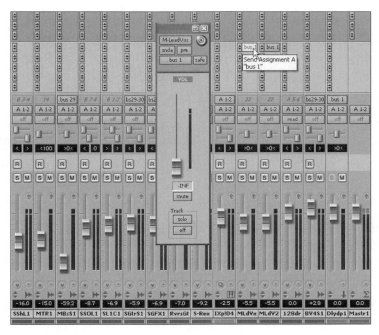

Clicking on the Send Assignment to open the Send window

2. Click the **SOLO** button in the Send A window to solo the M-LeadVox track.

3. Choose **WINDOW > MEMORY LOCATIONS** to open the Memory Locations window.

4. Click on **VERSE 2** to place the insertion point at the beginning of the second verse.

5. Press the **SPACE BAR** to begin playback.

6. While listening to the track, raise the level on the Send Fader to introduce the delay.

   The delay will play back while the M-LeadVox track is soloed because the Delay track is set to Solo Safe mode. Solo Safe mode is commonly used on Auxiliary tracks to prevent them from being muted when another track is soloed.

 You can place a track in Solo Safe mode by Ctrl-clicking (Windows) or Command-clicking (Mac OS) on the Solo button in the Edit or Mix windows.

 More information on Solo Safe mode can be found in the Pro Tools 110 course.

7. When you are satisfied with the results, press the **SPACE BAR** to stop playback.

8. Press the **SOLO** button to take the track out of Solo mode, close the Send A window, and close the Memory Locations window.

Enhance the Guitar Effect

In this part of the project, you will add some flanging and EQ to liven up the reverse guitar effect that you placed earlier. You will add flanging using an AudioSuite plug-in and add EQ using the 7-Band EQ III RTAS plug-in.

A Note about AudioSuite Plug-Ins

You will be using the DigiRack Flanger to modulate the sound effect. The DigiRack Flanger is an AudioSuite plug-in. These plug-ins behave differently from RTAS in that they are not real-time processors. AudioSuite plug-ins process and modify audio files on disk, rather than adding the plug-in effect in real time.

 More information on AudioSuite processing can be found in the Pro Tools 110 course.

Zoom in on the Rev Guitar Effect 2 region on the Reverse Guitar track:

1. Choose WINDOW > EDIT to switch to the Edit window, or press CTRL+= (Windows) or COMMAND+= (Mac OS).

2. If necessary, scroll the Edit window so that the Reverse Guitar track is visible on screen.

3. Click on REV GUITAR EFFECT 2 in the Region List to select the region on the Track Playlist.

4. Press E on your keyboard to activate Zoom Toggle and zoom in on the selected region. The region Rev Guitar Effect 2 will expand to fill the available space in the window.

Use DigiRack Flanger to process the region Rev Guitar Effect 2:

1. Choose AUDIOSUITE > MODULATION > FLANGER. The DigiRack Flanger plug-in window will appear on screen.

2. Verify that USE IN PLAYLIST is highlighted. If it isn't, click it to highlight it.

3. From the LIBRARIAN MENU, choose VOCAL FLANGE.

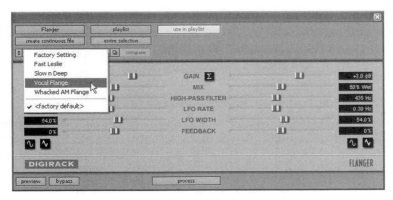

Select Vocal Flange from the plug-in Librarian menu.

4. To audition the effect, click PREVIEW. Adjust the effect parameters using the sliders, as desired.

5. When you are satisfied with the effect, click PROCESS to process the audio region. A new region will be generated, combining the source audio with the Flange effect and replacing the selected region.

6. Press E on your keyboard to return the session to the previous view.

7. Using the GRABBER tool, click on the second Reverse Guitar region on the track to select it.

8. Press **E** on your keyboard again to reactivate Zoom Toggle and zoom in on the currently selected region.

9. Click **PROCESS** in the Flanger plug-in window to apply the same flanging effect to this second instance of the Reverse Guitar effect.

10. Close the Flanger plug-in window to reduce on-screen clutter.

11. Press **E** on your keyboard once more to return the session to the previous view.

Save Work in Progress

Before continuing with work on your session mix, you should take this opportunity to save your work.

Save your work:

1. Choose **FILE > SAVE** to save your progress up to this point.

Mix the Project

The project is now ready for mixing to blend all of the tracks together. You will use the Volume Faders and Pan Sliders to create a stereo mix.

Getting Started

To get started, you will deactivate the click track and determine the contribution of each track to the overall mix by soloing each track individually. Some tracks, such as the Delay track, only process sounds that flow through them. Because they don't create any sound on their own, you will not be able to isolate such tracks by soloing them, making it more difficult to determine why they are important to the mix. Tracks that cannot be isolated by soloing can be muted and unmuted to determine their contribution.

Deactivate the Click track:

1. Scroll to the top of the Edit window so that the Click track becomes visible.

2. Right-click (Windows or Mac OS) or Ctrl-click (Mac OS) on the Click Track Nameplate and choose **MAKE INACTIVE** from the pop-up menu. The Click track will become grayed and will no longer play back.

Solo each track to isolate its contribution:

1. Press **CTRL+=** (Windows) or **COMMAND+=** (Mac OS) to toggle to the Mix window.

2. Click the **RETURN TO ZERO** button in the Transport window to place the insertion point at the beginning of the Timeline.

The Return to Zero button in the Transport window

3. Press the **SPACE BAR** to begin playback.

4. Solo each track for a few moments by clicking the **SOLO** button (labeled "S") above the Volume Fader in the Mix window.

   a. Consider how the track contributes to the overall mix, and make adjustments as needed by adjusting the Volume Fader.

   b. Toggle Solo mode on and off as needed to alternate between isolating the track and placing it in context within the mix to fine-tune the track.

   c. When you are satisfied with the results, take the track out of Solo mode and move on to the next track.

 Some of the tracks have audio only during specific parts of the song. To adjust the mix on these tracks, you might want to switch to the Edit window, select a region on the track, and listen to it in Loop Playback mode, toggling Solo on and off as you fine-tune the mix.

5. Use the Pan Sliders in the Mix window to help give some stereo separation to your mix. Pan select tracks to the left or right, using your discretion, to help distinguish each of the tracks in the mix.

6. When you are finished soloing each track, press the **SPACE BAR** again to stop playback.

Mute each track, as needed, to isolate its contribution:

1. If needed, click the **RETURN TO ZERO** button in the Transport window to place the insertion point at the beginning of the Timeline.

 *You can also press **ENTER** (Windows) or **RETURN** (Mac OS) on your keyboard to place the insertion point at the beginning of the Timeline.*

2. Press the **SPACE BAR** to begin playback.

3. Toggle MUTE on and off for each track, alternating between dropping the track out of the mix and adding it back in, to determine the track's contribution to the mix. Make adjustments to the track as needed.

4. When finished, press the SPACE BAR again to stop playback.

Completing the Mix

Complete this portion of the project using your discretion, experimenting until you are happy with the results.

Save Work in Progress

You have now created a complete mix for your project. You should take this opportunity to save your work.

Save your work:

1. Choose FILE > SAVE to save your progress up to this point.

Finishing Your Work

Once a project is mixed, you will often want to create an internal bounce, mixing down your session to a stereo Audio track. This will allow you to make high-level adjustments to the song at the native sample rate and bit depth.

For this part of the project, you will make a tempo adjustment using a previously created internal mix. You will then create an external stereo bounce of your session mix. This will enable the mixed song to be played back in a standard audio application and shared with others.

Lastly, you will archive your work. Through the process of creating this project, you generated many files, not all of which are needed for the completed session. By archiving your work, you are able preserve your work without taking up excess disk space due to unnecessary files.

Enable the Internal Mix

A mix of the project has previously been created on a hidden track in the session. To work with this mix, you will mute the source tracks, change the session view to hide the source tracks while displaying the mixed track, and unmute the mixed track.

Mute the source tracks:

1. Press **CTRL+=** (Windows) or **COMMAND+=** (Mac OS) to toggle to the Edit window.

2. Click on **SOURCE TRACKS** in the Edit Group List on the left side of the window to enable the Source Tracks group.

Enabling the Source Tracks group

3. Click the **MUTE** button on the S-Ride track to mute all of the tracks in the group.

4. Click the **MUTE** button on the S-Drums track to mute it as well. (This track is not a member of the Source Tracks group, since it was added later.)

Change the view and unmute the Mixdown track:

1. Choose **WINDOW > MEMORY LOCATIONS** to open the Memory Locations window.

2. Click on the **INTERNAL MIX** memory location to recall the display settings saved with this memory location. The source tracks will be hidden from view, and the Mixdown track will be displayed.

3. Click the **MUTE** button on the Mixdown track to unmute the track.

Add Tempo Change

The Mixdown track has been enabled for Elastic Audio, a new feature in Pro Tools 7.4 that allows audio to conform to tempo changes and other timing adjustments. In the next few steps, you will add a tempo change to the bridge section of the song using the Tempo Operations window.

 The Elastic Audio feature used in this section requires Pro Tools 7.4. Users on older systems can skip this section and proceed to the "Add Dither" section.

Select the bridge and add a tempo change:

1. In the Memory Locations window, click on the Bridge memory location.

2. While holding the Shift key, click on the Breakdown memory location. The area between the Bridge and Breakdown markers will become selected in the Timeline.

3. Choose Event > Tempo Operations > Scale to open the Scale page of the Tempo Operations window.

4. Set the parameters as follows:
   • Selection Start: 37|1|000
   • Selection End: 45|1|000
   • Average Tempo: 102.0000
   • Preserve tempo after selection: enabled (checked)

5. Click Apply to initiate the tempo change for the selection. The corresponding tempo change events will be added at the start and end of the bridge section.

6. Close the Tempo Operations window.

7. With the Selector tool, click on the Mixdown track at any point before the Bridge, and audition the tempo change by pressing the space bar.

8. When finished, press the space bar a second time to stop playback.

Add Dither

Next, you will make an external bounce of the finished project. The purpose of this bounce is to make a CD-quality stereo audio file (that you can burn to CD-R and play on your CD player, if you wish). For this, you will need to create a 16-bit audio file from your 24-bit session. To resolve the differences in amplitude resolution between these bit depths, you should add dither to the Master Fader. (For more information on bit depth, see the "Bit Depth and Amplitude Resolution" section in Chapter 1.) Dithering helps preserve the quality of your audio during the bounce, preventing low-level quantization errors and LSB clipping. The technical function and purpose of dither is beyond the scope of this book; however, the process of adding dither to your session is quite simple and straightforward within Pro Tools.

 As a rule of thumb, you should always add dither when bouncing to a lower bit depth.

Add dither to the Master Fader:

1. Press CTRL+= (Windows) or COMMAND+= (Mac OS) to toggle to the Mix window.

2. Click on INSERT SELECTOR A of the Master Fader track and choose MULTI-CHANNEL PLUG-IN > DITHER > POWR DITHER (STEREO). The POWr dither plug-in window will appear on screen.

3. Choose the following settings in the POWr Dither plug-in window:
   - 16 bit
   - Noise Shaping Type 3

4. Close the POWr Dither plug-in window.

Dither will now be added to your mix during playback.

Bounce the Song

You will use the Bounce to Disk command to make a stereo file of your session.

Make a 16-bit stereo bounce of your session:

1. Choose WINDOW > EDIT to switch to the Edit window.

2. With the SELECTOR tool, click anywhere in the session.

3. Choose WINDOW > MEMORY LOCATIONS to open the Memory Locations window.

4. Click on the SONG START memory location.

5. Press CTRL+SHIFT+ENTER (Windows) or OPTION+SHIFT+RETURN (Mac OS) to make a selection from the song start to the end of the session.

6. Choose FILE > BOUNCE TO > DISK. The Bounce dialog box will appear on screen.

7. Select the following settings in the Bounce dialog box:
   - FILE TYPE: WAV
   - FORMAT: Stereo Interleaved
   - RESOLUTION: 16 bit
   - SAMPLE RATE: 44100
   - CONVERT AFTER BOUNCE: Selected

8. Click BOUNCE. The Save Bounce As dialog box will appear on screen.

9. Select a location for the audio file in the Save In section of the dialog box, and type in a name for your file in the File Name field.

10. Click SAVE. You will hear playback begin as Pro Tools creates a 16-bit stereo mix of your session.

Archive Your Work

Now that your project is complete, you will need to back it up for storage. On a real-world project, you might also need to deliver the session to the client. Because many files are associated with a session, a potential exists for something to get lost if the archival process isn't completed properly. Fortunately, Pro Tools has many features to help ensure that you keep the files you need and remove the files you do not.

In this process, you will complete the following steps:

1. Remove unused audio files and regions. Because these files are not being used by the session, they are essentially wasting space on your hard drive or archive medium.

2. Use the SAVE COPY IN command to "collect" all of the audio and video files and copy them to a new location (preferably on a different hard drive).

3. Open the copied session to verify that it copied correctly.

4. Use the COMPACT SELECTED command to remove the unused portions of each audio file that is used in the copied session.

 This archival process will permanently remove any audio that is not currently being used in the session. Because this could potentially limit your creative possibilities (should you need to revise some aspect of this session in the future), you should complete this process only after the project work is complete.

Remove Unused Material

To remove unused audio files and regions, complete the following steps:

1. Click on the double arrow in the bottom-right corner of the Edit window to display the Region List.

2. Click on the REGION LIST pop-up menu and choose SELECT > UNUSED. All of the regions that are not included on a Track Playlist will be selected.

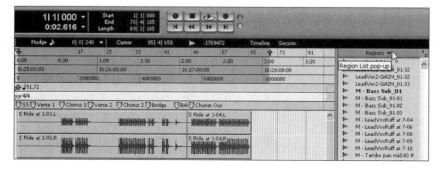

Click the Region List pop-up menu to select unused regions.

3. Click on the REGION LIST pop-up menu a second time and choose CLEAR. The Clear Regions dialog box will appear on screen.

4. Click REMOVE in the Clear Regions dialog box to remove the regions from your session. The audio files will be removed from the session without being deleted from the drive. If you later find that you need an audio file that has been removed, you can re-import it into your session.

Collect Session Files in a New Location

To save a copy of your session and all associated files, do the following:

1. Choose FILE > SAVE COPY IN. The SAVE COPY OF SESSION IN dialog box will appear on screen.

2. Choose a directory to store the session copy and name the copy of the session. If possible, it is best to choose a directory on a different drive from the current session.

3. In the ITEMS TO COPY area, select the following:
   - All Audio Files
   - Session Plug-In Settings Folder

4. Click the SAVE button. Pro Tools will begin processing the save, copying files as needed.

5. After the Save operation completes, choose FILE > CLOSE to close the original session. If you are prompted to save, choose OK to save your changes in the original session. (It will be saved with the unused material removed.)

You have now created a copy of the session file along with all of the audio and session plug-in settings files in the directory you chose.

Verify the Copied Session

To verify that the session copied correctly, do the following:

1. Open the new copy of your project, either by navigating to it or by using the search function in the Workspace browser as described in the "Locate the Session Using the Workspace Browser" section at the beginning of this project. Be sure to select the session copy that you created in the last section.

2. If you are prompted by a warning that the original disk allocation cannot be used, click NO when asked to save a report.

   After the session is open, there should be no offline regions.

3. Choose WINDOW > PROJECT to open the Project browser. You will use the Project browser to verify that every file referenced in this session is stored in the proper directory.

The Project browser provides powerful search and management tools for the files referenced in your current session, regardless of where they are stored.

4. In the left pane of the Project browser, expand the AUDIO FILES folder.
5. In the right pane of the Project browser, use the scroll bar to find the PATH column. Verify that the path for every file in the Audio Files folder leads to the new copy of your project's session folder.
6. Close the Project browser when you are finished.

Compact Your Session

Once you have verified that all of your files are properly referenced, you have one more step to complete your archive: compacting. Most regions in a session reference only a part of a larger audio recording. Because the session is now complete, it is safe to remove the unused parts. Compacting is the process of removing the audio from a file that is not used by any region. Hence, only the used portions of the audio files remain, reducing the amount of disk space being consumed.

To compact your project's audio files, do the following:

1. Click on the REGION LIST pop-up menu and choose SELECT > ALL. All of the regions in the Region List will be selected.
2. Click on the REGION LIST pop-up menu a second time and choose COMPACT. The Compact dialog box will appear on screen with a description of the compacting process.
3. Click COMPACT to compact the audio files. A dialog box will appear, indicating that an audio region in the session has been warped by a tempo change and cannot be compacted.
4. Choose SKIP to skip the warped file. Pro Tools will begin compacting the session files.
5. When finished, save your work by choosing FILE > SAVE and close your session by choosing FILE > CLOSE SESSION.

This concludes the Music Hands-On project.

Project 2

Post Hands-On Project

In this project, you will work with a 45-second commercial spot consisting of 20 tracks in rough form. To complete the project, you will create a new track and record a voice-over, import video footage as a QuickTime movie, import additional music and sound effects files, make various improvements and enhancements to the audio, and add effects processing to polish the mix.

The media files for this project are provided courtesy of Janne Anderson at Housework Sound Design:

- **PRODUCTION COMPANY:** Social Club, Stockholm
- **PRODUCER:** Markus Ahlm
- **DIRECTOR:** Axel Laubscher
- **AGENCY PRODUCER:** Lars Sundin Lowe, Copenhagen
- **CLIENT:** Lotto Denmark

 The audio and video files provided for this project are to be used only to complete the exercises contained herein. No rights are granted to use the files or any portion thereof in any commercial or non-commercial production or video.

Notes

Powering Up

To get started on this project, you will need to power up your system. It is important to power up your system *properly* because improper power-up procedures can lead to various problems and can possibly damage your equipment.

When using audio equipment, you should power up components in the order that the audio signal flows through them. The general process for powering up a Pro Tools M-Powered or LE system is as follows (see your system documentation for powering up a Pro Tools|HD system):

1. Power up external hard drives.
2. Verify connections and power up audio/MIDI interfaces.
3. Start your computer.
4. Power up your monitoring system, if applicable.
5. Launch Pro Tools.

Refer to Chapter 2 for more details on powering up your system.

Opening the Post Project

In this section of the hands-on project, you will open the Post project and prepare your session windows for the work you will be performing in this project.

The session that you will use for this project was created using a Pro Tools LE system with an Mbox 2 interface. When you first open a project session created on a different system, you are often prompted by several dialog boxes notifying you of setup differences. This is normal behavior; simply select the default options to close the dialog boxes and continue working.

Locate the Session Using the Workspace Browser

Pro Tools provides a number of ways to open a session. For instance, you can always navigate to the session folder in your Explorer or Finder window and double-click on the session file to open it. For the purposes of this project, however, you will locate and open the session file from the Workspace browser, just as you did for the Music project. Remember, the Workspace browser is your one-stop shop for finding, opening, and importing session-related files.

Locate and open the Post session from the Workspace browser:

1. Choose WINDOW > WORKSPACE to open the Workspace browser.

 You can also press ALT+; (Windows) or OPTION+; (Mac OS) to toggle the Workspace browser open and closed.

2. If necessary, click the RESET button to clear the results of your last search; otherwise, click the FIND icon (magnifying glass) to activate a search. The Find button will be highlighted, and the window will be split into an upper and a lower area.

3. Type **Post Hands-On Project** in the Name field.

4. Select SESSION FILE from the Kind pop-up menu.

5. Click the SEARCH button. After a few moments the session will display in the lower (green and white) area of the Workspace browser.

6. Double-click on the session to open it.

 Make sure you are opening the session copy from your hard drive and not the original from the DVD.

Refer to Chapter 3 for additional information on locating and opening sessions.

Dismiss warnings:

As the session opens for the first time, you could be prompted by two dialog boxes notifying you of changes in the system setup. Dismiss each of these by selecting the default options:

- **Playback engine not available.** Choose **OK** to continue with the current playback engine.

Example of the Playback Engine Notification dialog box

- **Disk allocation and I/O setup change.** Choose **No** to continue without saving a report.

The original disk allocation for this session cannot be used. Check the disk allocation window to see what's changed.

Your I/O setup has changed since the last time this session was saved. Check the I/O Setups window to see what's changed.

Would you like to save a detailed report?

No   Yes

Example of the disk allocation and I/O Setup Notification dialog box

Orient the Session Windows

When the session opens, you will see the Edit window displayed on your screen. (If you have closed the Edit window, choose **WINDOW > EDIT** to reactivate it.) You will use the Edit window for much of the recording and editing you will do in this project. You will also be using the Mix window and the Transport window throughout the project. Before getting started, you should open each of these windows and orient them on your screen. On Pro Tools 7.3 and later, you can do this using a Window Configuration that has been saved with this session:

1. Choose **WINDOW > CONFIGURATIONS > WINDOW CONFIGURATION LIST**. The Window Configurations List will open.
2. Click on the Window Configuration named "Main Windows." The Mix, Edit, and Transport windows will open on screen.
3. Close the Window Configurations List to reduce on-screen clutter.
4. Reposition/resize the windows as desired to maximize the use of your screen.

Nineteen tracks are visible in the session, displayed horizontally (left to right) as channel strips in the Mix window and vertically (top to bottom) as Track Playlists in the Edit window. You may need to scroll the active window to view all of your tracks. To view your Track Playlists, for example, you would activate the Edit window by clicking on it and use the scroll bar on the right side of the playlists to scroll the window up or down. (Note that there may be a separate scroll bar for the Region List, which will not affect your track display.)

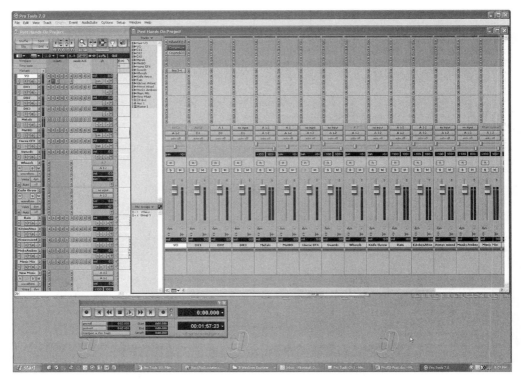

Session windows oriented for the start of the project

Set the Preferences

For this project, you will need to configure certain preference settings that affect the placement of the insertion point/selection during operation. Before continuing, make sure the following preferences are set accordingly.

 In Pro Tools 7.3 and earlier, some of the Preference options will be slightly different; users on older systems should use those settings that are applicable.

Check preferences settings:

1. Choose SETUP > PREFERENCES. The Preferences window will open.
2. Click on the OPERATION tab.
   - Verify that TIMELINE INSERTION/PLAY START MARKER FOLLOWS PLAYBACK is unchecked.
   - Verify that EDIT INSERTION FOLLOWS SCRUB/SHUTTLE is checked.
   - Leave all other settings unchanged.

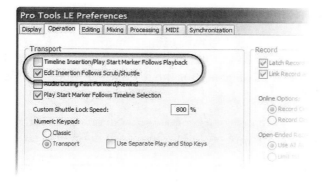

Preference settings under the Operation tab

3. Click on the **EDITING** tab.
   - Verify that **EDIT SELECTION FOLLOWS REGION LIST SELECTION** is checked.

4. In the Zoom Toggle section of the Editing tab, select the following settings:
   - Set both **VERTICAL MIDI ZOOM** and **HORIZONTAL ZOOM** to Selection.
   - Verify that **REMOVE RANGE SELECTION AFTER ZOOMING IN** is unchecked.
   - Set **TRACK HEIGHT** to Jumbo.
   - Set **TRACK VIEW** to Waveform / Notes.
   - Verify that **ZOOM TOGGLE FOLLOWS EDIT SELECTION** is unchecked.
   - Leave other settings unchanged.

5. Click **OK** to close the Preferences window.

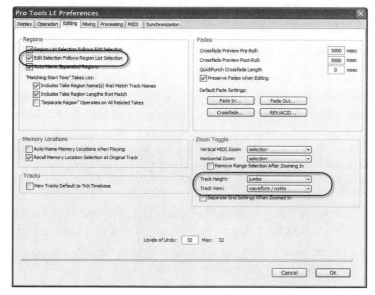

Preference settings under the Editing tab

Connect Input and Monitoring Devices

For this project, you will be recording a voice-over using a microphone. If you have an available microphone, you should connect it to your audio interface now. To do so, plug the microphone into the Mic connector for Input 1 of your Mbox 2 or other qualified interface.

If you do not have an available microphone or a compatible input on your interface, you can skip this step and follow the alternative procedures provided during the project.

If you have a monitoring system connected to the left and right outputs of your audio interface, you will use that to listen to the session playback. If you do not have a monitoring system, you can listen to the session playback using headphones on compatible audio interfaces. If your interface has an available headphone jack, plug in your headphones and test the playback level.

Creating New Tracks

In this section of the project, you will create a new track needed for the session. The information in this section is based primarily on the material in Chapter 3.

Create and Name a Track

For this project, you will need to create one new track that you will use to record a voice-over (also know as a VO). When creating tracks, you always want to select the track type and format based on how the tracks will be used. In this case, you will need to record a single human voice, so a mono Audio track will be appropriate.

Create a mono Audio track and name it New VO:

1. Scroll to the top of the Edit window and click on the VO Track Nameplate in the session Edit window to select the track. This will ensure that your new track will appear directly below the VO track, keeping all of the VO tracks together.

 Pro Tools always places new tracks below the lowest selected track in the session. If no tracks are selected, Pro Tools places the new track(s) at the bottom of the session.

2. Choose TRACK > NEW. The New Tracks dialog box will open, displaying Mono, Audio Track, and Samples as default selections from left to right.

3. Click CREATE in the New Tracks dialog box using the default settings. A new mono track will be added to the session, beneath the VO track.

4. Double-click on the track name (AUDIO 1) to open the Track Name dialog box.

5. Type **New VO** in the Track Name field and add comments to help identify the track function, such as "New Voice-Over."

6. Click **OK**. The track will display with its new name.

Renaming the Audio track

Save Your Session

After making any significant changes to a session, it is a good idea to save your work. That way, if something should disrupt your progress (such as a power outage), you will not have to redo any of your work. To preserve the original session for future use, use the Save As command at this point.

Save a copy of your session, adding your initials to the session name:

1. Choose FILE > SAVE AS. The Save As dialog box will open with the session name highlighted.

2. Click in the FILE NAME field after the session name and type your initials.

3. Click SAVE.

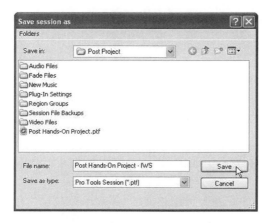

Saving the session with your initials after the session name

Now you have saved a copy of the session file with a different name. This new session continues to reference the original audio, video, and fade files. For more information on Save options, see Chapters 3 and 10.

Recording Audio

For this section of the project, you will use the concepts presented in Chapter 4 to record your voice-over. You will need to have a microphone connected to your Pro Tools system to complete these steps. Depending on the specific type of Pro Tools system you have, you might need to connect through an external preamp prior to routing to your audio interface in order to boost the microphone gain. (All Pro Tools LE products have built-in preamps on the audio interface.) Refer to the Getting Started guide that came with your audio interface for more information.

 If your interface or preamp has a Mic/Line switch, be sure to place it in the Mic position.

If you do not have an available microphone, you can skip over the live recording steps and use the alternative procedure noted. (This session has a hidden track that is designed to mimic audio from a microphone connected to the system.)

The general workflow you will use to prepare for your recording is as follows:

1. Check disk space.
2. Route the signal.
3. Record-enable a track.
4. Set input level.

In the sections that follow, you will work through each of these steps.

Check Disk Space

Because the audio signal is recorded directly to disk, the amount of free disk space that you have available is directly related to your total available recording time. Refer to Table 3.1 in Chapter 3 to determine the amount of disk space required for a project. If you have limited space on your hard drive, it is a good idea to verify that you have adequate free disk space before you start recording. You can access this information from within Pro Tools using the Disk Space window.

For this project, you will be recording only a few seconds' worth of material, so you will not need much available space. However, we recommend starting with a minimum of 300 MB of disk space available for any audio recording.

Verify that you have adequate free disk space:

1. Choose WINDOW > DISK SPACE. A small window will open, indicating the available space on each of your drives.
2. Check the available space for the drive you are using for the project.
3. If the available space is less than 300 MB, consider freeing up additional space on the drive or switching to another drive before continuing.
4. Close the Disk Space window when you are finished to minimize on-screen clutter.

Route the Signal

To record onto a track, you need to properly route the signal to the track. For this project, you should have a microphone connected to an appropriate input on your audio interface, such as Mic Input 1 on an Mbox 2.

To route the Mic signal to your New VO track, you also need to set the input on the track to receive the incoming signal by selecting the appropriate input of your audio interface.

Set the New VO track's input:

1. Press CTRL+= (Windows) or COMMAND+= (Mac OS) to toggle to the Mix window.
2. Click on the AUDIO INPUT PATH SELECTOR for the New VO track and choose the appropriate input for your microphone. [If your mic is plugged into Input 1 of your Mbox 2, choose INTERFACE > A 1 (MONO).]

   - Or -

   (Alternate) If you don't have a microphone connected, click on the AUDIO INPUT PATH SELECTOR for the New VO track and choose BUS > BUS 1 (MONO).

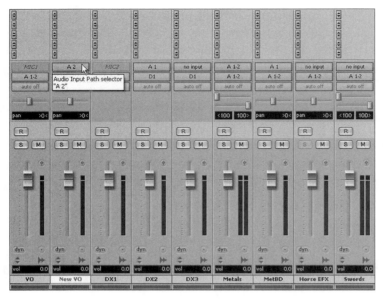

Click the Audio Input Path selector to choose the appropriate input for the signal to record.

Enable the Audio Track for Recording

You will be using the New VO track to record your voice-over for the project. Pro Tools allows you to record to a track or multiple tracks while playing back from others. To do so, you will need to record-enable the track.

Record-enable the New VO track:

1. Press CTRL+= (Windows) or COMMAND+= (Mac OS) to toggle to the Edit window.

2. Click on the TRACK RECORD ENABLE button (R) for the New VO track. The Record Enable button will begin to flash red.

Set the Recording Level

If you are not currently recording with a microphone, you can skip to the next section because you will not need to set the input level.

With the input of the track assigned and the track record-enabled, you will next need to set the record level such that the track receives an adequate signal without clipping. Speak into your microphone at the same volume you will use when recording the voice-over while visually monitoring the track's level meter. The level meter indicator should fluctuate in the top half of the meter, averaging about two-thirds up. The red portion of the meter should never light up.

If the signal is either too weak or too hot, you will need to adjust the input level of the microphone. If you are using an Mbox 2 or other Digidesign Pro Tools LE interface, you can adjust the level using the gain knob on the interface for the input that the mic is plugged into. If you are using a separate preamp, you will need to adjust the level on the preamp.

Record a Track

At this point in your project, you are ready to begin recording your voice-over. To do so, you will position the insertion point at the starting point for the recording, arm Pro Tools to record, and proceed with recording on the New VO track.

Place the insertion cursor at the starting point for the recording:

1. With the SELECTOR tool, click anywhere on the New VO track in the Edit window.
2. Choose WINDOW > MEMORY LOCATIONS to open the Memory Locations window.
3. Click the memory location labeled NEW VO START. The insertion point will move to the proper location.
4. Close the MEMORY LOCATIONS window to reduce on-screen clutter.

Record the new voice-over:

1. Click the RECORD (R) button in the Transport window. The Record button will flash red, showing that Pro Tools is armed and ready to record.
2. Press the SPACE BAR to start recording. The Record Enable button on the track will turn solid red. You will also see a red waveform being written on the New VO track.
3. Speak the words, "You traveled the world, now you must journey inwards," into the microphone, putting a dramatic pause between "world" and "now" for effect.

   (Alternate) If you do not have a microphone connected and have set the track input to Bus 1, allow the playback to complete the above phrase.
4. Press the SPACE BAR a second time to stop the recording.
5. Click the RECORD ENABLE button on the New VO track to disable recording on the track.

 If you are not satisfied with the take, you can choose EDIT > UNDO after step 4 to undo the recording and repeat the process. You might have to click on the New VO Start memory location to return the insertion point to the proper start location.

Rename Audio Files and Regions

The audio file/region you just recorded has a name similar to that of the track it was recorded on. This is one of the reasons for giving your tracks meaningful names before you start recording. However, at times you might want the audio file or region name to be different from the track name. For this project, you will rename the audio file and region to reflect the content that was spoken instead of the track name.

Rename the New VO audio file and region:

1. In the Edit window, select the GRABBER tool.
2. Using the GRABBER tool, double-click the region you recorded on the New VO track. A Name dialog box will appear.
3. In the Name the Region field, type **You Traveled**. Because this region represents the entire audio file (or whole-file region), the Name dialog box also gives you the option to either name the region only or rename both the region and the audio file.
4. Choose NAME REGION AND DISK FILE by clicking on the radio button.
5. Click OK.

You have now successfully recorded a new voice-over and renamed both the audio file and the region.

Save Work in Progress

Earlier, you created a copy of the session using the Save As command under the File menu. As you complete each main portion of the project, you should save your work in progress. To do this, you will use the SAVE command under the File menu. This will not create a copy of your session; rather, it will save your changes to the existing session that is currently open.

Save your work:

1. Choose FILE > SAVE to save your progress up to this point.

Importing Media

Not all of the media that is used in a Pro Tools session needs to be recorded from within the session. For instance, you might have a movie file that you would like to work with for post-production or existing audio files that you want to use to add background music and sound effects. In these cases, you will import the existing media files from your hard drive into the current session.

Pro Tools provides many ways to import media into your session. (Refer to Chapter 5 for detailed information regarding importing media.) For this project, you will import a movie and background music using the Import command, and you will import sound effects using the Workspace browser.

Import a Movie

For this project, you will import a QuickTime movie into your session and then enhance it with music and sound effects.

Import Red Dragon.mov into your session:

1. Choose FILE > IMPORT > VIDEO. A dialog box will open on screen, prompting you to choose a video file.

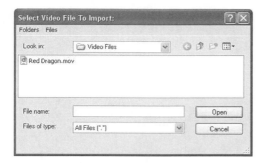

Dialog box for importing a video file

2. Navigate to the VIDEO FILES folder (found within the Post Project folder that you copied earlier).
3. Select RED DRAGON.MOV and click OPEN. The Video Import Options dialog box will appear.
4. Select SESSION START in the Location menu and click OK. The movie will be imported into your session and will open in a Video window. A Video track will also display in the Edit window.

The Video window as displayed after importing Red Dragon.mov

View the clip (optional):

1. Press ENTER (Windows) or RETURN (Mac OS) to move the insertion point to the beginning of the Timeline.
2. Press the SPACE BAR to begin playback. The movie clip will play back in time with the audio in the session.
3. When the clip ends, press SPACE BAR again to stop playback. The insertion point will return to the beginning of the Timeline.

The Video window during playback

Import Files to the Region List

Next, you will need to import some additional music into your session. When importing audio, you can choose to have it placed either into the Region List or directly onto a track. For this project, you will import music files to the Region List and later decide which file to use to replace the existing music.

Import music audio files to the Region List:

1. Choose FILE > IMPORT > AUDIO.
2. In the Import Audio dialog box, navigate to the NEW MUSIC folder (found within the Post Project folder that you copied earlier).
3. Select the four NEW MUSIC files (click on the first, then Shift-click on the last to select them all) and click the ADD FILES button. The files will be added to the Region Import area of the dialog box.

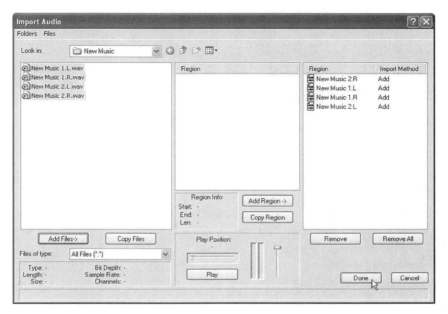

The Import Audio dialog box as it appears after clicking Add Files

4. Click **DONE**. The Audio Import Options dialog box will appear.

5. In the dialog box, select **REGION LIST** for the destination, and click **OK**. The regions New Music 1 (Stereo) and New Music 2 (Stereo) will be imported and will display in your Region List.

Upon import, Pro Tools intelligently links the left and right files of each split stereo file together, displaying them as two stereo regions rather than as four individual files. You can reveal the original files by clicking on the disclosure triangles to the left of the region name in the Region List.

Import Files from the Workspace Browser

As you've already seen, the Workspace browser is a great resource for locating, opening, and importing all sorts of media files. For this part of the project, you will use the Workspace browser to import a region group containing sword sound effects. A region group can be thought of as simply a collection of regions grouped together to look and act as a single region.

 Region groups are covered in greater detail in the Pro Tools 110 course.

For this project, all of the sword sound effects have been edited and spotted to the movie outside of the current session and grouped together as a single region group. You will need to drag the region group from the Workspace browser onto a stereo Audio track; the region group (along with all associated regions and audio files) will be automatically imported into your session.

Locate the region group file called "Sword Group" with the Workspace browser:

1. Choose WINDOW > WORKSPACE to open the Workspace browser. Reposition the windows as necessary so that the Workspace browser is not obscured by the Video window.

2. If necessary, click the RESET button to clear the results of your last search; otherwise, click the FIND icon (magnifying glass) to reveal the search fields. The Find button will be highlighted, and the window will be split into an upper and a lower area.

3. Type **Sword Group** in the Name field.

4. Select REGION GROUP FILE from the Kind pop-up menu. Make sure that there is a check next to the disk volume that contains the Post Project folder.

5. Click SEARCH. After a moment, the Sword Group file will appear in the lower pane of the Workspace browser.

Drag the region group to the Swords stereo Audio track:

1. Reposition the Workspace browser, if necessary, so you can see both the Swords track in the Edit window and the Sword Group file in the Workspace browser.

2. Drag the SWORD GROUP file onto the Swords track in the Edit window.

3. If necessary, use the GRABBER tool to drag the Sword Group to the very start of the session.

4. Close the Workspace browser to minimize on-screen clutter.

Audition the changes (optional):

1. If necessary, press ENTER (Windows) or RETURN (Mac OS) to move the insertion point to the beginning of the Timeline.

2. Press the SPACE BAR to begin playback. The movie clip will play back with the existing audio and newly added sword effects.

3. When the clip ends, press the SPACE BAR again to stop playback. The insertion point will return to the beginning of the Timeline.

Save Work in Progress

You have now imported and placed the movie, sound effects, and other audio files needed for the project. You should take this opportunity to save your work.

Save your work:

1. Choose FILE > SAVE to save your progress up to this point.

Editing in Pro Tools

With all of the media recorded and imported, it is now time to do some editing on your project. So far, you have used the Selector and Grabber tools. In addition to these, you will use the rest of the tools (Zoomer, Trim, Scrubber, and Pencil) to modify the project so that it sounds more complete.

View the Project

Before you begin editing this project, you should familiarize yourself with the movie. To do so, you will play back the movie and navigate along the Timeline to get a feel for the movie's progression and transitional points.

View the movie and play back the project:

1. If it is not already open, choose WINDOW > VIDEO to display the Video window.
2. If necessary, press ENTER (Windows) or RETURN (Mac OS) to place the playback cursor at the start of the session.
3. If you have not already done so, view the movie from start to finish:
   a. Press the SPACE BAR to begin playing the session. The audio on the Pro Tools tracks will play back in time with the video display in the Video window.
   b. When the clip ends, press the SPACE BAR again to stop playback.

After viewing the movie, you should review some of the transitional points to better understand how the sequence progresses. Because Pro Tools provides a nonlinear editing environment, you can instantly jump to any point on the Timeline at any time. You will use the Selector tool to click at different points within the project and use the Video window to view the action based on the location of the playback cursor.

Experiment with the Selector tool to update the Video window:

- Click on various parts of the Video track with the **SELECTOR** tool to get a rough idea where the main action transitions fall on the Timeline. Use the SPACE BAR to control playback.

- Experiment with making selections on the Video track and the Audio tracks; try to select a scene from beginning to end and play it back.

 The Video window will always reflect the start time of a Timeline selection. Because of this, when you are making a selection based on the Video track, you will find it beneficial to locate the end point first and select backward to the start.

Add Sound Effects

The session is currently missing some sound effects. During this part of the project, you will use various editing techniques to add the sound effects to your project. Refer to Chapter 6 as needed for details on editing techniques.

Add Cavalry Roar

The first sound effect that you will add occurs at the point in the movie when the horses are galloping. You will need to add the sound of a cavalry to match the action using the Horses Gallop Cavalry sound effect in your Region List.

Place the Horses Gallop Cavalry region onto the DX3 track and spot it to the proper location:

1. Select the **HORSES GALLOP CAVALRY** region in the Region List (Edit window). If necessary, use the scroll bar to scroll the list until the region is visible.

2. Drag the **HORSES GALLOP CAVALRY** region from the Region List to any open space on the DX3 track.

3. Click the **SPOT** button in the upper-left corner of the Edit window to activate Spot mode. (You might have to reposition the Video window first.)

4. With the **GRABBER** tool, click on the region that you just placed on the DX3 track. The Spot dialog box will open.

The Spot dialog box

5. Set the Time Scale to **TIMECODE** or to **MIN:SECS** if Timecode is not available.
6. In the Start field, type **00:02:32:15** (Timecode) or **0:34.750** (Min:Sec) and click **OK**. The region will move to the start time you typed.
7. Click the **SLIP** button to activate Slip mode.

Audition the sound effect:

1. Activate loop playback, if it is not already selected, by choosing **OPTIONS > LOOP PLAYBACK**. The Play button in the Transport window will display a looping arrow to indicate Loop Playback mode.
2. With the region still selected, press the **SPACE BAR** to play back the sound effect with the picture. During playback, you can solo the DX3 track by clicking the **S** button under the track name.
3. When you are finished, press the **SPACE BAR** again to stop playback, and click the **S** button if necessary to take the track out of solo mode.

Edit Cavalry Roar

The cavalry sound effect you've added is a little longer than the scene to which it corresponds. You will use this extra time before and after the scene to create a fade-in and a fade-out effect.

Create a fade-in and a fade-out on the Horses Gallop Cavalry region:

1. If it is not already selected, click on the **A...Z** button in the toolbar area of the Edit window to enable Commands Keyboard Focus mode. When selected, the button will be outlined in blue.

Clicking the Commands Keyboard Focus button

 Commands Keyboard Focus mode gives you access to many Pro Tools commands at the touch of a single key stroke. Focus keys are covered throughout the Pro Tools training coursework and are summarized in the Pro Tools 310M course.

2. Using the **GRABBER** tool, click the Horses Gallop Cavalry region to select it.
3. Press **E** on your keyboard to activate Zoom Toggle. The selected region will expand to fill the available space in the Edit window.
4. With the **SCRUBBER** tool, click and drag near the start of the region.

    Gradually move the mouse back and forth while viewing the Video window. Locate the point where the scene changes to the close-up of the woman on the horse. Release the mouse to position the insertion point at this spot.

5. Press **D** on your keyboard to create a fade-in.
6. With the **SCRUBBER** tool, click and drag near the end of the region.

    Gradually move the mouse back and forth while viewing the Video window. Locate the point where the scene changes to the profile of the woman starting to throw the knife. Release the mouse to position the insertion point at this spot.

7. Press **G** on your keyboard to create a fade-out.
8. Press **E** on your keyboard to activate Zoom Toggle again, returning the session to the previous view.

Add Knife Throw

The next sound effect you need to add is the Knife Throw. For this sound effect, you will need to sync the impact point of the sound effect to the point in the movie at which the knife hits the wall. To do this, you will use a Sync Point.

Place the Knife Throw sound effect on the Knife Throw track and identify a Sync Point:

1. Scroll the Edit window so that the Knife Throw track is visible on screen.

2. Locate the KNIFE THROW region in the Region List and drag it onto any open space of the Knife Throw track.

3. With the region selected, press **E** on your keyboard to activate Zoom Toggle and zoom in on the region.

4. With the SCRUBBER tool, click and drag across the region until you hear the sound of the knife making impact. Release the mouse to position the insertion point as close as possible to the beginning of the impact (about halfway into the region).

5. Choose REGION > IDENTIFY SYNC POINT. A small triangle will appear in the lower part of the region, under the insertion cursor, signifying a Sync Point at that spot.

6. Press **E** on your keyboard to activate Zoom Toggle again, returning the session to the previous view.

Having identified a Sync Point in the sound effect region, you will now need to create a memory location to mark the corresponding point in the movie.

Create a memory location:

1. With the SCRUBBER tool selected, click and drag on the Video track to locate the point when the knife hits the wall; position the insertion point at this spot. The impact should occur somewhere between 00:02:26:08 and 00:02:37:08 (Timecode) or 0:38.500 and 0:39.500 (Min:Sec).

2. Press ENTER on the numeric keypad or click the ADD MARKER/MEMORY LOCATION button (plus sign) at the head of the Marker Ruler to create a memory location. The New Memory Location dialog box will open.

The Add Marker/Memory Location button

3. Enter **Knife Hits Wall** in the Name field, and type the time from the Main Counter (Edit window) in the Comments field.

   Adding the time to the Comments field will allow you to hover your mouse over the marker in the Marker Ruler to view the exact time value in the pop-up information.

4. Click **OK**. The marker will be displayed on the Marker Ruler as a yellow diamond.

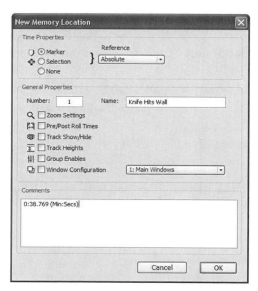

Enter Name and Comments in the New Memory Location dialog box.

Pop-up information showing the values entered for the marker name and comments

Spot the Knife Throw sound effect to the movie:

1. Click the **SPOT** button in the Edit window to activate Spot mode.

2. With the **GRABBER** tool, click on the **KNIFE THROW** region on the Knife Throw track. The Spot dialog box will appear.

3. In the Sync Point field, type the time that you noted in the Knife Throw marker. Be sure to use the same Time Scale in this dialog box that you used when noting the time previously.

If you don't remember the exact value, click Cancel and place your mouse over the marker to view the pop-up information. Click the Knife Throw region again when you are ready to reopen the Spot dialog box.

4. Click **OK**. The region's Sync Point will be spotted to where the knife hits the wall.
5. Click the Sʟɪᴘ button to return to Slip mode.

Audition the sound effect:

1. With the region still selected and loop playback enabled, press the sᴘᴀᴄᴇ ʙᴀʀ to play back the sound effect with the picture. During playback, you can solo the Knife Throw track if desired by clicking the **S** button under the track name.
2. When you are finished, press the sᴘᴀᴄᴇ ʙᴀʀ again to stop playback, and click the **S** button if necessary to take the track out of solo mode.
3. Press Eɴᴛᴇʀ (Windows) or Rᴇᴛᴜʀɴ (Mac OS) to return to the beginning of the Timeline.

Remove the Pop

The VO track for the project has a pop in the third region that needs to be removed. You will do this by using the Pencil tool to redraw the waveform at that point.

Remove the pop for the VO track:

1. Solo the VO track by clicking on the **S** button under the track name (Edit window).
2. Click on the third region on the VO track with the Gʀᴀʙʙᴇʀ tool to select the region.
3. Press the sᴘᴀᴄᴇ ʙᴀʀ to play the region. Listen for the pop between the words "heroes" and "are born."
4. With the region selected, press **E** on your keyboard to activate Zoom Toggle. The region will expand to fill the available space in the Edit window.
5. With the Zᴏᴏᴍᴇʀ tool, click and drag over an area of the region to zoom in closer on the silence between the spoken words. The pop will become visible as a sudden spike in the waveform.

6. Continue zooming in on the spike to display the magnification needed for editing the waveform of the pop. You will need to be able to see the path of the waveform displayed as a single line.

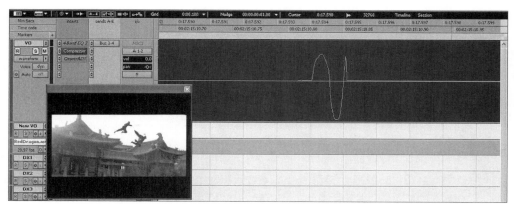

Zoom in to an adequate magnification level to edit the waveform.

7. Using the PENCIL tool, drag a horizontal line in the center of the track across the middle of the pop. The line doesn't have to be perfectly straight, but try to get it as close as possible.

8. If necessary, click the region with the GRABBER tool to reselect it.

9. Press the SPACE BAR to play the region and verify that the pop no longer exists. If needed, select UNDO and repeat the process to obtain the desired results.

10. When you're satisfied with the edit, press E on your keyboard to return the session to the previous view.

11. Unsolo the VO track.

Change the Music

Next you will turn your attention to the music for the project. You will need to replace the existing music for the project to give the soundtrack a different emotional undertone. To do this, you will select from the music that you imported to the Region List, place the selected music onto the New Music track, and trim the new music to the proper length.

Audition the music in the Region List:

1. Locate the New Music 1 and New Music 2 regions on the Region List. If necessary, scroll the REGION LIST until the New Music regions are visible.

2. ALT-CLICK (Windows) or OPTION-CLICK (Mac OS) on the New Music 1 region in the Region List. The audio region will play back as long as you hold down the mouse button.

3. Release the mouse button to stop the audition.

4. Repeat steps 2 and 3, auditioning the NEW MUSIC 2 region.

5. After listening to each music region, select the region that you feel is more appropriate for the project. We will refer to this as the New Music X region for descriptive purposes, but you can use either region to complete the project.

Place the selected region onto the New Music Audio track:

1. Locate the MUSIC MIX track in the Edit window.

2. Using the GRABBER tool, click on the MUSIC MIX_02 region on the track. The region will be highlighted.

3. Hold the START key (Windows) or CONTROL key (Mac OS) while dragging the NEW MUSIC X region (whichever you chose in step 3 in the previous task) from the Region List onto the New Music track. The region will appear on the track, aligned to start at the same time as the Music Mix_02 region.

 The New Music region you've chosen should be placed on the New Music track so that it appears below the Music Mix_02 region. Do not place it on the Music Mix track, as it will obscure the Music Mix_02 region; you will need to access this region in a later step.

 Holding the START key (Windows) or CONTROL key (Mac OS) while dragging a region from the Region List constrains its placement to begin at the start time of a selection or at the insertion point.

4. Mute the MIX MUSIC_02 region by selecting it and choosing REGION > MUTE/UNMUTE.

5. Press ENTER or RETURN to move the insertion point to the beginning of the timeline, followed by the SPACE BAR to play back the session with the new music track.

6. At the end of the clip, press the SPACE BAR a second time to stop playback.

The New Music X region is quite a bit longer than necessary. You will next use the Trim tool to adjust the region to the appropriate length.

Trim the end of the region:

1. Using the GRABBER tool, click on the MUSIC MIX_02 region on the Music Mix track.

2. Note the TIMECODE or MIN:SEC time displayed in the Edit Selection End field in the Counters display of the Edit window.

The Edit Selection End field displayed in the Edit window (Min:Sec Time Scale shown)

3. Click on the NEW MUSIC X region that you placed on the New Music track.

4. Press the SPOT button to place Pro Tools in Spot mode.

5. Using the TRIM tool, click on the right side of the NEW MUSIC X region. The tool should look like a "]" when you click. The Spot dialog box will open.

6. In the End field, type the time that you noted in step 2 and click OK. The region end will be trimmed to the length of the original music track.

7. Click the SLIP button to place Pro Tools into Slip mode.

Save Work in Progress

You have now completed the editing tasks for your project. You should take this opportunity to save your work.

Save your work:

1. Choose FILE > SAVE to save your progress up to this point.

Mixing in Pro Tools

Now that all of the editing is complete, you will use some of the mixing features in Pro Tools to add some real-time processing and blend all of the sound elements together.

Remove the Hum

The DAT.02.new.10.sine region on the DX2 track contains a low-frequency hum that you will now need to remove. Using some creative EQ, you can eliminate most of the hum. To do so, you will need to locate and zoom in on the region, insert an EQ plug-in on the track, and adjust the EQ settings to reduce the hum.

Locate and zoom in on the DAT.02.new.10.sine region:

1. Click on the **DAT.02.NEW.10.SINE** region in the Region List to select the region on the Track Playlist. If necessary, scroll the Region List until the region is visible (toward the top).

Click on the region in the Region List to select it.

2. Press **E** on your keyboard to activate Zoom Toggle and zoom in. The DAT.02.new.10.sine region will expand to fill the Edit window.

Insert the 1-Band EQ 3 on the DX2 track:

1. Choose **WINDOW > MIX** to activate the Mix window, or press **CTRL+=** (Windows) or **COMMAND+=** (Mac OS).
2. Locate the channel strip for the DX2 track.
3. Click on the **INSERT SELECTOR A** for the track and choose **PLUG-IN > EQ > 1-BAND EQ 3 (MONO)** from the pop-up menu. The 1-band EQ III plug-in window will appear.

The 1-band EQ III plug-in window

Adjust the EQ settings to reduce the hum:

1. Solo the DX2 track by clicking on the **S** button just above the Volume Fader in the Mix window.

2. Press the **SPACE BAR** to initiate playback. With loop playback enabled, the region will loop until playback is stopped.

3. In the 1-Band EQ III plug-in window, activate a **NOTCH** filter and drag the gray ball in the graphic display to the left until you hear the hum reduced (around 60 Hz).

4. Press the **SPACE BAR** to stop playback.

5. Close the plug-in window and un-solo the track.

6. Press **CTRL+=** (Windows) or **COMMAND+=** (Mac OS) to toggle to the Edit window and press **E** on your keyboard to return the session to the previous view.

Add Reverb

Next, you will need to add some reverb to the VO track to help it fit into the rest of the mix. This project includes an Auxiliary Input track that has already been configured with the D-Verb plug-in assigned and the track input assigned to Bus 3–4. Additionally, Send A on the VO track has already been assigned to Bus 3–4. Therefore, all you will need to do is to increase the level of the send on the VO track to add reverb to the mix.

Increase the Send A level on the VO track:

1. Press **CTRL+=** (Windows) or **COMMAND+=** (Mac OS) to toggle to the Mix window.

2. Click on **SEND ASSIGNMENT A** on the VO track (labeled Bus 3–4). The Send A window will appear.

3. Click the **SOLO** button in the Send A window to solo the VO track.

4. Press **CTRL+=** (Windows) or **COMMAND+=** (Mac OS) to toggle to the Edit window.

5. Using the **GRABBER** tool, click on any region on the VO track to select the region.

6. With loop playback enabled, press the **SPACE BAR** to begin playback.

7. While listening to the track, raise the level on the Send Fader to introduce the reverb.

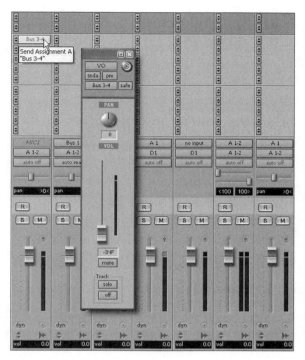

Clicking on the Send Assignment opens the Send window (foreground)

The reverb will play back while the VO track is soloed because the Reverb track is set to Solo Safe mode. Solo Safe is commonly used on Auxiliary tracks to prevent them from being muted when another track is soloed.

 You can place a track in Solo Safe mode by Ctrl-clicking (Windows) or Command-clicking (Mac OS) on the Solo button in the Edit or Mix windows.

 More information on Solo Safe mode can be found in the Pro Tools 110 course.

8. When you are satisfied with the results, press the SPACE BAR to stop playback.
9. Press the SOLO button to take the track out of solo mode and close the Send A window.

Enhance the Whoosh

This project includes a whoosh sound effect that sounds a bit dull. You will need to add some flanging and EQ to liven up the sound. You will add flanging using an AudioSuite plug-in and add EQ using the 7-Band EQ III RTAS plug-in.

A Note about AudioSuite Plug-Ins

You will be using the DigiRack Flanger to modulate the sound effect. The DigiRack Flanger is an AudioSuite plug-in. These plug-ins behave differently from RTAS in that they are not real-time processors. AudioSuite plug-ins process and modify audio files on disk, rather than adding the plug-in effect in real time.

 More information on AudioSuite processing can be found in the Pro Tools 110 course.

Zoom in on the Whoosh comp 2.1 region on the Whoosh track:

1. Select WHOOSH COMP 2.1 in the Region List (toward the bottom) to select the region in the Track Playlist.
2. Press E on your keyboard to activate Zoom Toggle. The Whoosh comp 2.1 region will expand to fill the Edit window.

Use the DigiRack Flanger to process the Whoosh comp 2.1 region:

1. Choose AUDIOSUITE > MODULATION > FLANGER. The DigiRack Flanger plug-in window will appear on screen.
2. Verify that USE IN PLAYLIST is highlighted. If it isn't, click to highlight it.
3. From the Librarian menu, choose SLOW N DEEP.

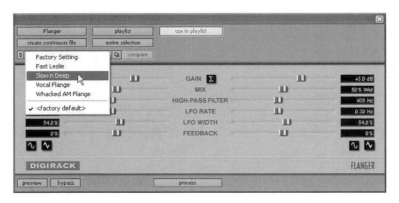

Select Slow n Deep from the plug-in Librarian menu.

4. To audition the effect, click PREVIEW. Adjust the effect parameters using the sliders, as desired.

5. When you are satisfied with the effect, click PROCESS to process the audio region. A new region will be generated, combining the source audio with the Flange effect and replacing the selected region.

6. Close the Flanger plug-in window to reduce on-screen clutter.

Add the 7-Band EQ III to Insert A on the Whoosh track:

1. Verify that LOOP PLAYBACK is still active. (The Play button of the Transport window should display a looping arrow.) If necessary, choose OPTIONS > LOOP PLAYBACK to enable loop playback.

2. Press the SPACE BAR to start playback. The Whoosh comp 2.1 region will repeat until playback is stopped.

3. In the Edit window, click on INSERT SELECTOR A for the Whoosh track and choose PLUG-IN > EQ > 7-BAND EQ 3 (MONO). The EQ III plug-in window will open.

Clicking an Insert selector in the Edit window

4. Experiment by raising and lowering the colored balls in the graphic display of the EQ III plug-in window.

5. When you are satisfied with the results, close the plug-in window and press the SPACE BAR to stop playback.

6. Press E on your keyboard to return the session to the previous view.

Mix the Project

The project is now ready for mixing to blend all of the tracks together. You will use the Volume Faders and Pan Sliders to create a stereo mix.

Getting Started

To get started, you will determine the contribution of each track to the overall mix by soloing each track individually. Some tracks, such as the Reverb track, only process sound that flows through them from external sources. Because they don't create any sound on their own, it might be difficult to determine why such tracks are important to the mix. Tracks that cannot be isolated by soloing can be muted and unmuted to help determine their contribution.

Solo each track to isolate its contribution:

1. Press CTRL+= (Windows) or COMMAND+= (Mac OS) to toggle to the Edit window.

2. Click the RETURN TO ZERO button on the Transport window to place the insertion point at the beginning of the Timeline.

3. Press the SPACE BAR to begin playback.

4. Solo each track for a few moments by clicking the SOLO button (labeled "S") beneath the track name in the Edit window.

    a. Consider how the track contributes to the overall mix, and make adjustments as needed. Toggle Solo mode on and off to alternate between isolating the track and placing it in context within the mix to fine-tune the track.

    b. When you are satisfied with the results, take the track out of Solo mode.

 Many of the tracks have short segments of audio, such as sound effects, that occur only at specific locations. To adjust the mix on these tracks, you might need to select a region on the track and listen to it in Loop Playback mode, toggling Solo on and off as you fine-tune the mix.

5. Use the Pan Sliders to help give some stereo separation to your mix. Pan selected tracks to the left or right, using your discretion, to help distinguish each of the tracks in the mix.

6. When you are finished soloing each track, press the SPACE BAR again to stop playback.

Mute each track as needed to isolate its contribution:

1. If needed, click the RETURN TO ZERO button on the Transport window to place the insertion point at the beginning of the Timeline.

2. Press the SPACE BAR to begin playback.

3. Toggle MUTE on and off for each track, alternating between dropping the track out of the mix and adding it back in, to determine the track's contribution to the mix. Make adjustments to the track as needed.

 Be sure to leave the Music Mix track muted to avoid a conflict with the New Music track that you've added.

4. When you are finished, press the SPACE BAR again to stop playback.

Completing the Mix

Complete this portion of the project using your discretion, experimenting until you are happy with the results.

Save Work in Progress

You have now created a complete mix for your project. You should take this opportunity to save your work.

Save your work:

1. Choose FILE > SAVE to save your progress up to this point.

Listen to the Automated Mix

Chapter 9 introduced you to basic automation features of Pro Tools. Although many of the automation features that Pro Tools provides are beyond the scope of this book, this portion of the project allows you to experience some of the power that automation offers by activating the preset automation included in the session.

Throughout this project, you have completed your work with all of the track automation modes set to Auto Off. Now you will switch the tracks to Auto Read mode and play back the session using the previously recorded Automation Playlists.

 All of the automation features are covered in detail throughout the courses in the Digidesign Certified Training Program.

Enable Auto Read automation mode for all tracks:

1. Choose WINDOW > MIX or press CTRL+= (Windows) or COMMAND+= (Mac OS) to activate the Mix window.

2. **ALT-CLICK** (Windows) or **OPTION-CLICK** (Mac OS) on the **AUTOMATION MODE SELECTOR** for any track and choose **READ**. All of the tracks in the session will switch to Auto Read mode.

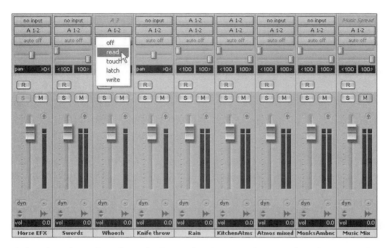

Selecting Auto Read mode from the Automation Mode selector (Mix window)

3. Maximize the Mix window to show all tracks in the session.

Mix window maximized to show all tracks

4. Press ENTER (Windows) or RETURN (Mac OS) to move to the beginning of the Timeline, followed by the SPACE BAR to play back the session. The Volume Faders will move automatically to help create a more dynamic mix.

5. When the clip ends, press the SPACE BAR a second time to stop playback.

6. Choose FILE > REVERT TO SAVED to return the session to your mix settings.

Finishing Your Work

Now that the project is mixed, you will need to create a bounce of the movie to add your version of the soundtrack to the movie file. This will enable the file to be played in a standard movie player application with the soundtrack you've created so that you can share your work with others.

Lastly, you will need to archive your work. Through the process of creating a project you generate many files, not all of which are needed for the completed session. By archiving your work, you are able preserve your work without taking up excess disk space due to unnecessary files.

Bounce the Movie

You will use the Bounce to Movie command to add your soundtrack mix to the movie file.

Bounce your mix into the movie file:

1. Choose WINDOW > EDIT or press CTRL+= (Windows) or COMMAND+= (Mac OS) to activate the Edit window.

2. With the GRABBER tool, click on the video region on the Video track to select it.

3. Choose FILE > BOUNCE TO > QUICKTIME MOVIE. The Bounce dialog box will appear on screen.

4. Click BOUNCE. A Save Bounce As dialog box will appear on screen.

5. Select a location for the movie file in the SAVE IN section of the dialog box, and enter a name for your file in the FILE NAME field.

6. Click SAVE. You will hear playback begin as Pro Tools creates a QuickTime movie containing your mix and the Video track.

Archive Your Work

Now that your project is complete, you will need to back it up for storage. On a real-world project, you might also need to deliver the session to the client. Because there are many files associated with a session, there is a potential that something could get lost if the archival process isn't completed properly. Fortunately, Pro Tools has many features to help ensure that you keep the files you need and remove the files you do not.

In this process, you will complete the following steps:

1. Remove unused audio files and regions. Because these files are not being used by the session, they are essentially wasting space on your hard drive or archive medium.

2. Use the Save Copy In command to "collect" all of the audio and video files and copy them to a new location (preferably on a different hard drive).

3. Open the copied session to verify that it copied correctly.

4. Use the Compact Selected command to remove the unused portions of each audio file that is used in the copied session.

 This archival process will permanently remove any audio that is not currently being used in the session. Because this could potentially limit the creative possibilities (should you need to revise some aspect of this session in the future), you should complete this process only after the project is complete.

Remove Unused Material

To remove unused audio files and regions, complete the following steps:

1. Click on the REGION LIST pop-up menu and choose SELECT > UNUSED. All of the regions that are not included on a Track Playlist will be selected.

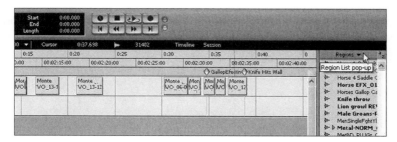

Click the Region List pop-up menu to select unused regions.

2. Click on the REGION LIST pop-up menu a second time and choose CLEAR. The Clear Regions dialog box will appear on screen.

3. Click REMOVE in the Clear Regions dialog box to remove the regions from your session. The audio files will be removed from the session without being deleted from the drive. If you later find that you need an audio file that has been removed, you can re-import it into your session.

Collect Session Files in a New Location

To save a copy of your session and all associated files, do the following:

1. Choose FILE > SAVE COPY IN. The Save Copy of Session In dialog box will appear on screen.

2. Choose a directory to store the session copy and name the copy of the session. If possible, it is best to choose a directory on a drive other than the one used for the current session.

3. In the ITEMS TO COPY area, select the following:
   - All Audio Files
   - Movie/Video Files

4. Click the SAVE button. Pro Tools will begin processing the save, copying the session file along with all of the audio and video files in the directory you chose.

5. Choose FILE > CLOSE to close the original session. If you are prompted to save, choose OK to save your changes in the original session. (It will be saved with the unused material removed.)

Verify the Copied Session

To verify that the session copied correctly, do the following:

1. From the File menu or the Workspace browser, open the new copy of your project.

2. If you saved your session to a different hard-drive volume, you might see a warning that the original disk allocation cannot be used. Click No when you are asked to save a report.

   After the session is open, there should be no offline regions.

3. Choose WINDOW > PROJECT to open the Project browser. You will use the Project browser to verify that every file that is referenced in this session is stored in the proper directory.

The Project browser provides powerful search and management tools for the files referenced in your current session, regardless of where they are stored.

4. In the left pane of the Project browser, expand the AUDIO FILES and VIDEO FILES folders.

5. In the right pane of the Project browser, use the scroll bar to find the PATH column. Verify that the path for every file in the Audio Files and Video Files folders leads to the new copy of your project's session folder.

6. Close the Project browser when you are finished.

Compact Your Session

Once you have verified that all of your files are properly referenced, you have one more step to complete your archive: compacting. Most regions in a session reference only a part of a larger audio recording. Because the session is now complete, it is safe to remove the unused parts. Compacting is the process of removing the audio from a file that is not used by any region. Hence, only the used portions of the audio files remain, reducing the amount of disk space being consumed.

To compact your project's audio files, do the following:

1. Click on the REGION LIST pop-up menu and choose SELECT > ALL. All of the regions in the Region List will be selected.

2. Click on the REGION LIST pop-up menu a second time and choose COMPACT. The Compact dialog box will appear on screen with a description of the compacting process.

3. Click COMPACT to compact the audio files. Pro Tools will begin compacting the session files.

4. When finished, save your work by choosing FILE > SAVE and close your session by choosing FILE > CLOSE SESSION.

This concludes the Post Hands-On project.

PART IV

Course Completion

Components

- Additional projects

- Final exam

Overview

Part IV of the Pro Tools 101 course can be completed in an instructor-led environment at an official Pro Tools training center. In this part of the course, you will have the opportunity to work with additional project material, including music sessions by major-label recording artists and post-production sessions for commercial television advertisements and/or movie trailers. Upon completing the coursework, you will be able to take the final exam and receive an official completion certificate through the training center.

Overview | Information for Course Completion

This section provides information for completing the Pro Tools 101 course through an official Digidesign Training Partner. Included are instructions for locating a training center, descriptions of the additional project material that is available, a description of the final exam and completion certificate, and information on the free plug-in promotion currently offered with enrollment in the Pro Tools 110 course.

Notes

Locating a Training Center

The Pro Tools 101 course can be completed at any of more than 100 facilities located in 25 countries worldwide.

Training facilities lookup page on the Digidesign website

Training centers offering the Pro Tools 101 course include the following:

- **Sponsored Schools.** These include colleges, trade schools, and high schools that offer beginning coursework in Digidesign hardware and software. Training at sponsored schools is generally provided for the Pro Tools 100-level courses only. With more than 60 locations in countries such as Australia, China, France, Germany, Ireland, Netherlands, Spain, Switzerland, the United Kingdom, the United States, and others, Sponsored Schools are available in many major cities worldwide.

- **Certified Training Locations.** These include colleges or technical programs that integrate Pro Tools coursework within a larger audio education program. Courses may span weeks or semesters, allowing you to learn Pro Tools within a broader curriculum. More than 20 Certified Training Locations are available in countries such as Canada, the United Kingdom, the United States, and others.

- **Authorized Pro Schools.** These institutions offer professional training in multi-day courses focusing solely on Pro Tools. Pro Schools offer the fastest way to get trained and certified in Pro Tools. More than 25 locations qualify as Authorized Pro Schools in Canada, the United Kingdom, the United States, and other countries.

A list of available training centers can be found on the Digidesign website at www.digidesign.com by clicking on the Training link and then clicking on Training Facilities.

Additional Projects

Additional project materials are available at official training partner facilities. As part of your Pro Tools 101 course completion and other Pro Tools courses that you enroll in, you will have the opportunity to work with many of these projects. (Check with the school for completion requirements and project availability.)

Some of the projects that are commonly available include the following:

- **Black Eyed Peas, "Hey Mama."** This project is a live recording of the band mixed through a Digidesign VENUE system and recorded as a multi-track session into Pro Tools.

- **The Time Machine.** This project, a movie trailer for the 2002 movie staring Guy Pearce, Samantha Mumba, Jeremy Irons, and Orlando Jones, features video footage from the movie along with dialog, music, and sound effects. Session and media files provided courtesy of Dreamworks, SKG.

- **Ugly Duckling.** This television commercial for Ugly Duckling Car Rental is an ideal beginning project for students interested in post-production applications for Pro Tools. Session and media files provided courtesy of Greg Kuehn at Peligro Music & Sound Design.
- **Devil's River.** This project, created for the Nature Conservancy to promote conservation of the Devil's River land area, includes audio backgrounds and some narration along with a QuickTime movie. Students can edit, sync, and mix this project to their own tastes to create a documentary fit for broadcast. Session and media files provided courtesy of Match Frame, San Antonio.
- **NewsRadio.** In this scene from the U.S. sitcom, one of the characters interviews fellow employees about sharing his apartment. The project contains video footage with audio that lends itself to editing dialog and replacing dialog. Footage produced by Brillstein/Grey Entertainment; session and media files provided courtesy of BGE.
- Session files of releases by popular recording artists, including:
  - Nine Inch Nails, "Only"
  - Paul Oakenfold, "Bleeder"
  - M83, "Don't Save Us from the Flames"
  - 311, "Don't Tread on Me"
  - Chevelle, "Send the Pain Below"
  - Romero/Rich Tozzoli, "La Vida Nueva"
  - Westside Connection, "Gangsta Nation"
  - Ozomatli, "Live at Fillmore"

Final Exam

The Pro Tools 101 exam consists of 50 multiple choice questions. The exam is conducted at Digidesign Training Partner facilities upon course completion. Students have a specified time limit to answer all questions. You will need to achieve a passing score to receive your Certificate of Completion.

Certificate of Completion

Upon successful completion of the coursework and final exam, you will receive a Certificate of Completion to formally recognize your accomplishment. The Pro Tools 101 completion certificate signifies your eligibility to enroll in the Pro Tools 110 course and continue your progress toward Operator or Expert Certification.

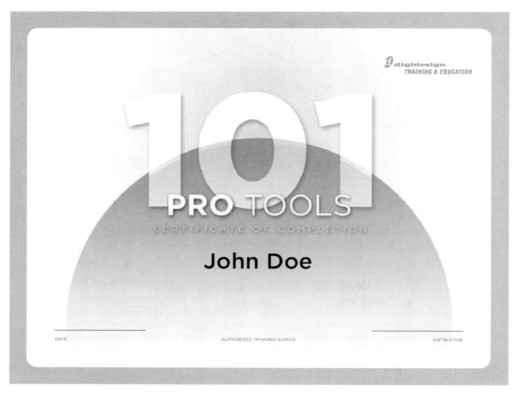

Pro Tools 101 Certificate of Completion

Pro Tools 110 Promotion

After completing the Pro Tools 101 course, you will be eligible to enroll in the next course, Pro Tools 110, at any Digidesign Training Partner facility. Digidesign is currently running a promotional offer that allows you to choose one free plug-in when you enroll and attend the Pro Tools 110 course at any official Digidesign Training Partner facility. Upon meeting the promotion requirements, you will receive an activation card with a special Pro Tools 110 activation code for the plug-in of your choice. Visit www.digidesign.com/trainingpromo for more information.

PT 110 Activation Card

To obtain a license for your PT 110 plug-in:

1. Visit www.ilok.com to sign up for an iLok.com account.

2. Visit http://secure.digidesign.com/activation/ to input your activation code, select your plug-in choice, and enter your iLok.com user ID. Your iLok.com User ID is the name you create for your iLok.com account. This process will transfer the plug-in license into your iLok.com account.

3. Visit www.ilok.com to transfer the licenses from your iLok.com account to your iLok USB Smart Key.

PT 110 Activation Code:

9340-56405-00 Rev.A

Receive a free plug-in with the Pro Tools 110 course.

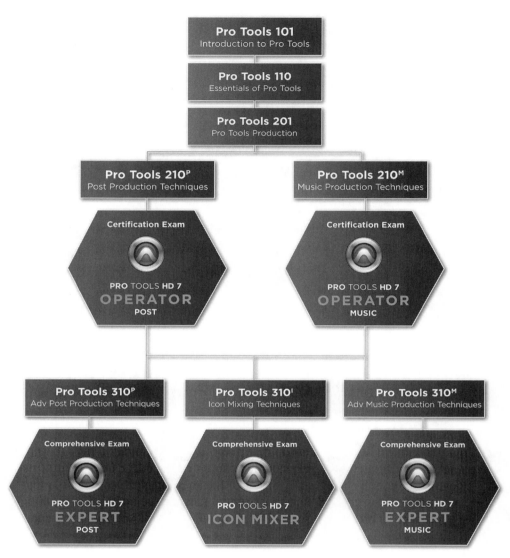

Coursework in the Pro Tools Certification Program

Index

folders. *See also* files
>   Region Groups, 49

formatting
>   files, considerations prior to importing, 121–123
>   plug-ins, 238
>   tracks, 89, 330–332

Frames view, viewing video, 132

frequency, 21
>   analog-to-digital conversion, 22

FX Designer, 9

G

Gotcher, Peter, 6, 7

Grabber tool, 68, 166
>   playlists, editing, 236
>   regions, editing, 205–207

GRAMMY award, 14

Grid mode, 71, 195
>   configuring, 196–197
>   regions, moving, 206

Grid Value selector, 196

guitar effects
>   adding, 301
>   optimizing, 312–314

H

hardware
>   configurations, 24. *See also* configurations
>   connections, checking, 104–105
>   powering up, 50–51

Hardware Buffer Size controls, 53

Hardware Setup dialog box, 104–105

HD Core card, 33–34

Heal Separation command, 204–205

help, navigating, 64–65

Help menu, 56

Hertz (Hz), 21

hiding columns, 59

Higher CPU Usage Limit settings, 53

Higher Hardware Buffer Size settings, 53

Horizontal Zoom In button, 179

Horizontal Zoom Out button, 179

host-based performance, optimizing, 52–54

hum, deleting, 350–352

human hearing, range of, 20

Hybrid, 39

HZ (Hertz), 21

I

ICON integrated console environment, 15–17

icons, picture-icon (picon), 131

Import Audio dialog box, 124–125

Import command, 126–127

importing
>   files
>> Region List, 338
>> Workspace browser, 339–340
>
>   media, 297–300, 336–341
>> audio, 124–130
>> considerations prior to, 121–123
>> video, 131–132
>
>   movies, 337–338
>   Region List, 128–129
>   region group to tracks, 299–300
>   REX files, 298–299
>   tracks, 129–130

Import Options dialog box, 127

incoming signals, configuring, 106

incompatible ASCII characters, 44

input, 223
>   configuring, 106–108
>   devices, connecting, 279
>   MIDI devices, enabling, 140
>   selectors, 226–228
>   signals, 226
>   tracks, enabling, 293–294

input/output (I/O), 24
>   configuring, 86
>   MIDI, 37
>   MIDI, checking, 141–142

Digidesign's support of the audio production community doesn't stop at great products. We also offer the most comprehensive set of training and education programs and resources in the industry. From Pro Tools 101 basics to Expert Certification in Pro Tools Music or Post, Digidesign's Training & Education Program and its partner facilities provide the fastest path to a marketable understanding of Pro Tools.

Visit training.digidesign.com to learn about all the options available to you today.

PRO TOOLS OPERATOR & EXPERT CERTIFICATION TRAINING PATHS

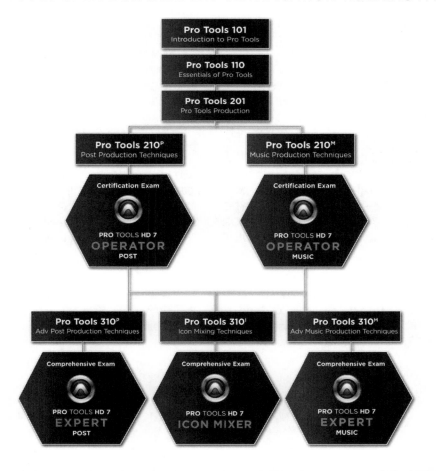

License Agreement/Notice of Limited Warranty

By opening the sealed disc container in this book, you agree to the following terms and conditions. If, upon reading the following license agreement and notice of limited warranty, you cannot agree to the terms and conditions set forth, return the unused book with unopened disc to the place where you purchased it for a refund.

License:
The enclosed software is copyrighted by the copyright holder(s) indicated on the software disc. You are licensed to copy the software onto a single computer for use by a single user and to a backup disc. You may not reproduce, make copies, or distribute copies or rent or lease the software in whole or in part, except with written permission of the copyright holder(s). You may transfer the enclosed disc only together with this license, and only if you destroy all other copies of the software and the transferee agrees to the terms of the license. You may not decompile, reverse assemble, or reverse engineer the software.

Notice of Limited Warranty:
The enclosed disc is warranted by Thomson Course Technology PTR to be free of physical defects in materials and workmanship for a period of sixty (60) days from end user's purchase of the book/disc combination. During the sixty-day term of the limited warranty, Thomson Course Technology PTR will provide a replacement disc upon the return of a defective disc.

Limited Liability:
THE SOLE REMEDY FOR BREACH OF THIS LIMITED WARRANTY SHALL CONSIST ENTIRELY OF REPLACEMENT OF THE DEFECTIVE DISC. IN NO EVENT SHALL THOMSON COURSE TECHNOLOGY PTR OR THE AUTHOR BE LIABLE FOR ANY OTHER DAMAGES, INCLUDING LOSS OR CORRUPTION OF DATA, CHANGES IN THE FUNCTIONAL CHARACTERISTICS OF THE HARDWARE OR OPERATING SYSTEM, DELETERIOUS INTERACTION WITH OTHER SOFT-WARE, OR ANY OTHER SPECIAL, INCIDENTAL, OR CONSEQUENTIAL DAMAGES THAT MAY ARISE, EVEN IF THOMSON COURSE TECHNOLOGY PTR AND/OR THE AUTHOR HAS PREVI-OUSLY BEEN NOTIFIED THAT THE POSSIBILITY OF SUCH DAMAGES EXISTS.

Disclaimer of Warranties:
THOMSON COURSE TECHNOLOGY PTR AND THE AUTHOR SPECIFICALLY DISCLAIM ANY AND ALL OTHER WARRANTIES, EITHER EXPRESS OR IMPLIED, INCLUDING WARRANTIES OF MERCHANTABILITY, SUITABILITY TO A PARTICULAR TASK OR PURPOSE, OR FREEDOM FROM ERRORS. SOME STATES DO NOT ALLOW FOR EXCLUSION OF IMPLIED WARRANTIES OR LIMITATION OF INCIDENTAL OR CONSEQUENTIAL DAMAGES, SO THESE LIMITATIONS MIGHT NOT APPLY TO YOU.

Other:
This Agreement is governed by the laws of the State of Massachusetts without regard to choice of law principles. The United Convention of Contracts for the International Sale of Goods is specifically disclaimed. This Agreement constitutes the entire agreement between you and Thomson Course Technology PTR regarding use of the software.